NORMS IN CONFLICT

NORMS IN CONFLICT

SOUTHEAST ASIA'S RESPONSE TO HUMAN RIGHTS VIOLATIONS IN MYANMAR

Anchalee Rüland

Copyright © 2022 by The University Press of Kentucky

Scholarly publisher for the Commonwealth,
serving Bellarmine University, Berea College, Centre
College of Kentucky, Eastern Kentucky University,
The Filson Historical Society, Georgetown College,
Kentucky Historical Society, Kentucky State University,
Morehead State University, Murray State University,
Northern Kentucky University, Spalding University,
Transylvania University, University of Kentucky,
University of Louisville, and Western
Kentucky University.

All rights reserved.

Editorial and Sales Offices: The University Press of Kentucky
663 South Limestone Street, Lexington, Kentucky 40508-4008
www.kentuckypress.com

Library of Congress Cataloging-in-Publication Data

Names: Rüland, Anchalee, 1990- author.
Title: Norms in conflict : Southeast Asia's response to human rights violations in Myanmar / Anchalee Rüland.
Description: Lexington, Kentucky : The University Press of Kentucky, [2022] | Includes bibliographical references and index.
Identifiers: LCCN 2021049410 | ISBN 9780813183701 (hardcover) | ISBN 9780813183725 (pdf) | ISBN 9780813183732 (epub)
Subjects: LCSH: Human rights—Burma. | International and municipal law—Indonesia. | International and municipal law—Malaysia. | International and municipal law—Thailand. | International law and human rights—Indonesia. | International law and human rights—Malaysia. | International law and human rights—Thailand. | International relations—Philosophy. | Burma—Foreign relations—Indonesia. | Indonesia—Foreign relations—Burma. | Burma—Foreign relations—Malaysia. | Malaysia—Foreign relations—Burma. | Burma—Foreign relations—Thailand. | Thailand—Foreign relations—Burma. | Burma—Politics and government—1988-
Classification: LCC JC599.B87 R85 2022 | DDC 323.4/909591—dc23/eng/20211123
LC record available at https://lccn.loc.gov/2021049410

This book is printed on acid-free paper meeting
the requirements of the American National Standard
for Permanence in Paper for Printed Library Materials.

Manufactured in the United States of America.

 Member of the Association of
University Presses

Contents

List of Abbreviations   vi

Introduction   1
1. Theorizing and Studying Response to Norm Conflict   9
2. Commitment to the Norms   33
3. Norm Reconciliation in Indonesia   56
4. Strategic Norm Replacement in Thailand   92
5. From Norm Reconciliation to Conflict Denial in Malaysia   125
Conclusion   160

Acknowledgments   181
Notes   183
Bibliography   225
Index   239

Abbreviations

AICHR	ASEAN Intergovernmental Commission on Human Rights
AIPMC	ASEAN Inter-Parliamentary Myanmar Caucus
Amnesty	Amnesty International
APCET	Asia Pacific Conference on East Timor
ASEAN	Association of Southeast Asian Nations
BN	Barisan Nasional (National Front)
CSIS	Centre for Strategic and International Studies
DAP	Democratic Action Party
DPR	Dewan Perwakilan Rakyat–Republik Indonesia (House of Representatives of the Republic of Indonesia)
ESCAP	UN Economic and Social Commission for Asia and the Pacific
EU	European Union
FPI	Front Pembela Islam (Islamic Defenders Front)
Fretilin	Frente Revolucionária do Timor-Leste Independente (Revolutionary Front for an Independent East Timor)
Golkar	Partai Golongan Karya (Party of the Functional Groups)
Hindraf	Hindu Rights Action Force
HRW	Human Rights Watch
IFHR	International Federation for Human Rights
IKIAM	Institut Kerjasama Islam Antarabangsa Malaysia (Malaysian Institute of International Islamic Cooperation)
ILO	International Labour Organization
IR	International Relations

IRT	International Relations Theory
ISA	Internal Security Act
KontraS	Komisi untuk orang hilang dan korban tidak kekerasan atau disingkat (Commission for the Disappeared and Victims of Violence)
Komnas HAM	Komisi Nasional Hak Asasi Manusia (Indonesian National Commission for Human Rights)
MAPIM	Majlis Perundingan Pertubuhan Islam Malaysia (Malaysian Consultative Council for the Islamic Organization)
MoU	Memorandum of understanding
NAM	Non-Aligned Movement
NGO	Nongovernmental organization
NHRC	National Human Rights Commission
NLD	National League for Democracy (democratic opposition party in Myanmar)
OHCHR	Office of the United Nations High Commissioner of Human Rights
OIC	Organization of Islamic Cooperation
PAN	Partai Amanat Nasional (National Mandate Party)
PAS	Parti Islam Se-Malaysia (Malaysian Islamic Party)
PDI-P	Partai Demokrasi Indonesia Perjuangan (Indonesian Democratic Party of Struggle)
PKR	Parti Keadilan Rakyat (People's Justice Party)
PKS	Partai Keadilan Sejahtera (Prosperous Justice Party)
PMI	Palang Merah Indonesia (Indonesian Red Cross)
RtoP	Responsibility to protect
SPDC	State Peace and Development Council (governing body in Myanmar until 2011)
SUHAKAM	Suruhanjaya Hak Asasi Manusia Malaysia (Malaysian Human Rights Commission)
UDHR	Universal Declaration of Human Rights
UMNO	United Malays National Organisation
UN	United Nations
US	United States
WFP	World Food Programme

Introduction

With the liberalization of some of the key member states of the Association of Southeast Asian Nations (ASEAN) during the third wave of democratization,[1] a tension developed in their foreign policies between commitment to human rights protection and promotion, and noninterference in the internal affairs of other member states. Ever since the formation of the regional organization in 1967, the norm of noninterference has been a sacrosanct standard of how states are to deal with one another in questions of state-society relations. The commitment to the norm not only reflects a shared security predicament across the postcolonial world—namely the imperative to prevent the repetition of colonial-era interventions by powerful states. In a highly heterogeneous and formerly conflict-ridden region like Southeast Asia, noninterference has also been valued as a means to build trust and stability among governments. Successive generations of ASEAN policymakers have thus been socialized into the norm of noninterference. At the same time, a number of countries in the region, including the Philippines, Indonesia, Thailand, and at times Malaysia and Singapore, began from the late 1990s onward to push past the exclusive understanding of sovereignty as authority, starting to emphasize notions of responsibility. This entailed a commitment to democracy, good governance, and the protection and promotion of human rights—not only at home but also at the regional level. ASEAN's more democratically advanced states therefore faced a dilemma: The norms of human rights protection and noninterference created conflicting obligations regarding their behavior in cases of extraterritorial human rights violations. They seemingly had to choose between compliance with two equally valid behavioral standards in cases of human rights violations within the region.

The case of ASEAN's democratizing states is representative of a larger problem. It shows that all states have multiple identities and manifold normative commitments. Sometimes these commitments are contradictory.

When they clash, the result is a norm conflict—a situation in which it is impossible to conform to two norms at the same time. Norm conflict creates a serious dilemma for decision makers who value norm following and want to be seen in a particular way by others. Where norm conflicts relate to the foreign policy of states, they constitute a huge source of uncertainty not only for the government itself but also for other actors within its region and the broader international society with which it engages. Especially in times of normative advancement, norm conflicts can be expected to be frequent, as old norms continue to coexist next to new ones for extended periods of time. It is thus important to understand how governments determine in practice which norm to follow and why they respond the way they do.

Interestingly, though, very little is known about state behavior in situations of norm conflict. This is particularly surprising from a constructivist perspective. Whereas scholars who embrace more materialist theory traditions, such as realism, have dismissed the impact of norms on state behavior, constructivism considers norms as motivational forces for state behavior. But constructivist scholars have largely circumvented the problem of norm conflict. One strand of theorizing has focused on showing how new international norms are *grafted* into an existing normative environment.[2] In order to fit into a state's set of preexisting normative ideas, norms have to be *contested* or *localized* domestically before being internalized.[3] Norm conflict in this scenario is understood as a tension between international and domestic norms. In a process of arguing, different actors pitch against each other the conflicting meaning of the norms involved.[4] As a consequence of the norms' localization, norm conflict, understood as mutually exclusive obligations within two equally internalized norms, does not arise. These theories ignore that overlap between two norms often only develops over time as identities evolve and contextual changes take place. In other words, norm conflict then sets in at a later stage than norm contestation or norm localization. Norm conflict takes as a premise that there is already commitment to both norms at the domestic level. Other constructivist approaches have simply assumed that as states accept and adopt new international norms, conflicting old ones are replaced, thus failing to recognize that old and new norms often coexist for substantial periods of time until eventually (if ever) one completely replaces the other.[5] Only a few constructivist scholars have explicitly recognized the problem of norm conflict. Ian Hurd most accurately describes norm conflict when stating that there can be "inconsistencies within an actor itself."[6] Alexander Wendt similarly observes that "many situations call up several identities that may point in different directions leaving us unsure how to act."[7] Unfortunately both authors leave open how these situations can be resolved. Vaguely referring to agent choice between the conflicting norms, they fall short of further inquiring how such choice is motivated and how it plays out in practice. The only more direct consideration of norm conflict is provided by Florini, who concludes that if neither of the competing norms has driven the other to extinction, decision-making agents are likely to follow one norm on some occasions and the competitor on others.[8] Yet without specifying the factors that lead to compliance with either of the two norms, this insight is of little help in determining how decision-making is likely to play out in situations of norm conflict.

In light of this gap within international relations (IR) literature, analyzing how actors behave in situations of norm conflict is the main theme of this book. It therefore aims to speak to a wide group of IR scholars interested in norms research. Even though this book follows the constructivist tradition of IR theorizing, which treats ideational phenomena, such as norms, as constitutive elements of world politics, it does not understand norms as independent causes for state behavior in situations of norm conflict. I argue that in situations of norm conflict, the alleged "independent" pull of norms, which the behaviorist strand of constructivism has emphasized, would necessarily lead to paralysis. Given that the behaviorist approach relies on a "logic of appropriateness" and conceptualizes this logic as a largely "unconscious" process, it provides no means for determining which of the two norms—both of which invoke notions of appropriateness—will be followed.[9]

In contrast, this book outlines a consequentialist but socially embedded logic to norm following. In this framework, decision makers remain in a conscious state of norm following. They are motivated by the anticipated future consequences of norm following on their domestic legitimacy and international reputation.[10] Instead of being free to pursue just any a priori defined interests, decision makers are constrained in their choices by the expectations for norm compliance set by their prior commitment to the norms. These expectations are articulated both at the domestic and international levels by the legitimizing audiences to which a government has to answer in order to preserve and consolidate its domestic legitimacy as well as international reputation. What therefore matters in situations of norm conflict is the perceived strength of domestic and international expectations for norm following with either of the two conflicting norms and how the government manages the social costs of violating one of these norms. In sum, while norms influence the government's decision-making by defining a realm of possible action, they do not explain the response to norm conflict independent of the social costs the government anticipates in violating a norm.[11] What is crucial therefore is the government's desire to minimize if not avoid the social costs of norm violation, which include domestic legitimacy and international reputation costs.

In some situations, domestic and international expectations pull in the same direction, privileging one norm, whereas in other situations, they can diverge. Given that "the people" still constitute the main legitimizing audience, I expect that in cases in which the domestic and international expectations conflict, governments are more likely to align their stance with the expectations articulated at the domestic level. Borrowing insights outlined by the "logic of arguing," the book contends that governments will use arguments and persuasion to address conflicting expectations of action and thereby minimize the social costs of norm violation.[12] As a consequence, response to norm conflict is conceptualized both as an *act of choice* as well as an *effort to manage expectations*. On the basis of this framework, I develop five possible responses to norm conflict, which will each be addressed in detail in the theoretical chapter of this book. They include norm prioritization, general norm replacement, strategic norm replacement, norm reconciliation, and conflict denial.[13] Which strategy governments chose in a situation of norm conflict depends on whether the domestic and international expectations converge or conflict; their intent to influence the behavior of others; the power resources available to a government; and (un)certainty regarding future expectations. The theoretical framework is intended to cover the entire universe of possible response strategies to norm conflict and thereby serve as a reference for other scholars working on norms-related research.

The empirical heart of this book illustrates and refines the theoretical propositions with the help of three case studies from Southeast Asia. It analyzes how the more democratically advanced governments of Indonesia, Thailand, and Malaysia respond to situations of gross human rights violations in Myanmar. In those situations, the norms of human rights protection and promotion, and noninterference in internal affairs both apply and conflict. In studying norm conflict in Southeast Asia this book deliberately focuses on a non-Western part of the world. This is primarily because most research on norms, and especially research analyzing cycles of normative change, has so far concentrated on the West.[14] But engagement with norms, and particularly confrontation with conflicting norms, also takes place in non-Western contexts—a fact that deserves and requires attention. In contributing generalizable norms research to the wider discipline of IR, this book attempts to address that need. At the same time, it aims to speak those scholars specializing in Southeast Asian regionalism. In specifically looking at the foreign policy making of three Southeast Asian states, the book addresses a significant weakness of the existing rich body of books and papers on ASEAN, namely the endless repetition of the mantra that distinct regional norms exist that guide the interests and actions of ASEAN as a (seemingly) collective actor.[15] Most authors neglect that, in the absence of a supranational quality, ASEAN does not "act" on its own but reflects the collective political will of its member states. The "ASEAN position" in international relations is thus the result of a constant process of negotiation among sovereign governments, all of which are subjected to a specific set of international and domestic norm expectations. There is a lack of studies that challenge the notion of homogeneous norms as the guiding principle of intraregional relations and instead emphasize the "power" of norms as part of the foreign policy formation at the level of individual member states. The theoretical framework presented in this book closes this gap in the literature in successfully bridging the analytical divide between international and domestic politics. The conducted research within the region shows that a deep analysis of foreign policy making requires a study of both a government's vulnerability to domestic pressures and its quest for social recognition at the international level.

Finally, this book is intended to speak to a third group of scholars, namely those interested in human rights and their accompanying discourse. By applying the consequentialist but socially embedded logic of norm following to Southeast Asia, we learn much, not merely about *any* situation of norm conflict, but possibly the most pressing one of the twenty-first century, as an increasing number of states have first democratized and committed themselves to universal human rights and as democratic norms are now increasingly coming under pressure again. As one of the most diverse regions in the world in terms of regime types, ASEAN as a regional organization groups together democratic states as well as authoritarian regimes of various shades that have poor human rights records. As a consequence, human rights violations within the region are unfortunately not uncommon. During the peak period of democratization and engagement with human rights in Southeast Asia (2003–2012), the prime offender against human rights within the region was Myanmar. Therefore, this book focuses on how ASEAN's more democratically advanced states responded to three instances of large-scale human rights violations in Myanmar: the Saffron Revolution in 2007; Cyclone Nargis in 2008; and the Rakhine Riots in 2012. Empirically the book contributes novel insights on the three cases of human rights violations within Myanmar, as well as the engagement with two norms of noninterference and human rights protection in three democratizing Southeast Asian states. Although there has been some work on ASEAN's collective response to events in Myanmar, especially to the Saffron Revolution and Cyclone Nargis, the ways in which individual member states responded to these crises have remained largely unexamined.[16] The case studies show how Indonesia, Thailand, and Malaysia emphasized very different aspects of noninterference and human rights protection in their application of the norms in the regional context, as well as in the justifications of their actions vis-à-vis dissenting audiences.

The subsequent chapters of this book theoretically and empirically flesh out how states respond to norm conflict in practice and trace the underlying motivational factors. I seek to show that the expectations governments face at the domestic and international levels matter in determining which responses they opt for. Following this introduction, I start with the design of a theoretical framework for explaining response to norm conflict (chapter 1), which is comprised of five parts: (1) a theoretical discussion of norms, how they work and the decision-making problem that arises in situations of norm conflict; (2) an analysis of the logic of actions international relations theory (IRT) provides and their shortcomings in explaining decision-making in situations of norm conflict; (3) the outline of a consequentialist but socially embedded approach to norm following; (4) an overview of the universe of possible responses to norm conflict on the basis of a consequentialist but socially embedded approach to norm following; and, finally, (5) a discussion of the methodology, including case selection and the research methods used for this study.

In chapter 2, I establish the normative context in the three case-study countries—Indonesia, Thailand, and Malaysia—which provides the foundation for identifying and studying responses to norm conflict. The chapter analyzes the degree of commitment to the two norms in Indonesia, Thailand, and Malaysia by relying on a threefold measure of norm commitment consisting of (1) *formal norm adoption*, (2) *norm implementation*, and (3) *norm compliance*. It highlights the sources that give rise to expectations for norm compliance at the domestic and international levels. In emphasizing the relevance of the domestic aspects of norm internalization, namely norm implementation and demonstrated commitment to a norm in practice, this study of norm conflict importantly differs from the bulk of norms research, which still mainly focuses on the international level, asking whether and why states formally adopt norms.[17]

From there, the book moves on to empirically illustrate responses to situations of norm conflict. Chapter 3 assesses the Indonesian response to norm conflict in situations of gross human rights violations in Myanmar. It shows that in light of a domestic expectation for norm compliance with human rights protection and an equally strong domestic desire to uphold the noninterference norm in cases of territorial disintegration, the government employed a strategy of norm reconciliation. To reconcile the conflicting norms, the Indonesian government reduced the meaning and application of the noninterference norm to instances involving a secessionist dimension. While generally acting in accordance with the human rights protection norm, it remained silent in cases in which a country's human rights violations were related to a struggle for secession or involved a risk of territorial disintegration, such as the later stages of the Saffron Revolution and the Rakhine Riots in Myanmar. Chapter 4 analyzes Thailand's response to the same instances of norm conflict. It illustrates that the government opted for strategic norm replacement by privileging noninterference over human rights protection. This response reflects a strong domestic expectation in Thailand for a prioritization of noninterference that conflicted with international and (at times) regional expectations for human rights protection. In order to justify its silence in the face of extraterritorial human rights violations, thus appearing to undermine the general validity of the human rights protection norm within the region, the government justified its policy by appealing to its "special position" in relation to Myanmar as a direct neighbor. Chapter 5 assesses the way in which the Malaysian government dealt with human rights violations in Myanmar. It shows that over time the Malaysian government altered its strategy, as domestic expectations regarding norm compliance with human rights protection and noninterference changed. The shift in domestic expectations reflected both the relatively low degree of internalization of human rights protection and promotion in Malaysia compared to Thailand and Indonesia, as well as the presence of a major domestic crisis that coincided with two of the three analyzed cases of human rights violations in Myanmar. Reflecting domestic expectations, successive Malaysian governments first tried to reconcile the norms and later switched to a strategy of conflict denial. In doing so, the government challenged the predominant Western interpretation of the situations, arguing that they were not cases of human rights violations but humanitarian disasters. It reframed the situation, and, in denying the existence of a norm conflict between noninterference and human rights protection, the Malaysian government resolved the tension between the two norms in those particular instances.

In the book's conclusion, I revisit the overall research objectives of this work and review the findings of the case studies in light of the expectations set out by the theoretical framework. The conclusion provides suggestions for further research to increase the generalizability of the findings and points out how the study of norm conflict can enliven and advance the research agenda of scholars focusing on norms and how normative change takes place. The research from Southeast Asia suggests that the outcome of norm conflict will not necessarily be full-fledged norm replacement. Instead, subtler normative adjustments are often made that allow for both norms to remain part of a state's normative environment and the broader complex of norms at the regional and international levels. Such a nuanced understanding of normative change more easily explains why "good" norms not only progress but also regress—sometimes within astonishingly brief periods of time, as vividly displayed in Southeast Asia.

1

Theorizing and Studying Response to Norm Conflict

Since the constructivist turn in the 1980s, IRT has dealt extensively with norms and agency in normative environments. Central elements of this literature have analyzed the impact of norms on state behavior,[1] their diffusion and localization,[2] as well as their evolution, contestation, and change.[3] Among scholars working on Southeast Asia, a norm-centered social-constructivist view of intraregional relations has in fact been so successful that constructivism has established itself as the mainstream approach to the study of ASEAN since the early 2000s.[4] Yet the issue of norm conflict has remained theoretically and empirically understudied both in IR theorizing generally and in regional scholarship more specifically. We have little understanding of the judgments governments make regarding compliance when the directives inherent in the norms to which they have committed appear to be mutually exclusive. This chapter addresses this lacuna by outlining a theoretical framework for explaining and empirically studying norm conflict in Southeast Asia and beyond. It spells out five ideal-type responses to norm conflict and the most important scope conditions for choosing a response that are generally applicable and can serve as a reference to other norm-related research.

NORM CONFLICTS AS DECISION-MAKING PROBLEMS

Constructivist research of the last decade has stressed the dual quality of norms as both "static and changing."[5] Both qualities are important, as we will see, to understanding the decision-making problem entailed in norm conflicts as well as the determining factors for their resolution. Without some sense of fixity, norms would not provide what they must, namely relatively stable standards of conduct to guide the choices of those subject to them.[6] As such they reflect patterned behavior that is prescribed and gives rise to normative expectations as to what ought to be done.[7] Yet, at the same time, norms are also constantly evolving, and their meaning is often subject to contestation. Only in leaving their meaning and validity open to arguing and justification is normative change possible.[8] As a result, norms must also remain flexible. Norm conflicts as decision-making problems arise from the relatively "stable" quality of norms, which makes them recognizable and enforceable prescriptions for behavior. As Sandholtz argues, all norms are regulative, but some additionally have a constitutive effect.[9] Given their regulative function, norms identify standards of conduct and create expectations for compliance. As a consequence, all norms have an important action-guiding function.[10] In norm conflicts this action-guiding function is seriously impaired. According to Pauwelyn, "two norms are ... in a relationship of conflict if one constitutes, has led to, or may lead to, a breach of the other."[11] Hence a norm conflict occurs whenever an actor finds itself in a situation in which its normative directives are inconsistent or not uniquely action-guiding.[12] Neither norm is applicable without conflicting with the other.[13] The clearest example can be found where one norm prohibits a certain behavior, whereas another norm obligates the same behavior. The norms' normative directives are then mutually exclusive.[14]

In the realm of foreign policy, norm conflicts first and foremost relate to the policymakers' beliefs, which are based on shared normative ideas. Socialization into those shared normative ideas may have previously occurred at both the domestic and international levels. In a norm conflict, which presents itself as a situation of choice, policymakers recognize conflicting normative directives that flow from the competing norms that regulate the relevant subject matter. The decision-making problem is this: it is only possible for a government to comply with one rule by failing to adhere to the other. To illustrate the point, let us return to the case of norm conflict in Southeast Asia: In the wake of their countries' democratic transformations, decision makers from ASEAN's more democratically advanced member states increasingly felt committed not only to noninterference in internal affairs but also to human rights promotion and protection. This created a dilemma in situations of gross human rights violations within the region in which both norms applied. Next to exemplifying the decision-making problem governments face in situations of norm conflict, the case also shows that often a conflict between two norms only arises as contextual changes take place, such as democratic transitions.

Norm conflicts always represent a source of uncertainty for state behavior and create serious challenges to the management of systems governed by norms.[15] Although all norm conflicts create a decision-making problem, those that involve norms with a constitutive effect additionally give rise to questions about identity commitments and might therefore be particularly difficult to resolve.[16]

EXPLAINING CHOICE IN INTERNATIONAL RELATIONS THEORY

IRT has focused on three logics of action in order to explain behavior in situations of choice, respectively centering on notions of appropriateness, arguing, und consequences. Each logic comes with its own difficulties in explaining choice in situations of norm conflict. Constructivists within the "behaviorist" tradition have tended to focus on the logic of appropriateness as a mechanism of norm following.[17] Actors not only follow norms because they have an interest in their general adherence by others but also because they have internalized those norms and conceive of themselves in a certain way, that is, as good global citizens.[18] In a situation of choice, actors therefore do what they see as appropriate for themselves given their identities.[19] As norms are "taken for granted," compliance becomes habitual. Norm compliance is therefore largely perceived as an unconscious process, and decision-making appears to become impossible in situations of norm conflict.[20] The attempt at norm compliance would lead to paralysis. The respective actor—the government—would be unable to act. It would do nothing, not because it actively decides to do so, but because it does not know which of the two norms—conflicting yet viewed as equally appropriate—to follow. In a world in which agents do not operate in complete isolation and normative commitments create expectations by others regarding compliance, paralysis would be an extremely unsatisfying outcome for any agent.[21] A government would be seen as indecisive or unreliable. Given the social costs of paralysis, it seems reasonable to assume that most governments will work hard to avoid such an outcome.

Addressing this weakness inherent in "behavioralist" approaches, constructivists of a more "reflexive" tradition have described an alternative mechanism of norm following known as the logic of arguing. Within the logic of arguing, agents leave the unconscious process of norm following and via a communicative act of argumentation try to adjudicate which norm to comply with. Norm following is then understood as an "informed choice," and paralysis can be avoided.[22] The logic of arguing not only describes a logic of action but also a mode of social interaction that enables equal participants in a deliberation to mutually challenge and explore the validity claims of the conflicting norms.[23] Validity claims can be based on the moral rightness of the norm's underlying argument, the truthfulness and authenticity of the speaker, and the norm's conformity with the perceived facts in the world.[24] In a situation of norm conflict they could be used as grounds to establish a hierarchy of order between the two conflicting norms. In theory, the logic of arguing as a mechanism of norm following thus provides the analytical tools to understand state response in situations of norm conflict. What makes the logic of arguing problematic is the scale of its scope conditions, which creates the image of decision-making as an all-inclusive and consensual process. Akin to a Habermasian "ideal speech situation," the participants in a discourse have to be open to being convinced by the better argument and seek to find a communicative consensus—in this case on with which of the two conflicting norms one should comply.[25] Therefore relationships of power and social hierarchies recede into the background. But politics rarely, if ever, delivers ideal speech situations. The logic of arguing as outlined by Risse ignores that the actual decision-making power lies with the government, which in its governing role has interests of its own—most fundamentally to remain in office. These interests remain outside the framework. Once we recognize that it is the government that is doing the actual decision-making, it becomes obvious that some arguments count more than others.[26] As Crawford rightly points out, even in a democratic context, preexisting power and authority are not entirely removed from the scene, and therefore it is not only the force of the better argument that prevails. To the contrary, political arguments occur in a decidedly unlevel playing field of discourse between differently powerful actors.[27] What constitutes the "best" argument for a government in a norm conflict is very much a question of *who* advocates compliance with the different norms and how supportive those groups are of the government and its policies. In order to explain government choice in situations of norm conflict, we thus need a framework that allows for a consequentialist rationale while at the same time taking norms seriously.

A CONSEQUENTIALIST BUT SOCIALLY EMBEDDED APPROACH TO NORM FOLLOWING

The logic of consequence explains action in situations of choice based on a cost-benefit calculation. Scholars using this logic have traditionally dismissed the effect of norms on state behavior or simply seen it as a reflection of exogenously given interests or state power,[28] a point most prominently made by Krasner.[29] In his framework the logic of consequence is equated with an entirely egoistic disposition toward others. But there is no reason to believe that this is the case. In what follows I outline a consequentialist but socially embedded approach to norm following. It allows leaders to remain in a conscious and rational state of norm following, while at the same time factoring in the social costs that follow from their commitment to the norms in their decision-making. In line with other realists, Krasner overlooks the fact that even though governments are not punished for their actions internationally by an international enforcement agency, they are constrained in what they do by the structure of their social relations at both the domestic and international levels. Because norms are shared, commitment to a norm creates expectations toward compliance by others. They are thus part of the material and ideational context in which actors make choices. Functioning like promises, normative commitments can only be overridden by exceptional circumstances and acts of justification.[30] Leaders therefore have to account for their actions vis-à-vis their relevant audiences through a process of *legitimization*. Relevant audiences are all those communities with which a government identifies and within which it tries to secure a particular social standing.[31] Although a government's primary source of legitimacy is still "the people" of its own state, other audiences at the international level also have to be considered.[32] It is the job of those in power to identify which audiences matter and how to speak to those multiple audiences.[33] As Jetschke points out, audiences act "as judges about the persuasiveness of arguments" and actions.[34] They respond approvingly to actors and their actions that are in line with the expectations they hold and penalize those that are not.[35] As a consequence, their approval or disapproval can help reduce the indeterminacy of norms in situations of norm conflict.[36] In situations of choice, a government's commitment to a norm will create expectations for compliance with the norm among some of its relevant audiences. In response to a situation of norm conflict, this implies that a decision in favor of compliance with one norm over the other can be made based on the perceived strength of the articulated expectations of relevant audiences and the social costs the government anticipates in leaving them unaddressed. In sum, the considerations of the consequences of action go beyond the conventional self-interested understanding of the logic of consequences. What is deemed possible and desirable depends on the social context. In this sense norms do not function like causes.[37] In shaping expectations they influence the government's decision-making. They define the realm of possibility but do not explain the response to norm conflict independent of the social costs the government anticipates in violating a norm.[38]

This socially embedded but consequentialist view of response to norm conflict does not negate the possibility that governments, as the decision-making agents, believe in the norms in question. Nor does it suggest that they never pursue actions based on their inherent sense of appropriateness. It simply argues that in situations in which notions of appropriateness are not uniquely action-guiding, governments have to resort to a conscious process of decision-making that relies on a different mechanism for norm following than appropriateness. Compared to the logic of arguing, a consequentialist but socially embedded approach to norm following has several advantages. First, it leaves the process of decision-making open to relations of power and influence, thereby recognizing that governments do not treat all expectations equally. Especially at the domestic level, where all governments to some extent have to legitimize their claim to power and continuously gather support for their rule, some voices will count for more than others. While this is surely most pronounced within democratic polities, extenuated forms of domestic legitimization take place within all systems of governance. What represents the "best argument" from the government's point of view can, therefore, reflect power relations. Second, by ascribing the act of decision-making to the government, this approach recognizes that often a quick response to international events is required, which leaves little time for deliberation about a norm's superior validity claim.[39] A consequentialist but socially embedded approach to norm following can capture patterns of relative stability as well as change in compliance by factoring in the internal transformations that states undergo, as well as normative changes in their surrounding international environment. In the following sections, this chapter elaborates on the consequentialist but socially embedded approach by outlining the social costs that can arise in the domestic as well as international spheres if a government fails to align its policy with the expectations set by the norms. I conceive of social costs as including a concern for domestic legitimacy as well as international reputation.

Domestic Expectations: Avoiding Legitimacy Costs

Why should governments as the decision-making agents care about domestic expectations regarding norm following? As Krasner rightly points out, rulers want to stay in power.[40] But, unwilling to open the "black box" of the state, he provides no explanation as to how the government's decision-making is linked to the objective of staying in power. Domestic legitimacy provides this missing link. Following Suchman, legitimacy can be defined as "a generalized perception or assumption that the actions of an entity are desirable, proper and appropriate within some socially constructed system of norms, values, beliefs and definitions."[41] Hence legitimacy is more than the capacity to act. It also comprises the right or entitlement to do so.[42] Accordingly, an actor is only endowed with legitimacy where its legitimacy claim has been recognized as rightful and has been consented to by relevant audiences.[43] To command domestic legitimacy, a government has to align its policies with the expectations within its community that express "collective beliefs about right and wrong, or means and ends."[44] These beliefs are formulated on the basis of the community's shared norms and interests. Based on the domestic expectations, governments identify the issues their audiences are concerned about and what actions are considered legitimate or possible in a policy area or given situation.[45] Once a legitimacy claim has been recognized, it continues to be assessed on the basis of the congruence of the government's actions with the audience's articulated expectations.

In return for endowing the domestic audience with the means of shaping action by expressing expectations, legitimacy imposes obligations on the community members. To the extent that people acknowledge power to be rightful, as validly acquired and appropriately exercised, they will feel a corresponding obligation to obey and support the government, without having to be bribed or coerced into doing so.[46] The people cooperate voluntarily.[47] Since actors in command of legitimacy can benefit from low levels of opposition to their rule, legitimacy fundamentally contributes to the stability and maintenance of order in a state.[48] In short, it reduces the costs of governing for those in power. As a consequence, it is not any power, but *legitimate* power, for which governments strive, and they can be expected to make "every effort to establish and maintain their legitimacy."[49] Legitimacy constrains power, but it also enables it.[50]

The enabling function of legitimacy is impaired when governments fail to align their policies with domestic expectations and legitimacy costs arise. As legitimacy erodes, voluntary cooperation will most likely decrease, and resistance to rule will increase. As a result, the efficiency of rule suffers, and the costs of maintaining order and stability are increased through, for example, more surveillance and coercive mechanisms.[51] In order to reestablish legitimacy, the government has to use persuasion or modify its policies. In a norm conflict the desire to avoid domestic legitimacy costs constitutes an important motivational force for the government, which can be expected to align its policy with the expectations for norm compliance articulated by the domestic group most supportive of its rule. This group represents the dominant domestic audience and has the most power to influence the government's decision-making. But decision makers are not only constrained by domestic expectations for norm compliance. They also seek approval for their actions by their peers on the international plane.

International Expectations: Avoiding Reputation Costs

From a constructivist perspective, international expectations matter not only because governments pursue international cooperation but also because they strive to obtain international recognition for the "identities" and "roles" according to which they would like their countries to be seen and judged by others.[52] In other words, they care about their standing within an existing structure of relations and institutions at the international level.[53]

Within that structure of relations, expectations express what is seen as legitimate conduct in relation to a shared normative system. This system can encompass the norms governing the international system at large or those of a subgroup of states. In his seminal work, Hedley Bull pointed out that, based on their identities, states associate with groups of states that share similar norms and values and "conceive themselves to be bound by a common set of rules in their relations with one another."[54] He famously called such a group of states an international society. While Bull saw international society as global, Buzan and Wæver rightly stressed that shared normative systems at a regional level can equally be conceptualized as international societies (for example, the EU, ASEAN, the African Union, the Arab League, etc.).[55] The structure of an international society embodies "rules for identifying who gets to count as a member" as well as rules about "what conduct is appropriate."[56] Membership within an international society thus entails an understanding among states on the "inside" that they are bound by some shared norms and work through common institutions to pursue their goals.[57] In identifying rightful membership and judging rightful conduct, international societies are essentially legitimist, similar to domestic communities.[58] They provide social recognition of an actor's conformity with the shared norms while at the same time creating an expectation toward compliance with those norms.

Scholars within the subdiscipline of foreign policy analysis have added that at the international level governments do not only seek social recognition for their identities from those within groupings of states that hold similar norms and values. They also pursue particular "role conceptions" that reflect how they see themselves and how they want to be seen by others in their foreign policy. A "role" is generally understood as a set of norms that is thought to apply to a person occupying a given position.[59] In applying the notion of roles to the realm of foreign policymaking, Holsti defined "role conceptions" as the functions that policymakers believe "their state should perform on a continuing basis in the international system or in subordinate regional systems."[60] Reflecting the shared worldviews, values, commitments, and objectives within a state, role conceptions flow from a state's identity and constitute its foreign policy culture.[61] Typical roles states can perform are, for example, those of a balancer, mediator, regional leader, democracy promoter, or peacemaker, to name just a few.[62] In committing to a set of norms and pursing the associated role conception internationally, governments again create expectations about legitimate conduct and appropriate behavior among their international peers.

Desiring recognition for their identities and the role conceptions they pursue, governments cannot afford to ignore their peers' expectations regarding legitimate action. The attainment of a government's objectives partially depends on the beliefs and opinions of others about them—in short, their reputations.[63] Ignoring the expectations of others could entail reputation costs for a government, relating not only to the likelihood of cooperation but also its standing within international society and those subgroups of states with which it identifies. Constructivists thus argue that states seek to preserve and consolidate their reputations as legitimate members of those groups.[64] This implies a relational understanding of reputation rather than viewing it as a property or asset that can be "owned, controlled, accumulated and spent" by an actor.[65] Reputation can thus broadly be defined as "the extent to which a state is considered to be an honourable member of the international community" or a subgroup of states.[66] When states leave international expectations concerning legitimate conduct unaddressed by violating shared norms, their action can provoke resistance, and a state's reputation as a reliable or "good" member of the group suffers.[67] A constructivist perspective would also argue that reputation concerns affect all states. In short, even the most powerful states in terms of capacity are not completely free in their choices.[68] Despite the fact that they are often able to transgress international rules of legitimate conduct without suffering adverse material consequences, they in fact rarely do so. And though they might be better able than the weak to bear the material costs of noncompliance with a norm (for example, sanctions), reputation costs are equally real and painful for the materially well endowed.[69]

Finally, bridging the two realms of legitimation—the domestic and the international—Finnemore and Sikkink point to another factor that facilitates a government's pursuit of a positive international reputation. They argue that a government's international reputation feeds back into its domestic basis of legitimation and consent.[70] By ignoring international expectations for norm compliance set by the government's commitment to a shared norm, not only would its international standing suffer but also its legitimacy at home. Hence international reputation loss has negative consequences at both the domestic and international levels. In a situation of norm conflict, governments can be expected to consider the expectations articulated by those international audiences with which it most identifies and in relation to which it wants to preserve and consolidate a good reputation for norm following. The following section addresses the question of how governments weigh domestic versus international expectations when they do not converge but are in conflict with each other.

MANAGING DOMESTIC AND INTERNATIONAL EXPECTATIONS

The argument developed above suggests that in situations that are governed by two conflicting norms, governments can be expected to consider the consequences that a policy in favor of either norm would have for its domestic as well as international standing.[71] Hence, from the government perspective norm conflicts are similar to the "two-level" game as described by Putnam.[72] The articulated expectations for norm compliance at either level shape what kind of action is perceived as legitimate in a given situation. In trying to minimize the legitimacy and reputation costs that can arise from norm violation, governments can be expected to conform to the norm that causes the least amount of resistance among its relevant audiences.

This situation makes response to norm conflict relatively simple where domestic and international expectations regarding legitimate action are compatible. In complying with the norm that reflects those expectations, governments avoid both legitimacy and reputation costs.[73] However, the decision-making process is complicated in cases in which domestic and international expectations conflict. The government has to determine whether it is more vulnerable in its standing domestically or internationally. Intuitively, it seems reasonable to assume that most governments have an inherent tendency to prioritize domestic expectations, since "the people" constitute their primary legitimizing audience.[74] But ultimately this remains a question that has to be studied empirically. What can be said with certainty is that one set of expectations remains unaddressed by the government's choice for compliance in situations in which domestic and international expectations conflict. In those cases, response to norm conflict always entails a justificatory element. In order to reduce the social costs of noncompliance with a norm, the government has to justify its actions with arguments that can address conflicting expectations.[75] In political arguments those who argue try to persuade an important audience that they are right.[76] More specifically, in situations of norm conflict, governments will try to persuade the audience whose expectations have remained unaddressed that its conduct does not actually represent a violation of the conflicting norm, or constitutes a justifiable exception to the rule.[77] As Jetschke shows in her study of human rights violations, whether or not a government gets away with their violation depends on "how persuasively and effectively they package or frame their action, and how acceptable that makes it to the relevant audiences."[78] In sum, the theoretical framework for this thesis sees a government's response to norm conflict as both an *act of choice* and an *effort to manage expectations*. Whereas the act of choice relates to the stable property of norms that make them recognizable and enforceable, the effort to manage conflicting expectations reflects their inherent flexibility. The meaning of norms in relation to a situation is open to interpretation, which can then be used, via arguments, to minimize the social fallout from noncompliance.

IDEAL-TYPE RESPONSES TO NORM CONFLICT

In the following, five ideal-type responses to norm conflict will be outlined, along with the likelihood of their adoption in a situation of norm conflict. Which strategy is chosen depends on whether domestic and international expectations convene or conflict, the power resources a government needs to convince others, its intention to influence the behavior of others, and its (un)certainty with regard to future expectations. As Sandholtz has pointed out, in order to successfully convince others and pursue normative change, power is important.[79] While "hard" coercive power, understood as the material capabilities of a state, often coexists with persuasive power, it is the latter that is crucial for normative change. Persuasive power enables an actor to influence and alter the beliefs of others.[80] But getting one's message out there will not be enough if the government intends to change the behavior of others. It has to be credible in its normative leadership and therefore also needs soft power. Which power resources a government needs depends on whether it "only" wants to influence expectations (persuasive power) or also desires to change the behavior of others (soft power).[81] The ideal-type responses outlined comprise both ad hoc policy responses that over time manifest in a response pattern, as well as response strategies that entail an element of future planning.

Norm Prioritization

The easiest and most straightforward response to norm conflict is consistent norm prioritization. From a consequentialist but socially embedded perspective of choice in norm conflicts, norm prioritization is most likely to be seen as a response to norm conflict in cases in which a government faces compatible domestic and international expectations that favor compliance with one of the two conflicting norms and that are likely to remain constant over time. In this situation, there is a reasonably "settled" interpretation of what constitutes legitimate action in the face of two conflicting norms. Domestic and international expectations are most likely to converge in cases in which there is relatively uncontested and strong normative leadership within the state's shared normative system and a firm domestic engagement with the global or regional culture has taken place. The compatible domestic and international expectations reinforce each other and raise the stakes of noncompliance with the supported norm.[82] By addressing those expectations and complying with the norm prioritized by its relevant audiences, the government avoids both legitimacy and reputation costs. Over time, response to norm conflict manifests as a uniform response pattern. One norm is consistently prioritized over the other. As a consequence of the compatible expectations, the experience of norm conflict is benign: the response to norm conflict involves no social costs. Accordingly, there is no need to plan for future situations of norm conflict by trying to actively influence the meaning of the norms and the attitudes of others toward them. Nevertheless, incrementally, normative change will take place. As a result of the consistent prioritization of one of the two norms, the perceived validity of the violated norm unintentionally diminishes. Observing audiences might start to question the norm's relevance and ultimately its status as a shared standard of behavior in the particular domain. As the norm degenerates, it loses its prescriptive status, and noncompliance becomes the rule rather than the exception.[83] If left unchecked, this process slowly removes the norm from the shared normative system. As a result, the consistently prioritized norm assumes an exclusive action-guiding function and stipulates what constitutes appropriate state behavior in future situations of choice.[84] Over time consistent norm prioritization can therefore lead to norm replacement.[85]

General Norm Replacement

As a response to norm conflict, general norm replacement, like consistent norm prioritization, manifests as a uniform response pattern, as the government consistently complies with the same norm. But unlike the former, it represents not only ad hoc policy decisions that over time manifest into a pattern but also a strategy with an element of future planning. It actively pursues normative change.[86] General norm replacement only makes sense for a government to adopt as a response to norm conflict if it faces conflicting expectations for norm compliance from the relevant audiences at the domestic and international levels. In addition, the government must be relatively certain that the audience supporting its course of action will continue to do so in the near future. Otherwise, removing one of the two norms from the normative environment would create more social costs than it would prevent. And finally, it must be relatively confident in its abilities to convince others of the benefits of compliance with the prioritized norm. In order to manage the social costs that can arise from leaving one set of expectations for norm compliance unaddressed, the government deliberately tries to undermine the validity of the violated norm within a shared normative system and to replace it with the rival. Thereby the norm conflict is resolved. The immediate goal of norm replacement is to invalidate conflicting expectations in the situation of norm conflict through arguments that justify action in accordance with the prioritized norm as opposed to compliance with its competitor. By undermining the validity of the conflicting norm and seeking to replace it, general norm replacement as a strategy also tries to prevent conflicting expectations for norm compliance in future situations of choice. While general norm replacement is attractive in that it resolves the norm conflict and thereby removes uncertainty, it is rather demanding as a successful response strategy to norm conflict. At a minimum the government needs to generate acceptance for its choice of norm following among the audience with dissenting views on legitimate conduct in the situation of choice. However, the ultimate goal is to shape the behavior of others in accordance with the selected norm so compliance becomes "normal" and does not require legitimation in every situation of choice. Not every government has the capacity to influence others within a shared normative system in such a way, and some norms that relate to and interact with the identity of others may be very difficult to replace. Their replacement requires simultaneous identity change, and thus resistance to their violation and ultimate replacement might be particularly strong. As a response to norm conflict, general norm replacement is a demanding strategy. To fully replace a norm within one's normative environment and thereby change the behavior of others, a government needs both considerable persuasive and soft power resources.

Strategic Norm Replacement

Similar to the previous two responses to norm conflict, strategic norm replacement over time manifests in a uniform response pattern. One of the two norms is continuously prioritized over the other. As a response strategy, however, it is most likely to be used where domestic and international expectations for norm compliance conflict, but where the government does not seek a *general* replacement of the violated norm within the shared normative system. In such a scenario, the government does not intend to undermine the violated norm's general validity and thereby potentially weaken the compliance of others with that norm. In short, it wants others to continue to abide by the violated norm, while accepting its own violation. To reduce its social costs, it strategically selects the norm stipulated by its most important audience and then tries to affect the expectations of the dissenting audience regarding its own behavior within a specific context. In order to shape the expectations of the dissenting audience, the government has to argue that under exceptional circumstances the abandonment of the norm and its replacement with the rival is a legitimate response that should not be socially sanctioned. In other words, within a specific context the violation of the norm has to be framed as a legitimate exception for this particular actor to its general validity.[87] To do so, the actor has to provide an argument that explains why its own behavior within a specific context should be regulated by only one of the two conflicting norms. This requires some persuasive power but no normative leadership and therefore no soft power. The actor is not trying to convince others to behave similarly. If the government remains consistent in its approach and the dissenting audience accepts its argument, a replacement of the violated norm within the specific context with the prioritized rival will be the result. In subsequent situations of choice, the remaining norm will exclusively regulate behavior and give rise to expectations for norm compliance.[88] Outside the specific sphere and for everyone else the two conflicting norms continue to coexist next to each other.

Norm Reconciliation

Norm reconciliation is most likely to be seen as a response to norm conflict where governments consistently face conflicting expectations for norm compliance, but the dissenting audience is unlikely to be convinced by complete norm replacement as a consequence of principled norm selection. The government lacks the necessary persuasive and soft power to convince others of full norm replacement. At the same time it wants a resolution of the conflict inherent in the norms, for itself and others, thereby differing from strategic norm replacement. Over time norm reconciliation manifests as a mixed response pattern in which both norms continue to be applied, but in accordance with a clear a priori defined logic. The government intends to alter their meaning in a way most acceptable to its various audiences. In sculpting the norms it tries to remove the overlap between the norms' obligations, thereby reconciling the two norms.[89] To do so, a "general" and a "specific" norm have to be assigned and a gap has to be created within the general norm.[90] At the same time, the specific norm needs to be derogated so that it henceforth only regulates the specific subject matter of the gap within the general norm. As a result of the sculpting, a hierarchy of order between the norms is created.[91] The general norm applies with the exception of a priori defined situations that are henceforth better regulated by the specific norm. Following the modification of the norms' meanings and the creation of a hierarchy between them, the reconciling agent will try to establish the norms in their new form as shared standards of behavior within its normative environment. Only if the derogated norm has been recognized as a legitimate exception to the general norm that deserves prioritization under the a priori defined circumstances in situations of choice will the social costs of norm violation cease to exist in future situations of choice. Norm reconciliation thus targets both the expectations of the relevant audiences toward the government and the behavior of others in future situations of norm conflict. To achieve this, norm reconciliation as a strategy requires some persuasive and soft power. Since norm reconciliation represents some sort of compromise between the two norms, which both continue to live on in the shared normative system, it appears more achievable for a larger number of actors than general norm replacement. Governments employing a strategy of norm reconciliation can be expected to justify their actions and engage in arguments with dissenting audiences in order to persuade them of the norms' reconciled meaning. The likelihood of acceptance of the modified norms and adjustment of behavior by others increases with the credibility of the reconciling agent, which is grounded in its own adherence to the new spheres of application. In doing so, it exercises normative leadership. The more governments within the shared normative system that support the attempt of norm reconciliation, the more likely it becomes that the strategy will be successful.

Conflict Denial

Another possible option for response to norm conflict where expectations for norm compliance conflict is conflict denial. If used over time, it should manifest in a uniform response pattern to support the credibility of the government. However, since conflict denial does not target the general validity of either norm and thereby does not affect future expectations for norm compliance, it appears less attractive as a long-term response strategy than others in dealing with conflicting expectations for norm compliance. Instead, it appears particularly suitable as an ad hoc policy response for governments that face conflicting expectations and are uncertain about future expectations. By targeting the interpretation of a particular situation as opposed to the general validity of a norm, it retains the flexibility to align its stance with expectations in favor of compliance with either norm in the future.

In managing conflicting expectations, conflict denial focuses upon the interpretation of a situation and challenges the conclusions about legitimate action that others have drawn from the perceived facts. In short, it rejects a particular framing of a situation that pitches two conflicting norms, to both of which the government has previously committed, against each other. Perhaps the most obvious example of conflict denial relates to the framing of situations as cases of systematic human rights violations, as opposed to humanitarian crises. The former can trigger expectations for action within a foreign jurisdiction without the host state's consent; the latter rules out such measures.[92] Thus for a government that does not want to interfere in the internal affairs of the concerned state, the framing of the crisis can be crucial.[93]

Conflict denial differs from norm contestation in that it does not question the validity of a norm per se or a shared understanding of its general sphere of application.[94] Instead, it rejects the perceived facts of a situation, which invoke the norm as a standard of behavior and thus assumes that norm conflict in the particular situation can be interpreted away. The government has to argue that the "wrong" conclusions have been drawn from the interpretation of the situation and that, in fact, only one of the two norms presents a legitimate standard for response to the crisis.[95] In order for conflict denial to be effective as a response strategy, the government has to provide a powerful counternarrative of the situation, which combats expectations toward compliance with a competing norm. To do so, the government needs persuasive power. Since it does not aim to impact the behavior of others, no normative leadership and thus

Table 1. Ideal-type responses to norm conflict

	Strategy	Necessary type of power resources of government	Intention of influencing behavior of others	Certainty regarding future expectation
Domestic & international expectations compatible	**Prioritization**	None	None	High
Domestic & international expectations incompatible	**General norm replacement**	Persuasive & soft power	Yes	High
	Strategic norm replacement	Persuasive power	None	High
	Norm reconciliation	Some persuasive & some soft power	Yes	High
	Conflict denial	Persuasive Power	None	Low

Source: Author's compilation

soft power is needed. The five possible responses to norm conflict are summarized in table 1. Bear in mind that over time, as expectations and their perceived strengths might change, governments can alter their strategy.

METHODOLOGY

This book qualifies as a comparative case study across both space and time. In analyzing the responses of three Southeast Asian states to three situations of gross human rights violations in Myanmar between 2007 and 2012, in which the norms of extraterritorial human rights protection and noninterference in internal affairs both applied, it aims to illustrate and refine the deductively derived theoretical propositions and response categories outlined earlier in this chapter. In doing so, this study is an iterative exercise in theory building. It is neither entirely deductive nor inductive in its approach but combines theoretical guidance with real-world explanatory power.[96]

Southeast Asia as a regional setting was selected as an "extreme case" of norm conflict.[97] The contradiction between the affirmation of universal human rights and the reaffirmation of state sovereignty has been a recurring

Table 2. Conceptualization of noninterference in ASEAN

Dimensions of noninterference	Indicators of violation
1. No critique of governments	– Negative comments regarding domestic events in another ASEAN member state – Expressing concern about a situation in another ASEAN member state – Making unrequested recommendations – Pressuring another ASEAN government – Threatening another ASEAN government
2. Critique of others' interference	– Failure to condemn an illegitimate act of interference by a member state
3. No support for rebel groups	– Invitation and reception of opposition groups from other ASEAN member states – Recognition of rebel groups – Financial and material support of rebels or opposition groups – Provision of sanctuary to rebels
4. Supporting counterinsurgencies	– Questioning an ASEAN member state's sovereignty or territorial integrity – Refusing to provide financial and material assistance for counter-insurgency measures – Refusing to mediate if requested

Source: Author's compilation based on Amitav Acharya, *Regionalism and Multilateralism: Essays on Cooperative Security in the Asia-Pacific* (Singapore: Times Academic Press, 2002).

point of contention in international affairs and has been particularly pronounced in Southeast Asia.[98] This is owed to ASEAN's conjoint strict interpretation of the noninterference norm. While in many other regions and organizations there are various levels of noninterference, within ASEAN the principle rules out any form of interference, including unsolicited comments, recommendations, and verbal condemnations.[99] Where even verbal comments are ruled out as a legitimate means of expressing discontent in situations of human rights violations, the conflict between extraterritorial human rights protection and noninterference becomes very difficult to "interpret away." Table 2 summarizes the four dimensions of noninterference as understood in ASEAN.[100]

Noninterference as understood within ASEAN therefore entails a commitment to not publicly embarrass another member state by commenting on its internal affairs. Open discussion of a member state's internal affairs and involvement of a third party only become possible by invitation from the conflicting parties.[101] Although the conflict between extraterritorial human rights protection and noninterference is relatively frequent in the region, gross human rights violations that endanger the life and liberty of domestic populations are still a matter of concern in various member states.

In choosing case-study countries for the study of response to norm conflict, only those ASEAN members that experience the conflict between the norms of extraterritorial human rights protection and noninterference in internal affairs in their foreign policies are deemed suitable. I treat democratization as a proxy for a greater concern for human rights among those in power in relation to their nationals as well as strangers.[102] Numerous studies have shown that democratization leads to a stronger emphasis on human rights protection and promotion in the states' respective foreign policies.[103] On the basis of insights from the Universal Periodic Review, Heupel shows that in fact most states care (to some extent) about their extraterritorial human rights obligations, thereby becoming more closely aligned with the universal nature of human rights.[104] From the universe of ASEAN's more democratically advanced member states, Indonesia, Thailand, and Malaysia have been chosen as the "most different cases."[105] They are most likely to experience differences in the expectation structure for norm compliance and in the power resources available. As such they are suitable to illustrate different categories of response to norm conflict.

Finally, three situations of norm conflict between human rights protection and promotion and noninterference in internal affairs were chosen to identify recognizable behavioral patterns over time. Within the Southeast Asian region, Myanmar has been the prime offender of human rights both in terms of the number and seriousness of violations in the past. As a consequence, the comparison of state responses to norm conflict undertaken in this book concentrates upon three instances of gross human rights violations in Myanmar. They include the Saffron Revolution in 2007, Cyclone Nargis in 2008, and the Rakhine Riots in 2012 that later evolved into the ongoing Rohingya Crisis. In all three cases the right to life and liberty of individuals was severely violated by Myanmarese state forces. The three instances of human rights violation in Myanmar will be introduced briefly in the following. This summary provides the backdrop to the three case-study chapters, which will each discuss the state response to norm conflict in one of three ASEAN countries.

The first within-case looks at the Saffron Revolution of 2007. On 15 August the Myanmarese government unexpectedly announced the removal of subsidies on fuel and natural gas. Following the 500 percent increase of commodity prices, nonviolent street protests commenced in Yangon.[106] In the following weeks, small groups of protesters demonstrated almost every day in various parts of the country. Early on in the protests, Amnesty International (Amnesty) reported beatings and intimidation by enforcement agencies of the State Peace and Development Council (SPDC). By the end of August, more than one hundred people had been confined, including many officials of the opposition National League for Democracy (NLD).[107] The peaceful marches soon went beyond the initial price protests, reflecting people's built-up anger and demand for political reform.[108] They reached a turning point on 5 September, when a group of Buddhist monks marched in Pakokku, a town in Central Myanmar. The army intervened, beating monks and bystanders with bamboo sticks. Security forces raided at least 130 monasteries in Mandalay, and hundreds of monks were disrobed and arrested. Some of them were sentenced to long prison terms.[109] In the following weeks the demonstrations exploded in size to an estimated 150,000 people shouting slogans for the release of Aung San Suu Kyi, who had been under house arrest since 1989.[110] The government reacted brutally. On 26 September, some one thousand people were detained. The army beat down unarmed demonstrators and initiated mass arbitrary arrests and shootings.[111] UN Human Rights Council's special rapporteur Paulo Sérgio Pinheiro said that independent sources had reported that thirty to forty monks and fifty to seventy civilians had been killed during the crackdown.[112] He later put the final, confirmed death toll at thirty-one.[113]

As a second case of gross human rights violations, Cyclone Nargis was chosen. Although the Cyclone Nargis case initially started as a humanitarian crisis, transnational human rights organizations agree that over time it quickly evolved into a case of widespread human rights violations. Referring to the UN Guiding Principles on International Displacement, Human Rights Watch (HRW) argued that by "deliberately blocking life-sustaining aid," the government of Myanmar had violated the human rights of its citizens to life, food, and health.[114] In May 2008, Myanmar was hit by tropical Cyclone Nargis, which was the worst natural disaster in the recorded history of the country. Making landfall on 2 May, the storm surge swept through the densely populated Irrawaddy Delta, causing catastrophic destruction. The cyclone destroyed entire villages, leaving hundreds of thousands of survivors without food and shelter.[115] It severely affected about 2.4 million people, with about 140,000 killed or missing and more than one million people displaced.[116] Instead of focusing on the disaster and relieving the human suffering, the government pursued its plans to have a constitutional referendum scheduled for 10 May 2008.[117] It denied the United Nations' request to waive visas for relief workers assembled in Bangkok in order to allow them to swiftly start their work in the affected areas. Foreign aid teams had to negotiate with the regime to get access, which barred the UN and most Western disaster assessment teams from entering the country.[118] Myanmar's Foreign Ministry insisted that the government would deliver international aid "with its own labor."[119] The first two planes dispatched by the UN, carrying high-energy biscuits, medicine, and other supplies, had to wait for two days while the organization negotiated with the junta to allow the material into the country.[120] As a result of the junta's isolationism, even seven weeks after the cyclone hit Myanmar, only 1.3 million of an estimated 2.4 million people affected had been reached by humanitarian agencies.[121]

In the final within-case, the study assessed state response to the Rakhine Riots of 2012. Three years after the cyclone, a now nominally civilian, but still heavily military-controlled, Myanmarese government was once again in the international limelight as violence erupted between the Buddhist and Muslim communities in the impoverished Rakhine State.[122] The violence had commenced in early June 2012 after reports spread on 28 May 2012 that a Buddhist woman had been raped and killed by three Muslim men. On 3 June a large group of Buddhist villagers stopped a bus and brutally killed ten Muslims, which caused thousands of Rohingya to riot. In return, Buddhist mobs burned down the homes of up to ten thousand Rohingya and non-Rohingya Muslims.[123] Local police and soldiers either stood by and passively watched the killings or became actively involved in the conflict through mass arrests and arbitrary violence.[124] As Human Rights Watch reported, police and military forces "opened fire on Rohingya with live ammunition."[125] On 10 June 2012 the government of Myanmar declared a state of emergency in its western province.[126] In instigating martial law, which gave the administration control of the region, it essentially handed over control to the military, which had a history of extreme brutality in its treatment of the Muslim minority in Rakhine.[127] After what appeared to be a brief cease-fire, violence recommenced in October 2012.[128] According to an official statement issued by the Myanmarese government in May 2013, the total number of casualties since June 2012 comprised 211, among them 152 "Bengalis," as the Rohingya are officially called in Myanmar.[129] Human rights organizations such as HRW considered these numbers to be grossly underestimated, with unofficial calculations ranging between 300 and 650.[130] Moreover, the UN high commissioner for refugees assumed that up to 140,000 Rohingya have been displaced since the outbreak of the riots, many of whom remain in displacement camps today.[131]

To complete the theoretical and methodological chapter, this section outlines the research methods used in this book. To uncover the motivational forces that determined the state responses to norm conflict, I relied on process tracing as a method. Process tracing is valuable in "carefully accumulating observations across time as well as space,"[132] and thereby tracing "the links between possible causes and observed outcomes."[133] For the purposes of this book, process tracing was used to carefully map the governments' desire to minimize the social costs of violating one norm and prioritizing the other. This included demonstrating a concern for domestic legitimacy and international reputation to explain the effect of domestic, regional, and international expectations for norm compliance on state responses to norm conflict.[134] In order to successfully trace a process, a large array of qualitative data needs to be gathered. For this purpose I drew on a wide variety of primary and secondary sources. The bulk of the data was collected with the help of a qualitative content analysis of the international, regional, and local media coverage of the events. It was complemented with published speeches and statements by key actors in the foreign policy realm and human rights sector, as well as seventy interviews with elite actors conducted in the region. The interviewees were chosen based on their ability to provide additional insights into the government's response to norm conflict, given their direct or indirect involvement in the decision-making process; their professional knowledge of the subject matter; and/or their own research activities. Asking questions to key foreign policy actors in the region proved particularly important in understanding their individual motivations and learning about events in ASEAN's often closed-doors negotiations.[135] In doing so, the research tried to compensate for the fact that important negotiations in ASEAN often lack an accompanying body of documentation.[136]

2

Commitment to the Norms

This chapter establishes the conflicting pull of human rights protection and promotion and noninterference as action-guiding forces for the Indonesian, Thai, and Malaysian governments in cases of extraterritorial human rights violations. This is not to say that noninterference has been observed absolutely in the past by Southeast Asian countries, or that the entire repository of human rights norms has been fully internalized within the three states.[1] Instead, the chapter shows that the governments of Indonesia, Thailand, and Malaysia have expressed a credible commitment to both norms that arguably creates legitimate expectations for compliance at the domestic, regional, and international levels in situations of norm conflict. Within the discipline norm commitment has traditionally been measured on a rather superficial level. Constructivist scholars have mostly focused on a state's acceptance of an internationally institutionalized norm through processes of formal adoption such as treaty ratification.[2] Once governments have signed and ratified treaties, the task of IR scholarship has implicitly been understood to be complete. However, by focusing on formal norm adoption only, constructivism can say relatively little about the actual level of commitment to the norm, which could fall anywhere on a spectrum from mere rhetoric to a deeply internalized belief in the appropriateness of the norm.

Among the first to criticize this shortcoming, Betts and Orchard have highlighted an "institutionalization-implementation gap," according to which the same levels of institutionalization of a given norm across states can manifest in radically different outcomes in terms of state practice.[3] In order to better account for the variation seen in how the same norms play out in practice, they focus on the domestic process of norm implementation. In showing how norms translate into domestic law through implementation, they make an important first step toward establishing the levels of actual norm commitment exhibited by a state and its government. Yet it is not enough to show how international norms translate into national law without also analyzing government efforts to comply with those laws. Without their actual enforcement, commitment to norms remains relatively hollow.

From the perspective of studying norm conflict, understanding the levels of "real" commitment to a norm matters first and foremost because it determines whether a state actually experiences a norm conflict. Although a norm conflict can exist on paper, where governments have adopted and ratified conflicting norms, it only manifests in decision-making and creates a dilemma if those in power actually believe in the conflicting norms and are expected by others at the domestic and international levels to comply with their normative directives. In order to establish a government's commitment to a norm on a deeper level than just formal norm adoption, this chapter suggests a threefold measure of norm commitment. Building on Betts and Orchard's emphasis on domestic processes, while going beyond their focus on norm implementation, I emphasize *norm adoption, norm implementation,* and *norm compliance.* I define formal norm adoption as an act that follows the institutionalization of a norm at the international level.[4] Through the act of ratification, norm adoption indicates the expression by a state of its consent to be bound and held accountable to the provisions of an international norm. Norm implementation in turn encompasses the steps taken to introduce a norm's obligations into formal legal and policy mechanisms within a state.[5] Hence it requires an investigation into how the norm's obligations have been incorporated into national law. Indicators of implementation include changes in public policy and the establishment of institutions to preserve and further particular norms. In the context of human rights norms, this could include, for example, the adoption or amendment of a bill of rights or of measures to strengthen the independence of the judiciary, or the establishment of a National Human Rights Commission.[6] Yet measuring commitment is not complete without also examining compliance with the norm in practice and discourse. The threefold measure of adoption, implementation, and compliance not only establishes commitment to a norm on a deeper level than usually practiced within the discipline, but it also allows one to determine differences in the degree of internalization of noninterference and human rights protection. In the final part of the chapter, commitment to the two conflicting norms in Indonesia, Thailand, and Malaysia will be analyzed, starting with the norm of noninterference and followed by the norm of human rights protection and promotion.

THE COMMITMENT TO NONINTERFERENCE

International Adoption of Nonintervention

Although the idea is often expressed that noninterference as a principle is peculiar to ASEAN, the norm has been influential for much longer and is internationally known as nonintervention.[7] Sovereign equality and nonintervention have underpinned the system of interstate relations since the Treaty of Westphalia in 1648.[8] As Western constructs that predated statehood in many regions of the world, the norms already governed the international system when Southeast Asian states gained independence in the twentieth century.[9] Following the horrors of the Second World War, they were enshrined in the United Nations Charter to govern interstate relations. In acquiring UN membership following their independence, "Third World" states not only accepted the dominant values of the Westphalian system as part of the terms of interstate relations, but their state elites also internalized them to a remarkable degree.[10] Along with the principle of state sovereignty, developing countries embraced the corollaries of sovereignty, namely rigidly demarcated and sacrosanct boundaries, mutual recognition as sovereign political entities, and nonintervention in the internal affairs of other states.[11] In doing so, the newly independent states tried to protect themselves from further Western interference after, in some cases, centuries of foreign intrusion, colonialization, and humiliation.[12] Internationally, developing states became the prime defenders of the noninterference norm and contributed to its further institutionalization in the international normative system.[13]

As members of non-Western groupings such as the Asian-African Conference and the Non-Aligned Movement (NAM), Indonesia and Malaysia, and to a lesser extent Thailand (which only joined NAM in 1993), were influential in the evolution of the norm. They helped reinvent the principal feature of what Acharya calls the "sovereignty game" by moving away from positive sovereignty, understood as the capacity to act independently through a balance of power system, toward negative sovereignty, defined as freedom from outside interference.[14] At the Bandung Conference sponsored by Indonesia in 1955, Asian and African states reiterated that respect for the sovereignty and territorial integrity, as well as abstention from interference in the internal affairs of another country, ought to be the central principles of good neighborly and friendly relations.[15] The Non-Aligned states produced similar documents at their summit meetings in Belgrade in 1961 and Cairo in 1964.[16] As part of a growing non-Western, developing-world majority in the General Assembly, Indonesia, Thailand, and Malaysia also contributed to the specification of the norm in numerous General Assembly Resolutions from the mid-1960s to the 1980s.[17]

The Birth of Noninterference as an ASEAN Norm

As an international principle, Southeast Asian leaders had already adopted nonintervention when ASEAN was founded in 1967. For ASEAN's five founding members (Malaysia, Indonesia, Thailand, Singapore, and the Philippines), nonintervention had become a central tenet to defend their newly found independence in a global system they perceived as hostile and biased to their disadvantage. With the exception of Thailand, all members of ASEAN have a long history of colonialism.[18] While interference in Thailand's case did not imply complete foreign domination, it still came at the cost of forced territorial transfers to Britain and France in the nineteenth century.[19] This legacy of foreign interference left Southeast Asian governments "with a strong distaste for coercive external influences" and the belief "that a state must have exclusive control over all that goes on within its borders."[20] Coupled with the geopolitical instability that characterized the region prior to ASEAN's establishment in 1967, it is thus of little surprise that upon ASEAN's formation its member states were primarily concerned with protecting their newly gained independence and statehood, instead of pooling it through integration.[21]

Accordingly, the Association emphasized diplomatic norms and practices designed to manage intergovernmental relations by discouraging member states from intruding into one another's domestic affairs. The Bangkok Declaration, the founding document of ASEAN, called Southeast Asian states to "ensure their stability and security from external interference in any form or manifestation."[22] Noninterference became a centerpiece of the "ASEAN Way," a decision-making process that favors a high degree of consultation and consensus as well as regional cooperation and interaction based on discreetness, informality, and nonconfrontational bargaining styles.²³ This set of social norms was perceived as a crucial standard for building trust among the member states and thereby overcoming regional foes.²⁴ As a "judge not and be not judged yourself" guarantee, noninterference allowed the member states to concentrate on nation-building without neighbors commenting on their internal affairs.²⁵ In fostering stability and trust among ASEAN's member states, the commitment to noninterference made cooperation possible, and the organization's success in maintaining stability within the region reinforced and solidified noninterference as a guiding feature of ASEAN interaction.²⁶ It became binding as an ASEAN principle with the ratification of the Treaty of Amity and Cooperation in 1976,²⁷ and effectively froze the existing national boundaries of 1976, officially recognizing state authority in contested territories such as East Timor, Irian (now Papua), Sabah, southern Thailand, and Mindanao.²⁸ Since the formation of ASEAN, the principle has been reaffirmed in all major documents, including the ASEAN Charter, which provides the organization with a legal status. It recognizes the "fundamental importance of amity and cooperation and the principles of sovereignty, equality, territorial integrity, non-interference, consensus and unity in diversity."²⁹ A reference to the principle can also be found in ASEAN's regional human rights mechanism, the ASEAN Intergovernmental Commission on Human Rights (AICHR).³⁰

The Implementation of Noninterference at Member-State Level

As a consequence of Southeast Asia's postcolonial identities and the continuous socialization of state elites into the noninterference norm within the ASEAN context, noninterference is well represented in the foreign and defense documents of Indonesia and Malaysia. It features slightly less prominently in Thailand. As a norm that was at least originally based on prudence and the desire to keep others outside their national jurisdictions, references to the safeguarding of *self-determination, national sovereignty,* and *territorial integrity* are treated as proxies for commitment to noninterference.

The principles of Indonesian foreign policy, described as "independent and active," were first summarized by Mohammad Hatta on 2 September 1948.³¹ They build on the Indonesian state philosophy, Pancasila, which stipulates the unity of Indonesia (Persatuan Indonesia). Under President Suharto, Indonesian foreign policy was further outlined, and the resolution setting out its main pillars is still used today as a policy document to guide the country's foreign relations.[32] The protection of the territorial integrity of Indonesia is stated as one of its three main objectives, next to support of national development and the preservation of internal and regional stability.[33] Following the downfall of Suharto's authoritarian New Order regime in 1998, the country's foreign policy was codified in Law No. 37/1999 on Foreign Relations. The preamble stresses that foreign relations are to be "conducted on the principles of equality, mutual respect, mutual advantage, and non-intervention in the domestic affairs of other nations."[34] As highlighted in Indonesia's Defense White Paper from 2008, the primary purpose of Indonesian foreign and defense policy is to protect its "vital interests," whose "upholding is absolute."[35] They include maintaining state sovereignty, territorial integrity, and the unitary state of the Republic of Indonesia as well as the safety of the entire nation from all forms of threat.[36] To realize these objectives, the white paper further states that "Indonesia will not allow any business that would interfere with the existence and integrity of the Unitary Republic of Indonesia."[37] In sum, the documents highlight a pronounced concern for the unity and territorial integrity of the Indonesian Republic, which interacts with the commitment to noninterference as a guarantor of its unity.

The norm of noninterference also features centrally in Malaysia's foreign policy documents. The Ministry of Foreign Affairs defines it as one of the fundamental principles that guide the country's relations with other states: "These [fundamental principles] refer to sovereign equality and mutual respect for territorial integrity, mutual non-aggression, non-interference in each other's internal affairs, peaceful settlement of disputes as well as mutual benefit in relations and peaceful co-existence."[38]

In formulating the prime objectives of Malaysian foreign policy, the Foreign Ministry, Wisma Putri, further states that "it is geared towards promoting a peaceful regional and international environment, which would give Malaysia space to achieve all its national objectives without disruption of external threats."[39] It highlights that "Malaysia has repeatedly stressed the importance of adhering to the especially important principle of non-interference in internal affairs."[40] In line with this, the Strategic Plan 2009–2015 (and revised Strategic Plan 2011–2015) emphasizes the importance of "safeguarding and protecting national sovereignty in the international arena" by presenting it as the first objective of Malaysian foreign policy.[41] Moreover, it reiterates that the guiding principles of Malaysia's foreign policy are, first, protection of Malaysia's sovereignty and territorial integrity, and second, adherence to noninterference in the internal affairs of other countries.[42] In the same manner, the country's National Defense Policy is geared toward defending "Malaysia's sovereignty, territorial integrity and economic prosperity."[43]

In comparison, the principle of noninterference features less prominently in Thailand's foreign policy documents, which might reflect the fact that the country has never formally been colonized. Thailand's national foreign policy is outlined under Article 77 of the 2007 constitution. While noninterference is not directly mentioned, the constitution states that "the state shall protect and uphold the institution of monarchy, the independence, sovereignty and integrity of the territorial jurisdiction of the state."[44] Further direct references to national sovereignty and territorial integrity can be found in the National Defense Policy sections of the Policy Statements of the Council of Ministers. The Policy Statement of 2008 states that the objective of national defense is to "strengthen and develop the national defence capability in safeguarding the independence, sovereignty and territorial integrity of the state."[45] Since norm commitment is incomplete without actual efforts to comply with the norm, the following section will review the ASEAN practice of noninterference as an important factor in shaping regional expectations for compliance with the norm.

Compliance with Noninterference in ASEAN Practice

Since the foundation of ASEAN, its elites, especially in the foreign policy sphere, have been continuously socialized into the "ASEAN Way" as part of their daily interactions. As a norm that regulates interstate relations, expectations for compliance with noninterference have been frequently articulated either by individual member states or the grouping as a whole. Acharya therefore argues that over time noninterference has become part of the ASEAN identity. Indeed, there is a wide consensus among scholars working on Southeast Asia that ASEAN nations have generally stuck to the noninterference principle.[46] Collectively, compliance with the norm is well documented in the organization's response to critical junctures such as Indonesia's annexation of East Timor in 1976, the Vietnamese invasion of Kampuchea (Cambodia) in 1978, and the UN humanitarian mission in East Timor in

1999.[47] Especially following the last round of ASEAN enlargement, which granted membership to the former Communist countries Vietnam, Myanmar, Laos, and Cambodia, a renewed emphasis has been put on the norm. This is due to the fact that less developed new member states regularly invoke the norm but also because noninterference is believed to sustain ASEAN solidarity in an increasingly heterogeneous environment.[48]

It is against this backdrop that the norm was reaffirmed by the majority of the member states in 1998, when Thai foreign minister Surin Pitsuwan, following the Asian financial crisis in 1997, suggested a review of noninterference as practiced in the region.[49] In order to be able to properly respond to the reality of globalization and the increasing interdependence within the region, Pitsuwan argued that ASEAN members needed to be able to more closely coordinate their policies on trade, investment, and finance, as well as cross-border security problems.[50] To do so, Thailand suggested a loosening of ASEAN's rigid interpretation of noninterference and its replacement with "flexible engagement,"[51] which would allow ASEAN member states to discuss each other's domestic affairs openly, if these had impact outside their borders.[52] However, Pitsuwan's initiative was criticized by other ASEAN member states. They accused Thailand of "carrying a Western agenda" and "trying to echo the US' foreign policy objectives."[53] Surin Pitsuwan recalled: "My colleagues were not willing to concede. It was the late foreign minister of Indonesia, Ali Alatas, who said 'I know where you are coming from Surin, but the phrase sounds a bit aggressive. Let us say from now on we will do enhanced interaction.' So the phrase enhanced interaction was somehow adopted—not formally—but it was used in order to avoid the complete rejection of the approach, thereby showing the world that we do evolve and transform."[54]

Accepted as a compromise, in practice "enhanced interaction" meant a continuity of the "ASEAN Way" and the regional noninterference policy. In view of the strong resistance to Pitsuwan's proposal, foreign ministers Shunmugam Jayakumar of Singapore and Abdullah Badawi of Malaysia praised the decision as the reaffirmation of a time-tested principle.[55]

However, this is not to say that compliance with the norm has always been absolute. As Tan aptly puts it, the "ASEAN Way," with its emphasis on noninterference, has not always prevented individual member states from "sabre rattling and unfriendly posturing in bilateral disputes."[56] But these instances of occasionally stretching or even breaching the norm have generally become immediate subjects of complaint, highlighting the common expectation that noninterference ought to be respected among member states. Actual and perceived violations of the norm usually led to unfriendly diplomatic exchanges, as a result of which apologies had to be made.[57] Moreover, outright breaches of the norm have generally been perceived as surprising and hence are seen as exceptions to the rule.[58] The continued commitment to the norm of noninterference is especially visible in discourse as a form of compliance, which will be addressed in the following.

Defending Noninterference Internationally

Despite occasional violations of the norm, Indonesia, Malaysia, and Thailand continue to defend noninterference and criticize the violation of Westphalian norms internationally. Indonesia was a staunch supporter of noninterference within the region and internationally during the period of its authoritarian New Order regime. Although it started to emphasize democratic values, including human rights protection, more frequently following its democratic transition in 1998, the importance given to Westphalian values, such as nonintervention, in international forums has not diminished. In 2003, Indonesia declared that the United Nations was still "bearing witness to a world beset by terror, civil wars, armed conflicts and violence, acts of aggression and interference in the internal affairs of states."[59] Following the Russo-Georgian War in 2008, Indonesia expressed its "great concern" in view of recent infringements of the principle of the territorial integrity and political independence of states. The conflict had led to the secession of part of a state and involved a major power:[60] "It is of the greatest importance to Indonesia and, I believe, to many developing countries that those recent cases do not set an ill-advised and dangerous precedent. Developing countries in the midst of nation-building and state-building would be extremely vulnerable to such precedents. The danger is that it takes only one misstep to kill principles that have been enshrined in the Charter of the United Nations, such as the principle of the sovereignty and territorial integrity of states."[61]

Indonesian president Susilo Bambang Yudhoyono concluded his speech at the UN General Assembly debate in 2008 by stating that "the sovereignty of states must be preserved if there is to be a democratic spirit in international relations."[62] When the South China Sea conflict once again flared in the region and reached the top of the regional agenda in 2012, Yudhoyono described ASEAN's approach to managing the territorial and sovereignty disputes as one of "restraint and confidence-building" in line with the long-cherished "ASEAN Way."[63]

Similar to Indonesia, Malaysia has long stressed the importance of noninterference internationally. This did not change after the retirement of Prime Minister Mahathir Mohamad in 2003 and the opening of greater political space under Prime Minister Abdullah Badawi. That same year, Malaysia emphasized at the UN General Assembly that there was much for which small nations like itself had to be grateful: "From being the colonies of the Europeans we are now independent and we are granted membership of the United Nations with the right to speak. As independent nations, we believe that we have a right to manage our internal affairs ourselves without foreign interference."[64]

Commenting on the need for reform of the UN as a world body, Malaysia declared in the following year that these changes had to take place "without sacrificing certain immutable principles, such as sovereign equality, non-interference in the domestic affairs of states, peaceful settlement of disputes and respect for international law."[65] It further highlighted that for Malaysia, as a small country, the United Nations was a crucial guarantor of the sanctity of its existence as a sovereign nation.[66] Along similar lines, Malaysia therefore criticized in 2007 "the repeated use of force by the powerful over the weak to secure strategic or territorial gains," describing those interferences as "wars of control and domination."[67] In explicitly referring to the Iraq War of 2003, Malaysia stressed that it was the international community's clear responsibility not only to assist the people of Iraq to achieve peace and stability but also to guarantee that the unity of Iraq as a nation was preserved and the territorial integrity of Iraq as a state was not compromised.[68] Similar to Indonesia, it expressed its concern in 2008 over "recent attempts of powerful member states to question the national law of countries and the administration of justice under those laws."[69] In his UN General Assembly speech, Malaysian prime minister Badawi stated the need to reemphasize that no state has the right to meddle in the conduct of the internal affairs of other countries.[70]

In comparison to Indonesian and Malaysian reaffirmations of Westphalian norms, Thailand's support for nonintervention internationally has been less pronounced. It was especially in regard to actual conflicts, such as the situation in Iraq, that Thailand prioritized the upholding of Westphalian norms. In 2003 it declared its support for the UN in "paving the way for the stability, security and sovereignty of Iraq."[71] Similarly, Thailand refused to define any of its domestic crises as cases that legitimized regional or international interference. In 2004, Prime Minister Thaksin Shinawatra responded angrily to international scrutiny of his crackdown on Islamic radicals in the southernmost provinces bordering Malaysia. When the UN high commissioner for human rights in Geneva asked Thailand to investigate the killings, citing international treaties that require security forces "to refrain from using force exceeding that strictly required by the exigencies of the situation," Thaksin responded: "Don't intervene. Please leave us alone. It is my job and we can cope with this matter."[72] At the regional level, he threatened to walk out of an ASEAN summit in 2004 should the foreign ministers attempt to address the matter even if done behind closed doors.[73] The need to reaffirm Westphalian norms including nonintervention also became a matter of concern during Thailand's presidency of the Human Rights Council in 2011. In the context of its task of reviewing the methods of work and operation of the forum, Thailand stressed that "every government must find its own solutions and move at its own pace in a manner appropriate to its specific context and conditions."[74] For its part, the role of the international community was to support and promote constructive dialogue and engagement, while respecting state sovereignty, territorial integrity, and the will of the people.[75]

Following this review of the commitment to the noninterference norm in the respective three countries and the highlighting of differences in the degree of internalization, the second part of this chapter will assess Indonesia, Thailand, and Malaysia's commitment to human rights protection at the domestic and international levels.

COMMITMENT TO HUMAN RIGHTS PROTECTION AND PROMOTION

International Adoption of Human Rights

In contrast to the Westphalian principles of sovereignty and noninterference, human rights as a matter of state concern is a much more recent development within the individual ASEAN member states and within the region as a whole.[76] Having experienced colonialism, ASEAN governments "believed that human rights were merely [another] tool of Western imperialism."[77] This is partly owing to the fact that at the time when universal human rights were first spelled out as "a common standard of achievement for all peoples and nations" in the Universal Declaration of Human Rights (UDHR) in 1948, Southeast Asian states were not well represented at the UN. With the exception of Thailand (Siam) and the Philippines, they had not yet become UN members. But even membership did not guarantee a say in the deliberations. As poor, small, and underdeveloped nations, their voices were essentially muted on matters other than decolonization and the self-determination of non-Western nations.[78] Western powers, by contrast, were in a central position to advance their ideas of human rights, which were therefore initially perceived as a Western concept, applicable first and foremost to Western societies.[79] The fact that other regions of the world were not given the chance to influence the deliberations leading to the UDHR has since then repeatedly been a matter of contention in the relations between the West and the Global South.[80] It was prominently raised during the "Asian values" debate of the 1990s, when Malaysia called for a review of the UDHR. Supported by China, Indonesia, and the Philippines, it claimed that the Declaration was outdated and unrepresentative of the larger global community, having been drafted by superpowers when a much smaller number of states existed.[81] Criticizing the individualism that underpinned the Western liberal democratic model and global agenda, former Malaysian prime minister Mahathir Mohamad stipulated a rights concept that centered on communitarian ideals of harmony and consensus.[82] The popularity of the concept, however, waned in the aftermath of the Asian financial crisis, when it became evident that the region lacked any comprehensive institutional mechanisms to deal with crises. Now, very few government officials within the region would regard human rights as being completely outside their national agenda, even if the emphasis put on economic, social, and cultural rights often still supersedes political and civil rights.[83] This is especially true for ASEAN's more liberal and democratically advanced societies, where a wide range of human rights are constitutionally guaranteed. Yet the general acceptance of the UDHR and recognition of the state's responsibility to uphold these rights within its jurisdiction has not translated into an equal endorsement of the accompanying international human rights treaties. While Indonesia and Thailand have ratified almost all of the nine core international human rights treaties, Malaysia lags behind, having ratified only three.[84]

Regional Implementation of Human Rights

Until the 1990s, human rights agendas were largely absent in ASEAN diplomacy.[85] The first time that the question of human rights was addressed was at the 1993 ASEAN Ministerial Meeting in Singapore. The joint communiqué "reaffirmed ASEAN's commitment to and respect for human rights and fundamental freedoms as set out in the Vienna Declaration."[86] Practically, however, the document had little impact on member states' behavior, which mostly continued to subordinate human rights protection to considerations of national sovereignty, territorial integrity, and noninterference.[87] It was only with the democratic transition of some ASEAN states—particularly Indonesia—that universal human rights started to matter as a subject of debate in Southeast Asia. In the following decade, officials from Indonesia, in tandem with their counterparts from the Philippines and Thailand, were active in pushing for change on the matter of human rights in the region.[88] With the adoption of the ASEAN Charter in 2007 and its ratification by member states in the following year, democratic norms, including the promotion and protection of universal human rights, entered the body of shared norms within the Association. The Charter expressly requires the member states to commit themselves to the protection of these values.[89] It also established the ASEAN Intergovernmental Commission on Human Rights (AICHR), which started its work in 2009.[90] AICHR was followed by the adoption of an ASEAN Human Rights Declaration in 2012. The Declaration further details ASEAN nations' commitment to human rights and acknowledges their endorsement of the main international human rights instruments.[91] The ASEAN Human Rights Declaration stands as the first ever Southeast Asian Charter of human rights and contains commitments not only to economic, cultural, and social rights but also to far more contentious civil and political rights.[92] Even if international human rights standards are far from being met in many ASEAN countries, the regional human rights instruments signal that "human rights are indeed legitimate and right for Asian countries" and a matter of regional concern.[93]

Domestic Implementation of Human Rights

In order to demonstrate that the commitment to human rights within their own jurisdictions is not merely superficial but has been followed up by legal efforts to enshrine these rights in national laws, the following sections briefly outline the implementation of human rights and their enforcement in Indonesia, Thailand, and Malaysia. This shows that the institutional safeguards and the range of constitutionally guaranteed rights still vary across the three countries.

In the wake of its democratic transformation, following the downfall of former president Suharto in 1998, Indonesia has considerably adjusted its national human rights protections to be more in line with international human rights standards. Amendments to the constitution were introduced in a four-stage process (1999, 2000, 2001, 2002), most importantly adding ten entirely new human rights articles, which set forth the basic rights and obligations of Indonesian citizens. These constitutional safeguards stand at the apex of the hierarchy of all Indonesian legislation and take the form of a Bill of Rights closely modeled along the lines of the UDHR.[94] As Clarke (2003) argues, the amendments represent the first meaningful protection of human rights in Indonesia and stand for a "radical shift in Indonesia's constitutional philosophy from essentially authoritarian to more liberal-democratic model."[95] Thereby the constitutional coverage of protection is far-ranging and arguably more extensive than that of many developed countries.[96] Next to the rights guaranteed in the constitution, a complementary piece of legislation exists that further elaborates on Indonesia's human rights obligations.[97] The legal prosecution of violations is regulated by the Indonesian Penal Code and Special Human Rights Courts that can be convened to deal with cases of torture or crimes against humanity.[98] Next to these courts, the National Human Rights Commission (Komnas HAM) exists as a national accountability institution in relation to human rights protection. Following Indonesia's democratic transition, its mandate was considerably broadened to independently investigate human rights abuses.[99] Komnas HAM holds UN accreditation and even during the Suharto era fostered a reputation as "an independent, forthright and diligent national human rights institution" that often directly criticized government policies.[100] While Indonesia's human rights track record is far from perfect, in many areas the far-ranging shifts in Indonesia's legal human rights framework were accompanied by an "unprecedented level of substantive change in rights infrastructure and governance."[101] The post-Suharto government released political prisoners and trade unions multiplied, as the International Labour Organization Convention was not only enshrined in law but also applied in practice.¹⁰² Moreover, the institutional changes opened space in the decision-making process to a wide number of actors. Today the country has a diverse and vibrant media sector and civil society, including many effective, outspoken human rights groups.¹⁰³ Moreover, the judicial branch has shown its will to defend constitutionally guaranteed rights.¹⁰⁴

Thailand's path to democracy since the first elections were held in 1932 has not been smooth. It has been repeatedly interrupted by coups and lengthy periods of military rule.¹⁰⁵ While engagement with democracy and human rights has a much longer history than in other ASEAN states, it was not until the ratification of the so-called People's Constitution of 1997 that a juncture in terms of human rights protection was reached in Thailand. For the first time it introduced an extensive catalogue of rights. Following the 2006 military coup, the People's Constitution was replaced by the 2007 Constitution, which then comprised the primary source of human rights protection. It provided a large range of constitutional guarantees, including the right to life and liberty.¹⁰⁶ It has since then been replaced by a much less human rights–friendly document, enacted after the latest coup in 2014, which reinstalled a military regime in Thailand. To oversee the state's compliance with the human rights addressed in the constitution and to investigate possible violations, the Thai government in 1999 established a National Human Rights Commission (NHRC). It was a reaction to clashes between pro-democracy demonstrators and the military in May 1992 and came into force in June 2001.¹⁰⁷ Its main task is "to examine and report on the commission or omission of acts which violate human rights or which do not comply with the obligations under international treaties to which Thailand is a party."¹⁰⁸ The 2007 Constitution additionally empowered the NHRC to take cases directly to court, in its own name and on behalf of those whose rights had been violated.¹⁰⁹ In a significant step underlining the Commission's independence at the time, the NHRC cooperated with the UN Human Rights Committee in undertaking a joint review of Thailand's compliance with the International Covenant on Civil and Political Rights.¹¹⁰ Prior to the military coup of 2014, Thailand had generally been viewed as nurturing a human rights–friendly environment. The constitutional guarantees for political participation allowed a vibrant civil society and free media to develop. Infringements of human rights were most often the result of violent political conflicts between the two polarized political camps, the so-called Red and Yellow Shirts, and clashes between Muslim insurgents and the Thai security forces in southern Thailand.[111] In 2006, following the military coup d'état, the interim government apologized for the violations previously committed by the state and announced a new counterinsurgency strategy in the wake of which the number of abuses committed by security forces dropped considerably.[112]

In contrast to Indonesia and Thailand, Malaysia has not ratified an extensive number of international human rights treaties, but its constitution nevertheless protects basic rights that mirror those in the UDHR. In Malaysia fundamental liberties are set out in Articles 5 to 13 of the constitution.[113] However, such rights are not absolute but subject to limitations. This primarily affects freedom of expression, association, and assembly, where derogations from the constitutional guarantees are permitted on the grounds of national security, public order, and morality.[114] The Malaysian government has continued to insist that Malaysia's multi-ethnic society is too fragile to sustain genuine freedom of assembly and expression or full due process rights for all suspects.[115] Nevertheless, the country did experience a number of human rights improvements during the period analyzed in this book. In 2007, the Criminal Procedure Code was amended to provide increased protection to people under arrest.[116] Among Malaysia's most problematic regulation was the Internal Security Act (ISA), which permitted long-term detention without trial. In September 2011 Prime Minister Seri Najib Tun Razak announced the government's intention to repeal the law. It was replaced by the Security Offences Act in 2012, which reduced the limit on initial detention without charge and required that a suspect be charged in court or released thereafter.[117] The Malaysian government has also taken steps to implement the rights of special groups, including the human rights of women, children, and people with disabilities, in line with the international human rights treaties it has ratified. To incorporate its international obligations into national law, Malaysia included gender equality in the constitution, and passed the Child Act in 2001 and the Persons with Disabilities Act in 2008. Malaysia also acknowledges the need for a human rights protection mechanism. The government therefore established the Malaysian Human Rights Commission (SUHAKAM) under the Human Rights Commission of Malaysia Act 1999, which began its work in April 2000. Its mandate includes the promotion of human rights education, advice on legislation and policy, and conducting of investigations.[118] Although the Commission has been criticized for its lack of independence, as members are appointed either by the king or on the recommendation of the prime minister, it has put forth a large number of human rights recommendations to the government and has openly expressed its concern over several laws. As Tan highlights, it has frequently released press statements and reports on human rights abuses such as punishment in schools, abuse of the ISA, and has called for a review of human trafficking laws. It has also investigated the long-standing problem of corruption and abuses within the Malaysian police force.[119] Although in practice human rights problems persist, especially in the area of civil and political rights, due to their constitutional limitations, Malaysia has experienced a noticeable liberalization of society following the retirement of Prime Minister Mahathir Mohamad in 2003. With the appointment of Abdullah Badawi as his successor, pressure on human rights groups and lawyers decreased considerably.[120] The clearest manifestation of this trend was the reversal of the judiciary's verdict on former deputy prime minister Anwar Ibrahim, which led to his release from prison.[121] Since then Malaysia has witnessed the growth of an active civil society. There is now a large number of public interest groups and NGOs that concentrate on human rights in Malaysia and that have established a public dialogue on the key values contained in the UDHR.[122]

While implementation of and compliance with human rights in national law are important parts of demonstrating credible commitment to the norm, focusing on the internalization of human rights at home is not enough to establish the norm conflict between noninterference and human rights protection in cases of human rights violations in foreign jurisdictions. The following section will therefore discuss how far domestic recognition of human rights protection extends to a concern for the rights of strangers in the region and beyond by examining references to the norm in the foreign policy statements of the three states.

From Domestic to Extraterritorial Human Rights Protection

Since the end of the Cold War, the discussion on human rights has shifted from being solely a domestic affair to being a matter of legitimate international concern.[123] One illustration of this development is the unanimous adoption of the UN World Summit Outcome Document in 2005, which establishes and endorses the terms of Responsibility to Protect (RtoP). Articles 138 and 139 of the Document claim that both national governments and the international community bear the responsibility for protecting populations from genocide, war crimes, crimes against humanity, and ethnic cleansing.[124] While it would be false to argue that ASEAN states have been enthusiastic about the initiative, Indonesia, Thailand, and Malaysia have all expressed support for the principle. Around the same time, ASEAN itself saw an impressive amount of human rights institution building.[125] The ASEAN Charter not only requires the member states to commit themselves to the protection of these values, but it also gives the organization a role in their protection and promotion. It states that, among others, "the purposes of ASEAN are ... to strengthen democracy, enhance good governance, and the rule of law, and to promote and protect human rights and fundamental freedoms."[126] A regional concern for human rights protection and promotion has also been reflected in the advocacy of some member states, leading to the establishment of the AICHR, which started its work in 2009.[127] Together with the ASEAN Human Rights Declaration, it "depicts the ultimate expression of concern for human rights" in Southeast Asia and provides an important link between domestic and regional human rights issues.[128] All three case-study countries have been supportive of the human rights clause in the ASEAN Charter and the establishment of AICHR. In the following section their individual positions on human rights protection outside their own domestic jurisdictions will be analyzed.

Following its democratic transition, Indonesia also started to internationally act upon its democratic values.[129] Although commitment to human rights protection on a regional or global scale is not explicitly spelled out in the country's national laws, the laws state that Indonesia's foreign policy shall be based on a "just and civilized humanity" and "democracy promotion."[130] The mainstreaming of democracy and human rights as part of the country's foreign policy has been more explicitly articulated as part of the Foreign Ministry's Strategic Plan 2010–2014, which identifies "realizing the advancement and protection of human rights" as an objective.[131] Regionally, democracy and human rights became a foreign policy focus in 2003, when Indonesia assumed the ASEAN chairmanship.[132] President Megawati's administration, spearheaded by Foreign Minister Hassan Wirajuda, pushed the principles in the region via the concept of the ASEAN Political-Security Community.[133] The idea was to supplement the already existing economic cooperation with a political pillar to push democratization in the region. Believing that "democracy works best in a democratic environment," former foreign minister Hassan Wirajuda tried to actively foster the growth of democratic values in Indonesia's neighborhood.[134] This goal was furthered particularly during President Susilo Bambang Yudhoyono's two consecutive terms (2004–14). In his first foreign policy speech given to the Indonesian Council on World Affairs in 2005, Yudhoyono outlined Indonesia's responsibilities as the world's third-largest democracy.[135] He stressed that in its upcoming function as chair of the reformed Human Rights Commission, Indonesia would strive to do as much as it could to advance "all human rights all over the world."[136] Within its own region, it was Indonesia's intention to help ASEAN develop and nurture common values, particularly those that reflected due reverence for human dignity and freedom. "The cause of democracy and human rights will thereby be advanced in this part of the world," Yudhoyono proclaimed.[137] Accordingly, the Indonesian Foreign Ministry campaigned for the inclusion of democratic norms, including good governance, the rule of law, and protection and promotion of human rights and fundamental freedoms in the ASEAN Charter and the establishment of an ASEAN human rights body in line with international standards.[138] Looking back at the period, Yudhoyono recalled that Indonesia's hard work behind the Charter had been fueled by its determination to ensure that its members were committed to democracy and democratization, and to the promotion and protection of human rights.[139] "In our time, we in ASEAN can no longer afford to be allergic to democracy and human rights," he said.[140]

Yudhoyono continued to emphasize the importance of human rights promotion and protection within the region throughout his tenure as president. In a keynote speech delivered to the ASEAN Forum in 2007, he stressed that the concept of security had greatly broadened, no longer just implying defense of the state but extending to what is called "human security": "This means that we have a common obligation to protect the physical integrity and the dignity of the human being, whether alone or part of a group, against all attackers. The human being must be protected even when—perhaps especially when—the assailant is the state, which is supposed to protect him. And if we are going to have an ASEAN that is a 'community of caring societies' then it must care not only about the livelihood and the social amenities but also about the fundamental rights of the human being."[141]

To promote an environment in Asia that fostered respect for human rights, in 2008 Indonesia launched the Bali Democracy Forum to establish a central point where mainly Asian countries could share their experiences of democracy building and human rights protection.[142] As ASEAN chair in 2011, Indonesia reiterated its commitment to human rights protection. The foreign minister at the time, Marty Natalegawa, stressed that during its chairmanship Indonesia would continue to foster an ASEAN community "that serves as the vanguard for the promotion of democratic values, human rights and tolerance at the global level."[143] Indonesia also actively participated in the international human rights framework, successfully making its first bid for membership on the UN Human Rights Council in 2006. It argued that its candidacy was a "reflection of its strong commitment to the promotion and protection of Human Rights."[144] Its membership has since then been renewed several times.

As Thailand is one of the United States' prime allies in the Southeast Asian region, Thai technocrats and politicians have long been seen to practice a more or less liberal political stance.[145] As Lynch points out, successive generations of Thai elites have eagerly borrowed Western models to reorganize domestic governance arrangements.[146] Following the end of the Cold War and in response to the effects of the Asian financial crisis of 1997, this increasingly entailed the inclusion of human rights, not only domestically but also as part of the country's foreign policy. As a consequence, Thailand's foreign policy became one of the most liberal among developing countries, with the broadest appeal internationally.[147] The Democrat-led government under Chuan Leekpai in 1997 issued a seven-point foreign policy that emphasized the universal value of human rights and democracy, as well as good governance.[148] It was against this backdrop that Surin Pitsuwan, in his function as Thai foreign minister in 1998, suggested a review of ASEAN's noninterference norm. Defending the initiative against criticism from within the region, Thai commentators wrote that "Thailand cannot back down" as the initiative was about Thailand's determination to implement a "human and principled diplomacy and to enhance and expand ASEAN's reputation and its international leverage."[149] While successive governments have positioned their commitment to democracy and human rights protection less centrally in their foreign policies, policy statements still emphasize human security as a priority.[150] In his 2004 UN General Assembly speech, Foreign Minister Surakiart Sathirathai stressed that Thailand has long advocated a balanced development with "freedom from fear and freedom from want as the two inseparable prongs of human security."[151] The following year he reiterated that as chair of the Human Security Network, Thailand was pleased that a human-centered approach to security had been embraced as an integral part of the new collective security consensus.[152] The foreign policy section of the Policy Statement of 2006, moreover, explicitly mentions human rights. It reads that Thailand will "play a constructive role in the framework of the United Nations as well as other multilateral frameworks in the promotion of peace, democracy and human rights."[153] In its 2012 Annual Report, the Foreign Ministry reiterated that Thailand's foreign policy direction "has been based on cooperation with other countries in addressing new security challenges such as . . . human rights and democracy."[154] In line with its expressed commitment, Thailand acted as a strong promoter of human rights during the ASEAN Charter negotiations. Despite the domestic turmoil following the military coup in 2006, Thai negotiators maintained that ASEAN needed a human rights mechanism that could promote the principles of democracy, good governance, and human rights in the region.[155] In the wake of restructuring the organization, Thailand insisted that ASEAN had to become a more "rule-based" and "people-centered" organization, and membership had to carry with it both rights and obligations.[156] As the ASEAN chair in 2009, Prime Minister Abhisit Vejjajiva, furthermore, stressed that ASEAN needed to become a more sharing and caring society, ensuring that the human security needs of its people were met.[157] Following the establishment of the ASEAN Intergovernmental Commission on Human Rights, the Thai government appointed Sriprapha Petcharamesree, an experienced civil society leader, as the Thai representative and endowed her with an independent mandate.[158]

The final part of this section will look at human rights protection and promotion within Malaysia's foreign policy. In an important policy shift from Mahathir's "Asian values" approach, successive Malaysian governments have come to adopt a more open-minded attitude toward human rights, including in their foreign policies. Human rights for the first time became a matter of concern under Prime Minister Abdullah Badawi. Emphasizing a people-centered approach to domestic policymaking, he transferred those ideals into the foreign policy sphere. As a consequence, foreign policymaking under Badawi moved toward a policy in favor of human rights protection and good governance, especially in relation to ASEAN affairs and within the Muslim community.[159] In line with this, the Malaysian foreign minister insisted in 2004, at the Second East Asian

Forum in Kuala Lumpur, that the ASEAN security community perspective had to be expanded to include the new challenges faced by states in the region, including human rights issues.[160] When suggesting the concept of the ASEAN Charter in his capacity as ASEAN chair in 2005, Prime Minister Badawi therefore called for a bottom-up consultative process. ASEAN had to be transformed to become a more "people-centered" community, he argued.[161] At the ASEAN ministerial meeting in 2006, the prime minister went on to argue that "there must be adherence, by community members, to a common set of community values."[162] At the top of this list of values had to be the acceptance of good governance in ASEAN countries and societies. Moreover, member states had to be allowed to take a role in assistance when fellow member states faced humanitarian crises.[163] That same year, Malaysian foreign minister Syed Hamid Albar stated that "humanitarian intervention has become necessary with increased human security concerns, more so since globalization has made such issues borderless."[164] Albar stressed that the "protection of human life and the promotion of human dignity should not only be the preserve of domestic governments"; instead, "the international community too has a role and responsibility to play in this regard."[165] Accordingly, Malaysia backed Indonesia, Thailand, and the Philippines in the establishment of a regional human rights mechanism when negotiations came to a deadlock in 2007 between supporting and opposing member states.[166] Following the resignation of Prime Minister Badawi in 2009, the Foreign Ministry introduced a new strategic plan, which stated that protection and promotion of human rights will continue to be of concern for Malaysia's foreign policy.[167] It acknowledged that "as a result of globalization and free access to information, human rights and democracy have become prominent issues in global discourse."[168] Next to the maintenance of international peace and the tackling of security issues, the protection of human rights would therefore constitute one of Malaysia's interests in the international arena.[169]

In summary, this chapter has demonstrated a commitment to both noninterference and human rights protection in Indonesia, Thailand, and Malaysia while simultaneously highlighting differences in the degree of internalization of both norms. Unlike most traditional norm research within the discipline of international relations, which tends to equate a state's commitment to a norm with its adoption at the international level and subsequent treaty ratification, this chapter established norm commitment on a deeper level, including norm implementation and compliance. For research on norm conflict, the establishment of a credible commitment to both norms is necessary in order to demonstrate that a particular government actually perceives situations to which both norms apply as a norm conflict. Therefore, their commitment needs to go beyond rhetoric and involve an actual effort to adhere to the normative directives. In tracing the commitment to both norms, the chapter showed that noninterference evolved over the decades to become an integral part of the states' regional identity. As such, it can be expected to create a strong expectation for compliance among the ASEAN member states. In contrast, the commitment to human rights protection has been driven by a bottom-up process, following domestic demands for societal change. The analysis shows that the degree of internalization slightly differs between the states, with human rights protection and promotion being more thoroughly internalized in Indonesia and Thailand than Malaysia. The measures taken to protect and enforce human rights at the domestic level in tandem with references to human rights protection in the states' foreign policies represent an important source for international and domestic expectations regarding action on behalf of human rights within the region and beyond.

3

Norm Reconciliation in Indonesia

As the first of three case studies, this chapter assesses how the Indonesian government in practice responded to situations of norm conflict in its foreign policy. It analyzes the Indonesian response to three crises in Myanmar: the Saffron Revolution in 2007, Cyclone Nargis in 2008, and the Rakhine Riots in 2012. Each of these crises was internationally framed as a case of large-scale human rights violations, thereby pitting the behavioral standards inherent in the two norms against each other. This first section of the chapter systematically analyzes the government's response to the three instances of human rights violations in Myanmar. It shows that the Indonesian government at first complied with the human rights protection norm during the Saffron Revolution in 2007 but, later in the crisis, shifted to a policy of noninterference. It again prioritized human rights protection in the aftermath of Cyclone Nargis in 2008, but it complied with the noninterference norm during the Rakhine Riots in 2012. The second part of the chapter explains this response pattern as an attempt to reconcile the two norms in view of conflicting expectations for norm compliance and limited persuasive and soft power to convince others of a general norm replacement.

NORM FOLLOWING IN INDONESIA

The Saffron Revolution: From Human Rights Protection to Noninterference

Following a month of large-scale pro-democracy protests, on 26 September 2007 the military government of Myanmar violently cracked down on the demonstrating monks and civilians. The initial response of the Indonesian government to the junta's use of force against the protestors was critical and very outspoken. It openly condemned the state violence and individually as well as in concert with its ASEAN colleagues called for restraint. In commenting on the events unfolding in Myanmar and making a judgment on the appropriateness of the government's treatment of its citizens, Indonesian authorities violated the noninterference norm as interpreted in the ASEAN context and complied with the human rights protection norm. However, as the conflict progressed, the Indonesian government altered its stance and switched to a policy of noninterference.

In view of the state-orchestrated violence, Indonesian foreign minister Hassan Wirajuda stated as early as 25 September that "Indonesia urges Myanmar not to resort to coercive measures in handling the peaceful rallies."[1] He suggested that the latest developments in Myanmar proved that the so-called road map to democracy was at a standstill despite the junta's repeated promises of progress. Stressing that it was "premature to discuss the deployment of peace-keepers to Myanmar," Wirajuda instead suggested that "taking the junta to the UN Human Rights Council would be a good move."[2] The foreign minister expressed a preference for engagement and promised that the foreign ministers of ASEAN would table a debate on Myanmar to discuss the issue.[3] What followed was an uncharacteristically frank and critical ASEAN statement issued on 27 September 2007 at the sidelines of a UN General Assembly debate in New York. The ASEAN foreign ministers urged Myanmar's authorities to exercise restraint and find a political solution for national reconciliation without resorting to violence.[4] They collectively expressed their "revulsion to Myanmar Foreign Minister Nyan Win over reports that the demonstrations in Myanmar are being suppressed by violent force and that there has been a number of fatalities."[5] The collective ASEAN stance was strongly reaffirmed several days later by Indonesia's representative to the UN, Marty Natalegawa, who urged the authorities in Yangon to resume national reconciliation with all parties working toward peaceful transition to democracy and to release all political detainees, including Aung San Suu Kyi: "On the part of Myanmar itself we again urge the government to exercise restraint and to urgently work to substitute the climate of fear with the power of democratic persuasion and inclusive dialogue."[6] In addition to the collective action by ASEAN, the Indonesian Foreign Ministry sent a strong signal to the junta on 28 September, when ministry officials staged an act of solidarity with the protestors. Wearing red clothes, the color of the monks' robes, they gathered together and observed a period of silence in Jakarta.[7]

While the Indonesian government initially chose to favor the human rights protection norm by repeatedly condemning the violence and staging highly symbolic acts of support for the protestors, in the course of the conflict this stance changed and became more cautious. Moving away from directly criticizing the regime, on 6 October Indonesian foreign minister Wirajuda suggested the introduction of a transition period in which Myanmar's military could share power with a civilian leadership for five years, after which time the country could hold a democratic election. Building on Indonesia's experiences during its own democratization process, Wirajuda argued that the power-sharing arrangement might ease the "insecurity feelings the junta must be harboring."[8] In a meeting with UN special rapporteur Ibrahim Gambari on 18 October, Wirajuda expressed a concern about potential regime disintegration and state breakup. He stressed that in addition to human rights concerns, the anxieties of the regime had to be addressed.[9] Wirajuda's warning came shortly after the US ambassador to the UN, Zalmay Khaalilzad, had said it was "time to prepare for a transition" in Myanmar.[10] In line with Wirajuda's statement, the Indonesian defense minister, Juwono Sudarsono, cautioned the following day that "instant democracy in Myanmar could create another Iraq," by facilitating a power struggle between the country's ethnic minorities, many of which were still armed.[11] In line with its now more cautious stance, the Indonesian Foreign Ministry underlined that it had no plans to table the Myanmar issue at the UN during its presidency of the Security Council in November.[12]

It was only on the sidelines of the ASEAN summit that Indonesian president Susilo Bambang Yudhoyono addressed the issue again in a forty-minute private "heart-to-heart" talk with Myanmar's prime minister, Thein Sein. The *Jakarta Post* reported that during an informal "family dinner" on 19 November they discussed how reform could be introduced gradually to benefit Myanmar.[13] Even though Yudhoyono instructed Foreign Minister Wirajuda to follow up on the discussion with his Myanmarese counterpart, the Indonesian government effectively took no further steps to address the conflict.[14] Moreover, after the informal meeting, presidential spokesperson Dino Patti Djalal reiterated vis-à-vis the media the position that "reforms should not be applied by revolution" and that the "process of democracy must maintain Myanmar's territorial integrity."[15] The Indonesian government also emphasized the noninterference norm when backing Prime Minister Thein Sein's objection to a briefing with UN special envoy Gambari on the situation in Myanmar as part of the ASEAN summit.[16] Furthermore, at the end of the ASEAN summit, the Indonesian government stressed that it would not join other countries in imposing sanctions on Yangon in connection with the political and human rights situation in Myanmar.[17]

In sum, the Indonesian response to human rights violations during the Saffron Revolution shifted from initially favoring human rights protection, which involved a condemnation of the crackdown and the highly symbolic act of exhibiting sympathy with and support for the protestors, to a more cautious stance of noninterference.

Cyclone Nargis: Prioritizing Human Rights Protection

On 2 May 2008, Myanmar was hit by tropical Cyclone Nargis, which severely affected at least 1.5 million people, leaving them without shelter or access to food and medicine. Despite the destruction and the magnitude of human suffering, the junta refused to allow international relief workers to enter the country and to help deliver aid. Indonesia's individual response and the role it took within ASEAN to pressure the junta to open up to a coordinated relief effort proved to be in line with its commitment to the human rights protection norm.

Among the first countries to react following the cyclone, Indonesia announced on 6 May that it would donate aid worth US$1 million to Myanmar.[18] As presidential spokesperson Dino Patti Djalal stated, "The tragedy has reminded the President of the December 2004 tsunami in Aceh," and thus Indonesia immediately decided to offer help to Myanmar.[19] Addressing concerns regarding the junta's willingness to cooperate with the international community in the disaster relief efforts, Djalal emphasized that Indonesian president Yudhoyono would vigilantly monitor the situation on the ground and continuously request information from the government of Myanmar about the needs of the people.[20] In "requesting information" from Myanmar, the president effectively violated the terms of noninterference as defined within the ASEAN context.

On 9 May, Indonesia dispatched two Hercules aircraft carrying 24.8 tons of emergency relief supplies to Yangon.[21] Despite the junta's refusal to issue visas for foreign observers and to allow relief teams to enter the country, the Indonesian president insisted on an Indonesian delegation to accompany the aid. It included officials not only from the ministries of Public

Social Welfare Coordination, Foreign Affairs, and the National Coordinating Board for Disaster Management but also from the Indonesian Armed Forces. It was the only delegation to enter the country at this early stage.[22] The aid arrived in Yangon together with a letter from President Yudhoyono to Myanmar's military junta leaders, addressing some "lessons learned" from Indonesia's relief experience in the aftermath of the tsunami in 2004.[23]

But despite aid deliveries from several ASEAN countries and Myanmar's direct neighbors, the humanitarian situation in the affected areas worsened. The junta continued to deny access to any international aid workers, and cooperation with the UN had stalled. In view of the deadlock, a special meeting of ASEAN foreign ministers was convened in Singapore on 19 May.[24] During the intense negotiations with the Myanmarese representative, it was Indonesian foreign minister Wirajuda who took the lead and "broke the barrier."[25] This recollection by Wirajuda illustrates Indonesia's broader policy of interference:

> At that meeting I said that I would give Myanmar three options: Number one, Myanmar should follow in Indonesia's steps in how we dealt with the tsunami in Aceh. We opened Aceh for everyone, even foreign troops with light arms. As a result we succeeded in the process of rehabilitating the region. But knowing how isolated Myanmar was, I didn't think this was a realistic option for the country. Option two therefore suggested that Myanmar agree to an ASEAN-led mission, which meant that ASEAN would stand between Myanmar and the international community. I said this is the best option, because Myanmar would not need to deal directly with the international community—ASEAN would do that. I said this is a good option, and I recommend you [Myanmar] do this. Thirdly, you do nothing. But then you should ask yourself what the purpose of you joining ASEAN is, if you only create problems, even when your people are suffering.[26]

Wirajuda's statement underlines that Indonesia did not only make unsolicited recommendations. The foreign minister denounced Myanmar's chosen path of isolation in view of the suffering population. At least implicitly, he also threatened Myanmar by questioning the purpose of its ASEAN membership.[27] "ASEAN is blamed for what you do. So don't forget that we, the other ASEAN members, will also assess what the advantage is of having you

Norm Reconciliation in Indonesia 61

in the Association," Wirajuda stressed in the discussion with his Myanmarese counterpart.[28] Verifying Wirajuda's account of the ASEAN meeting, Singapore's foreign minister, George Yeo, recalled in an interview with the *Straits Times* that the Indonesian foreign minister "intervened passionately" when asking the basic question of what ASEAN means to Myanmar and what Myanmar means to ASEAN.[29] At the ASEAN-UN International Pledging Conference in Yangon, which followed on 25 May 2008, Foreign Minister Wirajuda reinforced the pressure on the junta by calling on them directly to open up: "In return for the good will of the international community to help, the Myanmar Government should be more open by giving greater access, not only to humanitarian relief and goods to enter Myanmar and distribute them to the families of the victims, but also granting access to humanitarian relief workers, be they of government or non-governmental organizations."[30] Overall, Indonesia clearly prioritized human rights protection over noninterference in the case of Cyclone Nargis. In the face of Myanmar's determination to continue its isolation and keep international aid workers out of the country, the Indonesian foreign minister intervened passionately. He not only pointed out the junta's role in aggravating the suffering of its people but also questioned the country's status within ASEAN as a means of pressuring the generals to open up.

The Rakhine Riots: Prioritizing Noninterference

Following the deadly clashes between the Muslim Rohingya and Burmese Rakhine in western Myanmar, violence against the Rohingya community intensified in the fall of 2012. It increasingly included deadly force executed by the state's enforcement agencies themselves against the Rohingya. The Myanmarese government failed to stop the discrimination and persecution of the Rohingya, which led to numerous deaths and the displacement of large groups of Rohingya across the entire region. But despite the scale of human suffering involved in the crisis, the Indonesian government opted for a policy of noninterference in response to the Rakhine Riots.

On 31 July, Indonesian foreign minister Marty Natalegawa made the first official statement on the crisis. It came more than a month after the sectarian violence had started in Myanmar and the Myanmarese government had declared a state of emergency. Natalegawa stated that Indonesia would emphasize its opposition to any kind of human rights violations. Yet he shied away from directly criticizing the human rights abuses against the Rohingya.[31] Instead, President Yudhoyono claimed on 4 August that Myanmar "had done its best to handle long-lasting tensions between ethnic Rakhine and Rohingyas."[32] Yudhoyono further stressed that the violence in Myanmar had nothing to do with religion and that no ethnic cleansing was taking place in the country.[33] He went on to state that Indonesia had done whatever was necessary to help settle the issue, particularly through diplomatic relations as well as international forums such as ASEAN, the Organization of Islamic Cooperation (OIC), and the UN.[34] He did not offer a plan of action beyond calling on Indonesians to "help provide humanitarian aid to our Rohingya brothers."[35] The official Indonesian stance did not change despite renewed fighting in October 2012 that proved to be even more intense.

The Indonesian government only became involved in the crisis after Myanmar, following the ASEAN summit in November 2012, issued a formal invitation asking the Indonesian government for help.[36] Since by definition interference in the domestic affairs of a foreign state only happens *without the consent* of the host state, by issuing an invitation, Myanmar accepted Indonesian involvement in the Rohingya crisis.[37] The invitation was followed by a meeting between the governments in early January 2013.[38] During a dialogue with the minister of border affairs, Lt. Gen. Thein Htay in Sittwe, Foreign Minister Natalegawa discussed the possibility of assisting Myanmar's government in dealing with the issue of citizenship of the Rohingya people.[39] At the same time, he stressed that the conflict between the Rakhine and Rohingya was an internal problem of Myanmar. Natalegawa underlined that Indonesia was not interfering in Myanmar's domestic affairs but was only responding to an invitation.[40]

In sum, the Indonesian government chose to interfere as little as possible in the Rohingya crisis until the junta issued an official invitation. Even after this point the government explicitly stressed that in supporting Myanmar it was not violating the ASEAN norm of noninterference. The Indonesian government therefore prioritized noninterference over human rights protection in its response to the Rakhine Riots.

EXPLAINING INDONESIA'S RESPONSE TO NORM CONFLICT

The above analysis of Indonesia's response to the three situations of norm conflict in Myanmar shows that the Indonesian government continued to apply both norms in its foreign policy. In this section, the variation in Indonesia's compliance with the two norms will be explained in light of the structure of domestic, regional, and international expectations set by Indonesia's commitment to the two conflicting norms and Indonesia's power resources to influence the expectations and behavior of others. In what follows, I argue that in light of conflicting expectations regarding legitimate action, primarily articulated at the domestic level, the government adopted a strategy of "norm reconciliation" to minimize the legitimacy and reputation costs of its response to norm conflict.

Early Saffron: Indonesian Solidarity with the Protestors

Following the junta's brutal use of force against the peaceful protestors, there was a strong public outcry in Indonesia. In particular, Indonesian legislators and human rights activists expressed their horror regarding the events in Myanmar. Responding immediately, the Indonesian House of Representatives (DPR) asked President Yudhoyono, on 24 September, "to direct the UN General Assembly's attention to the mounting tension in Myanmar" and thereby force the military junta to restore democracy.[41] Highlighting the extent of human suffering in Myanmar, Indonesian legislator Djoko Susilo demanded that the Indonesian president urge the military junta to return to the negotiation table with the NLD. Susilo's call was supported by Theo Sambuaga, chairman of Komisi I, the parliamentary commission for foreign affairs, who encouraged Yudhoyono to take "the initiative . . . to ask the junta to engage in national reconciliation" as the country was on the brink of civil war.[42] He argued that the Indonesian president should assign a special envoy to Myanmar to discuss with the junta the concrete measures that could be taken to end the tensions. In order to isolate the junta, Sambuaga also called on the government to lobby other ASEAN member states and exclude Myanmar from the next ASEAN summit in Singapore.[43]

In line with the demands put forward by Komisi I, legislators from Golkar and the National Mandate Party (PAN) contended that the mounting tensions in Myanmar were no longer Myanmar's internal affair, and thus ASEAN and the UN had to take concrete measures to end the human rights abuses. To achieve this, it was argued, Indonesia, the United States, and other democratic countries had to intensify their lobbying of China,

Russia, and India to abandon their support for the junta. In addition, the legislators demanded that Indonesia, as a nonpermanent member of the UN Security Council, should play an intensive role in issuing "a resolution imposing firm sanctions on the military junta."[44] The following day, 25 September, the DPR's strong condemnations were followed by a letter from Indonesian legislators and members of the ASEAN Inter-Parliamentary Myanmar Caucus (AIPMC) in which they urged the Indonesian government to take a stronger role in ensuring that the military junta refrained from using repressive approaches in handling the mass protests.[45] The legislators insisted that in order to solve the political crisis peacefully, the regime in Myanmar had to release Aung San Suu Kyi and other political prisoners and "come together to start a dialogue for peace, reformation and national reconciliation in order to secure democracy in Myanmar."[46]

However, pressure for action on behalf of human rights protection did not only emanate from the government's domestic audience. It was reinforced at the international level as a concerned international community, headed by UN secretary-general Ban Ki-Moon, forcefully condemned the violence. In his opening address to the annual UN General Assembly debate on 25 September 2007, he urged the authorities in Myanmar to exercise utmost restraint and to engage without delay in dialogue with all the relevant parties in the national reconciliation process.[47] Numerous Western heads of state reiterated his message to the junta while speaking to the Assembly that same day. In his speech, US president George W. Bush, for example, underlined that "Americans are outraged by the situation in Burma," announcing further economic sanctions against the regime.[48] Bush appealed to the authorities in Myanmar directly "not to use violence against their fellow citizens."[49] Addressing the international community, the US president emphasized that every civilized nation had a responsibility to stand up for people suffering under dictatorship. Therefore, he urged the UN and all nations to use their diplomatic and economic leverage to help the Burmese people reclaim their freedom.[50] The condemnations issued by the international body and representatives of the Western world clearly framed the Saffron Revolution as a case of extraterritorial human rights protection. The international response served as a reference point for the Indonesian government, as it indicated what kind of action the international community perceived as appropriate for responding to the crisis. It suggested that Indonesia, as a state committed to human rights protection and promotion, should not remain silent in view of the state violence in Myanmar. The Indonesian government thus faced strong expectations for compliance with the human rights protection norm at the domestic and international level. Hence, in prioritizing human rights protection in accordance with those expectations, the Indonesian government avoided both domestic legitimacy and international reputation costs.

"Of course we heard the call," Dewi Fortuna Anwar, foreign-policy advisor to the Indonesian vice president, said: "Ever since our democratization process started, there have been strong domestic voices asking the president to push for democratic reform in Myanmar. At the same time, we have started to look towards the West for assistance and orientation in our democratic transformation. Following the Saffron Revolution the world was outraged and, of course, this meant that we, too, could not remain silent."[51] In view of the strong domestic and international predisposition toward human rights protection, the Indonesian government instantly made a statement on 25 September 2007 condemning the violence. Elaborating on his motivation to speak up on the matter, Foreign Minister Hassan Wirajuda said: "At the Second World Conference on Human Rights in 1993, we had all agreed that gross violations of human rights are a matter of international concern. Accordingly, I believed that it was wrong to claim that the human rights violations in Myanmar were an internal affair, like my Burmese colleague had previously argued. Of course, they did not want us to comment on the matter. But I decided to speak up, because I did not agree with this static conception of non-interference. Our intention was not to harm, but to help."[52] On the same day Wirajuda also announced that despite Myanmar's call for noninterference, ASEAN would table a debate on the issue. While ruling out a peacekeeping mission as premature, he suggested to take the case to the UN Human Rights Council. This move is striking, given that ASEAN member states have traditionally opposed even non–legally binding and primarily symbolic collective UN measures against their ASEAN peers. However, as a member of the UN Human Rights Council, the Indonesian government on 2 October supported a resolution issued by the body that strongly deplored "the continued violent repression of peaceful demonstrations in Myanmar," and urged "the Government of Myanmar to exercise utmost restraint and to desist from further violence against peaceful protestors."[53] In backing the resolution, the Indonesian government demonstrated its acceptance of human rights protection as a legitimate matter of international concern, even where a fellow ASEAN member state was concerned.

Following Indonesia's initial statement on the crisis, international pressure continued. In a joint statement on 26 September, the European Union (EU) and the United States (US) expressed that they were "deeply troubled by reports that security forces have fired on and attacked peaceful demonstrators and arrested many Buddhist monks and others."[54] Similar statements were issued by, among others, UK prime minister Gordon Brown, French president Nicolas Sarkozy, the Japanese Foreign Ministry, EU foreign policy chief Javier Solana, and UN high commissioner for human rights Louise Arbour.[55] By 27 September, international pressure started to shift toward ASEAN and its role in response to the human rights violations occurring in one of its member states. At first, it was only transnational human rights organizations that targeted ASEAN, but Western governments soon followed suit in calling the regional organization to action.[56] On 27 September French foreign minister Bernard Kouchner and British foreign secretary David Miliband asked the ASEAN member states to use their influence on the Myanmarese generals.[57]

These international expectations were reinforced domestically. On the same day the *Jakarta Post* wrote that it would be shameful if the leaders of ASEAN continued their "obsolete indifference toward the brutality of their colleagues in Myanmar."[58] Indonesia especially, it argued, as the largest member of the regional grouping, should not wait for thousands of people to die before taking action to stop the generals from killing civilians who have lost their patience with oppression and poverty. The paper not only appealed to Indonesia's self-perceived leadership role in the region but also referred to the government's international ambition to be seen and recognized as a rising democracy. The *Jakarta Post* called upon President Susilo Bambang Yudhoyono to take the crisis in Myanmar as an opportunity to act on his favorite topic, namely boosting the country's international image. The paper suggested that as a retired army general, Yudhoyono should remind his colleagues in Myanmar not to use violence against citizens.[59]

Responding to the international pressure now directed squarely at ASEAN, on 27 September 2007 the member states followed up on Foreign Minister Hassan Wirajuda's announcement of an ASEAN debate on the topic. It resulted in an exceptionally strong collective ASEAN statement that openly condemned the junta's violent crackdown. For the Indonesian government the collective statement was a way of addressing the strong expectations regarding action on the domestic and international levels. The statement, which was a clear violation of the regional noninterference norm, instantaneously prompted loud protest from Myanmar. The Indonesian secretary-general of the Foreign Ministry at the time, Imron Cotan, remembered Myanmar's resistance to the informal ASEAN meeting: "Of course they were not happy. My colleagues in Myanmar tried to lobby Cambodia, Vietnam, and Laos. And at the initial stage, some of them were very reluctant, arguing that Indonesia cannot put another ASEAN member on the spot like this."[60] Despite initial reluctance, ultimately a consensus could be reached among the attending ASEAN representatives. Giving in to Indonesia's arguments, they accepted the human rights framing of the crisis and the collective interference. Internationally the unusually open and frank collective ASEAN statement was met with widespread recognition. French foreign minister Kouchner described the regional grouping as "the strongest tool" to deal with the crisis and its "tough declaration"[61] as "a victory for the pro-democracy movement in Myanmar."[62] In line with this, US secretary of state Condoleezza Rice called the ASEAN reaction "a very good statement," when concluding a meeting with the ASEAN ministers on the same day.[63] The Security Council also welcomed the statement, stressing "the important role played by the ASEAN countries in urging restraint, calling for a peaceful transition to democracy, and supporting the good offices mission."[64] Even Human Rights Watch commended ASEAN for its "strong statement."[65]

On the following day the Indonesian government once more underlined its support for the protesting monks in Myanmar, as the Foreign Ministry staged an act of solidarity by wearing red and observing a minute of silence for the protestors. One of the organizers of the Foreign Ministry initiative, Umar Hadi, at the time director for public diplomacy, recalled: "We were frustrated with what was happening in Myanmar and the normal [ASEAN] way of responding to the situation would not have been sufficient. That was why I grabbed about two hundred people from the Foreign Ministry. We were all wearing red batik, and we all stood in front of Monas in solidarity."[66] In siding with the pro-democracy protesters and condemning the crackdown, the Indonesian government aimed to give a clear signal to the world, as Hadi stressed: "After staging the act of solidarity with the protestors, we were asked by the West to step up when things went wrong in Myanmar. They knew exactly how we felt about the crackdown and that we have ideals we want to address."[67]

In sum, Indonesia's initial forceful response to the Saffron Revolution reflects the presence of strong domestic and international expectations regarding action in favor of human rights protection. By addressing the articulated concerns, the government avoided both legitimacy and reputation costs at the domestic as well as international levels. Running a comparatively weak coalition government, whose actions at the time were painstakingly scrutinized by a highly active parliament and a critical Komisi I, Indonesian decision makers were extremely vulnerable and responsive to domestic expectations. Following the country's democratic transition, respect for human rights in particular had become a central element of political legitimacy in Indonesia, as highlighted by former presidential spokesperson Wimar Witolar: "Every president bent over backwards to show sensitivity to human rights in order to legitimize himself or herself. It was just not politically viable anymore to ignore demands for human rights, be it at home or in the region."[68] Within the region, Indonesian parliamentarians and civil society activists focused in particular on the situation in Myanmar. The government's stance toward the recalcitrant regime had become a measure for its own commitment to and credibility as a democracy and human rights promoter in the region.

In a situation in which domestic pressure was coupled with Western expectations regarding action on behalf of human rights protection, a strong case for compliance by the Indonesian government with the human rights protection and promotion norm could be made. After decades of international scrutiny during the New Order regime of former president Suharto, improving the country's international reputation by joining the "democratic club" represented an important motivational force in Indonesia's foreign policy.[69] Following Indonesia's democratic transition, the established democracies and representatives of the so-called West thus became the country's main international audience. "In understanding Indonesian foreign policy, its evolving sense of self-awareness as a democracy, I think, is critical," ASEAN scholar See Seng Tan argued.[70] In addition, Indonesia has always fostered a sense of leadership within the region. Whereas previous leadership ambitions were based primarily on the country's sheer size and demographic characteristics, following Reformasi a set of more normative ambitions was incorporated.[71] With Indonesia having successfully transformed itself from an authoritarian into a democratic regime, its foreign policymakers justified the country's self-perceived role as a regional leader with reference to its democratic credentials and its democracy and human rights activism within the region.[72] In order to gain the recognition it desired from its democratic peers on the international level, it was crucial for the Indonesian government to live up to its stipulated role and address Western expectations regarding human rights protection, especially when they occurred in its own backyard. Internationally, Indonesia's transformation and its role within ASEAN have not gone unrecognized. Following Indonesia's successful bid in the Security Council elections in 2006, US president George W. Bush, for example, described Indonesia as an "example of how democracy and modernization can provide an alternative to extremism." Supporting Indonesia's growing international role, the US president lauded Yudhoyono's leadership and democratic credentials, which made "Indonesia strong" and enabled the country "to play a positive role in Southeast Asia and the world."[73] Similarly, Indonesia's "positive role within the Association of Southeast Asian Nations" was also acknowledged by transnational human rights nongovernmental organizations (NGOs).[74] HRW repeatedly endorsed Indonesia's efforts to strengthen ASEAN's human rights body, the AICHR, and the appointment of an independent expert as the Indonesian representative.[75] But despite this recognition in the eyes of many Indonesians, the country has not yet received the international recognition it deserves. Today a feeling of being internationally "underrated, undervalued, and underrepresented" remains, which fuels continued striving for an international reputation as a good democracy.[76] The following statement by Imron Cotan, former secretary-general of the Foreign Ministry, speaks to this feeling: "We are a maturing democracy. We need recognition, and we deserve it, as we have successfully moved from an authoritarian regime toward democracy. Someone should tap our shoulder for once and say, 'hey you are doing well.'"[77] This lingering sense of a lack of recognition made the country particularly eager to impress on the international stage. Thereby a positive international reputation as a good democracy and promoter of democratic values, especially within the region, was pursued not only as a motive in its own right but, importantly, because it was believed to also feed back into the government's domestic assessment and perceived legitimacy.[78]

Taken together, the government's vulnerability to domestic pressures and its quest for social recognition internationally made Indonesia particularly responsive to domestic and international expectations for compliance with human rights protection. Within the region Indonesia justified its interference by referencing the region's acceptance of the Vienna Convention and highlighting its own previous behavior. In doing so, it presented interference in cases of human rights violations as acceptable, and "normal" within the region.

From Solidarity to Noninterference in the Saffron Case

In order to explain the government's change in response from human rights protection to noninterference during the Saffron Revolution, a shift in the perceived strength of expectations for compliance with the norms in question must have occurred. This shift led the government to reassess the social costs involved in compliance with either norm. The following sections will provide evidence that Indonesia's change in response was motivated by the deteriorating situation in Myanmar, which increasingly involved a risk of ethnic conflict and territorial disintegration. This new territorial dimension to the conflict spoke to a strong domestic expectation for a continued validity of noninterference in cases involving secessionism or the risk of territorial disintegration, which the Indonesian government considered stronger than the simultaneous domestic and international expectations for compliance with human rights protection.

Indonesian interference in the interest of human rights protection came to a halt after the passing of the UN Human Rights Council resolution on 2 October 2007. However, domestic pressure on the Indonesian government to go even further in its support of the peaceful protesters did not subside. On 1 October Rizal Sukma, executive director of Indonesia's most influential foreign policy think tank, the Centre for Strategic and International Studies (CSIS) Jakarta, argued that if ASEAN could not manage the situation, "Indonesia should break away from the long-cherished tradition of solidarity within ASEAN."[79] He further stated that Indonesia should learn "to disagree with other ASEAN countries that lack the nerve to stand up for the people of Myanmar," adding: "It is also time for Indonesia to show other ASEAN members, and the international community, that we are now a different country from the one ruled by the authoritarian New Order regime. If Indonesia's government really believes in democracy and human rights, then it is our business to oppose any attempt by anyone, anywhere, to kill democracy and murder human rights."[80]

Similarly, representatives of religious interfaith organizations in Indonesia insisted that Indonesia should facilitate peaceful dialogue between the conflicting parties and condemned the military junta for its "irresponsible use of force."[81] Din Syamsuddin, chairman of Indonesia's second-largest Muslim organization, Muhammadiyah, demanded on 2 October that the Myanmarese government release every prisoner taken during the demonstration period. The representative of the Indonesian Bishops Conference, Benny Susetyo, added that given the situation unfolding in Myanmar, abstention in the Security Council on votes relating to Myanmar could no longer be an option for Indonesia. Since democracy had "a strong pull on the collective conscience of the Indonesian people—stronger, in fact, than does its ASEAN identity," the Indonesian government had to do more.[82]

But instead of further pressuring the junta, the Indonesian government grew more cautious in its response. The increasingly pronounced secessionist dimension to the crisis constituted a crucial impediment toward a more human rights–centered Indonesian response. The violent handling of the antijunta demonstrations had resulted in growing tensions within the Myanmarese authoritarian regime. There had been desertions among police and military personnel as well as a wave of cabinet reshuffles. In the process, the regime's internal stability started to crumble. While international observers increasingly saw the crisis as a window of opportunity for regime change in Myanmar, the junta's renewed fighting with Myanmar's armed ethnic minorities reinforced Indonesian fears of a balkanization of the country in the wake of violent ethnic conflict and separatism. This was discussed as the so-called Iraq scenario.[83] Under no circumstances did the Indonesian government want to get caught up in a domestic conflict with separatist dimensions by further interfering on behalf of the protestors. Its reluctance to be perceived as a violator of the noninterference norm by its regional peers in instances that featured a risk of territorial disintegration reflects a deep-seated fear across Indonesian society of the unitary Indonesian state suffering territorial losses through secessionism. This fear is based on the collective memory of disintegrative forces threatening Indonesian unity ever since its independence. Since then, Indonesia has faced five major separatist movements and many smaller ones.[84] Two of the major trouble spots in the past were Aceh, where a peace agreement was reached in 2005 after more than thirty years of civil war, and East Timor, which became independent in 2002 following a UN-sponsored popular referendum in 1999 and the deployment of an Australian-led international peacekeeping force. The loss of East Timor (now Timor Leste) represented a traumatic experience in Indonesian history.[85] Since then, Indonesia has been preoccupied with maintaining the integrity of the republic, determined not to allow East Timor to become a precedent for further secession.[86] As *Jakarta Post* editor Endy Bayuni stressed, Indonesia's bitter experience of secessionism has led its government to vow "to defend all its territory to the death."[87] This attitude was reinforced as ethnic and religious tensions mushroomed in the immediate wake of lifting the authoritarian controls of the Suharto regime.[88] Bayuni added: "We don't have any ambitions to expand, but we are very strong about defending our existing territory. I think this is where Papua comes in. Indonesia is not willing to give up one inch of its territory. This is very much in the heads of Indonesian politicians and society at large, as it is also embedded in our schools: 'Never give up an inch of your territory.'"[89]

Since the transfer of administration of New Guinea (now Papua) from the Netherlands to Indonesia in 1963, the Free Papua Movement has been active and continues to advocate for independence. A secessionist conflict still lingers in the region today. Many Papuans do not consider themselves part of an Indonesian state and nation due to ethnic differences and their history of being differently administered by the Dutch.[90]

The Indonesian fear of territorial disintegration, and the related domestic expectation for the government to prohibit external interferences in Indonesia that could facilitate secessionism, crucially mattered in explaining the government's shift in response to the Saffron Revolution. In order to live up to the domestic expectation of maintaining Indonesia's territorial integrity, the government had to prioritize the noninterference norm over human rights protection in a human rights case with secessionist dimensions. In complying with the noninterference norm, the government avoided the creation of precedents that could one day be put to use in relation to Indonesia's own internal affairs and ensured that noninterference remained the regional standard of behavior in secessionist conflicts or cases involving a risk of territorial disintegration. While advocating for a more relaxed interpretation of the noninterference norm, external meddling in cases of secessionism was meant to remain a regional taboo. "Indonesia remains strongly opposed to the idea of interference which could endanger the territorial integrity of the member states," the foreign-policy advisor to the vice president, Dewi Fortuna Anwar, pointed out, highlighting the evolution of Indonesia's interpretation of the norm's meaning:

> Noninterference was taken to the extreme in Southeast Asia because most of its member states for a long time were not previously democratic. Any form of criticism was seen as an act of interference. But in today's normative environment, a democratizing Indonesia argues that the relationship between state and society matters, and democracy as well as human rights protection within the region are now a concern of ours. We believe that it is permissible for us to talk about the problems within other ASEAN states, such as bad governance, a lack of democracy, and human rights violations. But noninterference remains important in the sense that it is not acceptable for others to interfere directly in another state by assisting rebels and supporting secessionist movements.[91]

Confronted with conflicting domestic expectations that were set by Indonesia's simultaneous commitment to human rights protection and noninterference as the corollary of respect for territorial integrity, the government had to choose between the norms by assessing the anticipated legitimacy costs of noncompliance with either norm. In order to determine which path of action to pursue, the Indonesian government had to make a judgment regarding which of the underlying objectives its domestic audience valued more: the protection of the rights of non-nationals in Myanmar or the safeguarding of Indonesia's territorial integrity by maintaining the validity of noninterference in secessionist conflicts within the region. The fact that few Indonesians are willing to discuss the human rights violations occurring in the course of the secessionist conflict in Papua—a case that features the rights not of strangers but rather of Indonesian *nationals*— suggests that the maintenance of territorial integrity was the overriding value.[92] Even for Indonesian NGOs that work in the human rights sector, Papua, as a case of potential secessionism, is treated as a very sensitive issue, as Malaysian human rights activist Adrian Pereira has highlighted: "Instead of defending human rights, when it comes to Papua, they refuse to discuss rights abuses at the ASEAN people's forum."[93] Former Indonesian ambassador Wiryono Sastrohandoyo summarized the rationale:

> We are still growing into the nation we aspire to be; more solid; not threatened by separatism. For those who are critical of Indonesia it does not matter whether there are two or three Indonesias. But we are confronted with the problem of preserving the nation. We don't want people to say things that could inspire separatism. Those countries that don't have any [separatist] problems, for them it is easy to speak up, but not for us. We do show openness. But if it is about the country's survival, its unity, we are nationalistic.[94]

President Yudhoyono experienced such nationalist sentiments firsthand in 2005 after a peace agreement had been signed in the separatist conflict in Aceh. He faced intense criticism at home when he permitted foreigners into the tsunami-devastated province to monitor the implementation of the peace agreement. Domestic critics accused Yudhoyono of internationalizing a problem that they argued should have been handled as a domestic issue. Responding to the criticism, Yudhoyono justified his decision, arguing that the presence of foreign monitors from the EU and ASEAN was not a foreign interference into Indonesia's domestic affairs, as they were only overseeing the implementation of an already concluded agreement meant to end the separatist fighting and the risk of secessionism.[95] At the same time, he ruled out any foreign involvement in the resolution of the Papua conflict, thereby addressing fears of foreign interference in the province. "The issue of Papua is our own domestic issue. We decline foreign interference in settling that issue," Yudhoyono said.[96] Previously Indonesian parliamentarians and the media had expressed concerns over criticism from external actors. Members of the US Congress especially had repeatedly questioned the integration of the vast province into Indonesia's territory in the late 1960s.[97]

Given these past experiences with Indonesian reactions to external involvement in its conflict areas, the government anticipated that even though less tangible at the moment of choice, the potential legitimacy costs of creating a regional environment that allowed for interference in secessionist conflicts were more severe than occasionally not acting upon its human rights commitment when human rights violations also involved a risk of territorial disintegration. Hence, as the Saffron Revolution developed a risk of territorial disintegration, the Indonesian government changed its initial stance of human rights protection to a policy of noninterference. In view of continued domestic pressure in favor of interference, Foreign Minister Wirajuda justified Indonesia's now cautious position by stating that "Myanmar's problems are not just about dictatorship and human rights abuses," but that "secessionism launched by minority tribes and security issues faced by the military junta are also of concern."[98] These insecurities had to be considered and addressed in the country's response to the crisis. As Myanmar's internal stability continued to deteriorate, the Indonesian shift in response became more and more obvious.

On 12 October, the prime minister of Myanmar, Gen. Soe Win, died, which led to another cabinet reshuffle and the appointment of Lt. Gen. Thein Sein as his successor.[99] At the same time, pro-democracy protests in Myanmar flared up again as new groups of activists formed. In addition, many monks resumed antijunta demonstrations and boycotts.[100] As a consequence, even Myanmar experts started to warn of a possible balkanization of Myanmar in the event of sudden regime change. As Myanmar expert Bertil Lintner predicted at that time, "the transition to civilian rule is bound to be extremely difficult, given the fact that the country has not had a truly civilian government since 1962."[101] The greatest challenge was perceived to be the prevention of fresh outbreaks of the insurgencies among ethnic minorities, which have been a constant in modern Myanmar. Former UN official Thant Myint-U reiterated this point: "Rebuilding these [state] structures at the same time as easing the army out of its overall government role is an almost unprecedented task. It's hard for me to think of another situation in which that has happened peacefully."[102] Both the Indonesian president and his foreign minister believed that in order to prevent Myanmar's internal conflicts from escalating in the wake of an overthrow of the government, an equally strong new government would be needed to replace the junta—something unlikely to be achieved democratically in an ad hoc fashion.[103] Accordingly, the reformist general Agus Widjojo, whom the Indonesian government had assigned as its special envoy to Myanmar, argued that Indonesia and other democratic countries had to expose the isolated junta to democratic values first, before regime change and civilian rule would be possible. For real change to happen, it was argued, the transition had to begin with reform of the military: "The best bet, the shortest and least violent way, is if the military can voluntarily transfer power through a transitional mechanism and finally hand it over to a democratic government. The key words are voluntary intent from the military for a transitional period of power-sharing and an agreed reconciliation process with the people of Myanmar."[104]

As the ASEAN summit in November 2007 approached, Singapore as the acting ASEAN chair invited UN special envoy Gambari to attend the summit and give a report on the situation in Myanmar. Myanmar's prime minister, Thein Sein, told the ASEAN leaders that Gambari should only report to the UN Security Council and not to ASEAN or the East Asia Summit. He thereby vetoed the chair's initiative to bring the special envoy in for a briefing.[105] In view of Myanmar's resistance, the Indonesian government, which had previously shown little concern for the country's complaints, rejected the Singaporean initiative, reflecting the desire not to create a precedent for interference in the internal affairs of a state facing a secessionist challenge. In order to maintain the regional validity of the noninterference norm as a standard of behavior in internal cases that featured a risk of territorial disintegration, the Indonesian president opted for what he called "a soft approach."[106] This entailed the rejection of further interference, especially in the form of sanctions or Security Council action. In view of the strong domestic and international expectations toward interference on behalf of human rights protection, Yudhoyono justified the Indonesian policy of noninterference by arguing that Indonesia, like Myanmar, was facing threats of national disintegration with minority tribes fighting for separation. In doing so he emphasized the norm's continuous importance for Indonesia in the context of territorial integrity.[107] Following the ASEAN summit, the initially strong collective ASEAN position in favor of human rights protection also softened. ASEAN chair Lee Hsien Loong from Singapore stated in a press conference that Myanmar did not need ASEAN to bring about a solution to its political problems, as the situation in the country was a domestic affair and the junta was capable of handling the issue itself.[108] At least at the regional level, Indonesia was once again successful in generating acceptance for its preferred application of the norms and their altered meaning. By complying with noninterference and thereby respecting Myanmar's expectations, Indonesia tried to maintain the validity of noninterference as a behavioral standard in such cases and to avoid anticipated domestic legitimacy costs caused by external interference in Indonesia's own secessionist conflict. The government attempted to justify the choice in relation to its domestic and international audiences, by highlighting the territorial dimension of the conflict and the continuous importance of noninterference in cases of secessionism within the region.

Leading by Example: Human Rights Protection during Cyclone Nargis

Similar to its initial response in the Saffron Revolution, the Indonesian government took the regional lead in addressing the crisis caused by Cyclone Nargis and the junta's subsequent failure in responding to the humanitarian disaster. The Indonesian response once again reflected the presence of domestic and international expectations for compliance with human rights protection. Although domestic voices supported this cause, during Cyclone Nargis it was primarily Indonesia's international audience that articulated expectations for interference in Myanmar on the basis of human rights protection.

As part of the AIPMC, Indonesian parliamentarians stated on 5 May that the group "strongly urges ASEAN leaders to take a direct approach to ensure that their counterparts in Myanmar . . . allow international aid agencies full access . . . to provide aid."[109] Moreover, a large number of Indonesian human rights NGOs, united in the group called Indonesian Solidarity for the People of Burma, expressed their support for the people of Myanmar by staging protests in front of Myanmar's embassy in Jakarta on 9 May 2008. They urged the military junta to immediately grant access to international aid groups, arguing that "the junta can neither afford the necessary relief, nor is it experienced in handling this kind of disaster."[110] These domestic voices, which condemned the junta's lack of action to support its people, were echoed at the international level.

Following Cyclone Nargis, Western governments quickly responded to what was initially seen as a humanitarian crisis in the aftermath of a natural disaster. Among the first to react was the US government, which in the past had led a drive for economic sanctions against the regime but now stated that it would provide aid.[111] On 7 May US president George W. Bush said that Washington was prepared to use the US Navy to help search for the dead and missing.[112] The junta, however, would not accept a US military presence on its territory. Moreover, it refused to issue visa approvals to UN relief specialists, with several dozen employees of UN agencies and the US Disaster Assistance Response Team waiting in Bangkok for visas to enter Myanmar.[113] As the US and other Western countries continued to be denied access to cyclone-ravaged Myanmar, on 8 May French foreign minister Bernard Kouchner urged the UN to invoke the principle of the "responsibility to protect" as the basis of a resolution to force delivery of aid into Myanmar, if necessary against the objections of the military government.[114]

Against that backdrop, HRW called upon ASEAN members directly to convince Myanmar's government to lift the restrictions on international assistance. Brad Adams, director of HRW's Asia Division, added that "Burma's inhuman response to the cyclone is yet another embarrassment for ASEAN." He urged the organization to "formally consider expelling Burma from the regional club" should Myanmar not "reverse course on this epic tragedy."[115] In support of Kouchner's position, Javier Solana, the EU's high representative for the common foreign and security policy, later stated that the international community "should use all possible means to get aid through to victims of Myanmar's cyclone."[116] Adding to the international pressure, British prime minister Gordon Brown argued that the national disaster had been turned into "a man-made catastrophe" because of the junta's negligence, thereby clearly framing it as a case of human rights protection.[117] Kouchner went so far as to describe the regime's reaction as a crime against humanity and condemned the junta's continued limitation of aid.[118] In agreement, US defense secretary Robert Gates claimed that Myanmar was guilty of "criminal neglect" for blocking large-scale international aid to cyclone victims.[119]

While Western powers and the UN were unable to contact the military leadership in Myanmar, ASEAN ministers still enjoyed high-level discussions with the junta.[120] On 10 May, in light of the deadlock, the UN therefore directly approached Indonesia to take the lead in the region to help the reclusive country cope with the disaster.[121] Highlighting Indonesia's credentials, Noeleen Heyzer, secretary-general of the UN Economic and Social Commission for Asia and the Pacific (ESCAP), referred to Indonesia's own exemplary response when in 2004 it was hit by a tsunami: "Indonesia did amazing work in responding to the tsunami in Aceh and has become a leader in effective natural disaster response. Therefore, I would like ESCAP to facilitate a strong Indonesian role in Myanmar."[122] The hope was that the Indonesian government could convince the generals to open up by sharing best practice as a country that had experienced an international humanitarian relief mission following the deadly tsunami in 2004.[123] Readily accepting the internationally assigned role, the presidential foreign policy advisor Ali Alatas remarked that Indonesia had already started to take action in addressing the junta's concerns over foreign interference. Alatas referred to a letter to Myanmarese prime minister Thein Sein in which Indonesian president Yudhoyono had discussed Indonesia's experience in managing foreign aid.[124] The Indonesian government thereby addressed both domestic and international expectations in favor of human rights prioritization and avoided legitimacy as well as reputation costs resulting from noncompliance.

Although willing to take responsibility and fulfill a leadership role, the Indonesian authorities criticized the threats put forward by the West of using force to intervene in the reclusive country based on the international community's "responsibility to protect" (RtoP).[125] Indonesian ambassador to the UN Marty Natalegawa argued that RtoP was not meant to apply to natural disaster situations and that delivering international aid to Myanmar without governmental consent would further politicize the situation.[126] Indonesia's rejection of an RtoP-based intervention in Myanmar highlights that even though the country was among those in Southeast Asia accepting and promoting international concern for human rights, it was far from welcoming Western intervention, especially by military means, within the region. "Indonesia was willing to interfere and if necessary also do so-called naming and shaming," the secretary-general of the Foreign Ministry, Imron Cotan, said.[127] "We let Myanmar know that what they did was unacceptable, but there are limits. We do not accept interference in the sense that the West had in mind, by military means."[128] Looking back at centuries of Western domination in Southeast Asia, Indonesia's rejection of the RtoP framing of the crisis reflects the shared aversion to Western intervention in the region. It also mirrors a repeatedly articulated Southeast Asian concern in regard to the concept of RtoP, which in the eyes of many decision makers within the region is liable to be abused by the powerful. In forcefully rejecting a framing of the crisis in terms of RtoP, the Indonesian government tried to maintain the prerogative of interpretation within its own region and avoid the creation of precedents for Western military intervention in a region rife with crises and natural disasters.

Instead of supporting a Security Council–based mission, the Indonesian government opted for action within the ASEAN framework, after Singapore, as the ASEAN chair at the time, called for a special ministerial meeting on 19 May 2008. "When the cyclone happened in Myanmar, ASEAN was sandwiched between Myanmar, whose government rejected any international offer to assist, and the international community," Indonesian foreign minister Wirajuda explained.[129] "Millions of Burmese were suffering, and once again ASEAN was blamed by the international community, arguing that a crisis happened in one of our member countries and we did nothing," he added.[130] The regional dimension of the norm conflict meant that for those ASEAN member states committed to both norms, the costs of noncompliance with human rights protection increased. They could suffer reputation costs individually as well as collectively through international shaming of ASEAN as an organization. This was additional motivation for Indonesia to act. "So I could not remain silent," Wirajuda explained.

Former ASEAN secretary-general Surin Pitsuwan, who was present at the emergency meeting, remembered the international pressure on the regional heads prior to the meeting: "The British diplomat Malloch Brown made phone calls to everyone in advance of the ASEAN meeting, saying that ASEAN cannot miss this opportunity to show that it cares."[131] According to Australian foreign minister Stephen Smith, his prime minster, Kevin Rudd, made similar calls prior to the gathering. As Smith stressed, the purpose was to "speak to those nations whom we thought might have a better chance of persuading the regime than Australia."[132] As Surin recalled, it was "because of the phone calls, because of the widespread expression of concern and because of the conscience-shocking dimension of what happened" that ASEAN, led by Indonesia, pressured the junta to agree to an ASEAN-led relief mechanism of unprecedented dimensions.[133] Surin added:

> The world was once again held in suspense as to what we would do; if ASEAN could not handle this, it would have been a stigma on ASEAN. That was what drove us. By the time I reached Singapore and rushed into the meeting, the foreign ministers were pretty much convinced that this was an existentialist test for ASEAN. Facing the crisis we were paralyzed, but the world was ready to come in as Kouchner had argued that this was a case for RtoP and we had three Western war ships in the region ready for intervention no matter whether there was a yes or no from Yangon.[134]

According to Umar Hadi, director of public diplomacy at the Indonesian Foreign Ministry, the analogies used by Foreign Minister Wirajuda throughout the crisis managed to keep the generals engaged and listening: "Their first reaction was to shut down. So Hassan told them to look at what we did in Aceh a few years before, following the tsunami. We chose to have ASEAN come in, which meant that there was precedent for what we then did with Nargis. What Hassan did was leading by example, showing the generals that no harm was done by letting ASEAN in."[135] But in making the case for an ASEAN-led mission, the Indonesian foreign minister did not shy away from also backing his arguments with the potential use of more coercive means. In the meeting, he emphasized how the regional organization had time and again shouldered blame in order to protect Myanmar. A point had been reached, he contended, at which the remaining ASEAN members had to reflect upon the purpose of having Myanmar as a member, particularly if by rejecting the offer of an ASEAN-led relief mechanism, Myanmar was again creating nothing but trouble for the organization. While the regional dimension of the crisis increased the costs of noncompliance by creating an additional level of international pressure, the anticipated collective reputation costs for ASEAN also served as a powerful and more acceptable justification for interference in discussions with member states of the organization that were less committed to human rights. Following Wirajuda's interference, Myanmar finally agreed to an ASEAN-led relief effort to channel international aid into the country.[136] This episode once again shows that Indonesia had the necessary power resources within the region to convince others of its preferred action and at a minimum accept that human rights protection and promotion was a legitimate regional concern.

Given the strong international expectations for Indonesia's compliance with the norm of human rights protection, expressed by the United Nations and representatives of several Western states, coupled with its own positive experiences with international relief missions in Aceh following the tsunami in 2004, Indonesia felt particularly comfortable with taking the lead in the negotiations with Myanmar. Expectation at the domestic and international level coincided, and Indonesia had the necessary power resources to convince others of its choice of action. With regard to Myanmar and those ASEAN members in support of noninterference in the crisis, the Indonesian government justified its interference with reference to the collective reputational damage for ASEAN as an organization in case of a continued deadlock.

Secessionism and Ethnic Conflict during the Rakhine Riots

As in the later stages of the Saffron Revolution, the Indonesian government abstained from interfering during the Rakhine Riots in 2012, which underlines the continued importance of noninterference for Indonesia in cases with a secessionist or territorial dimension. Indonesia's prioritization of the noninterference norm was also facilitated by the relative lack of Western pressure for human rights protection during the crisis. Although Western governments voiced some initial concern, they quickly expressed contempt for the measures taken by the new reform-minded Myanmarese government.[137]

Following the reinforcement of military divisions in Rakhine, the imposition of a curfew, and the sentencing of two Muslim men for the rape and murder of a Buddhist woman, the US praised Myanmar's response to the sectarian fighting.[138] Despite harsh criticism by rights groups such as Amnesty International, according to which Muslim Rohingyas were still fleeing arbitrary arrest and persecution by border forces, Michael Thurston, the US embassy chargé d'affaires in Myanmar, stated on 19 June that the government was "trying to help everybody who needs it."[139] Similarly, the EU had announced even earlier, on 11 June, that it was satisfied with Myanmar's handling of the conflict. Maja Kocijanic, spokeswomen for EU foreign policy chief Catherine Ashton, said that the EU believed that the security forces were dealing with the violence "in an appropriate way."[140] The relative lack of Western international expectations regarding action on behalf of the Rohingya was contrasted with an unprecedented domestic outcry in Indonesia following the human rights violations against the Rohingya Muslims in Myanmar. Indonesian civil society, the media, academia, and parliamentarians all argued strongly in favor of interference to protect the Rohingya, as human rights concerns and religious solidarity among the majority Muslim population in Indonesia merged to create a strong call for action. In Jakarta, regular demonstrations were held against the treatment of the Rohingya in Myanmar.[141] Following the declaration of the state of emergency on 10 June 2012, Indonesia's leading daily English-language newspaper, the *Jakarta Post,* called upon ASEAN to act: "Although the ASEAN

Charter states that no neighbor has the right to meddle in another's domestic affairs, ASEAN should nevertheless press the regime in the same way it has these past few years, to live up to the humanitarian values and principles enshrined in the Charter."[142] In line with this, Indonesian human rights activists forcefully stated as early as 13 June 2012 that they were "deeply alarmed by the continued sectarian violence in Rakhine state."[143] The human rights violations against Rohingya Muslims led to particularly extreme reactions among the more radical elements of Indonesia's civil society. Instead of justifying their call for interference on the basis of general human rights protection, they primarily framed the crisis as a case of Muslim solidarity. Following riots against the Rohingya, on 13 July two Indonesian hard-line Islamic organizations, the Islamic Defenders Front (FPI) and Jemaah Anshorut Tauhis, protested in front of Myanmar's embassy in Jakarta, threatening to storm the building.[144] Shortly afterward, the hard-line organization Hizbut Tahrir Indonesia called for Indonesian Muslims to help the Rohingya. "What are the Muslim armies in Bangladesh, Indonesia and Malaysia waiting for?" they asked. "Can't they see the massacre and expulsion of their brothers?"[145] Speaking for Indonesia's moderate Muslim community, on 18 July Slamet Effendy Yusuf, chairman of Nahdlatul Ulama, Indonesia's largest Muslim organization, urged the president to take the initiative. He stated that "it would be great if the Indonesian government was not just a spectator in this issue" as it was not only an ASEAN member and a democracy but also the largest Muslim country in the world.[146]

Given the strong popular support for the Rohingya, Indonesian legislators soon joined the public in addressing the crisis and calling for interference. The parliamentarians thereby used both human rights–centered arguments and arguments grounded in Muslim solidarity to justify interference. Among the first to publicly raise the issue was Nurhayati Ali Assegaf, president of the Parliamentary Women's World, who on 24 July urged the Inter-Parliamentary Union to take a firm stance on the "massacre of Rohingya Muslims" in Myanmar.[147] She was followed by Eva Sundari, at the time president of AIPMC and legislator for the Indonesian Democratic Party of Struggle (PDI-P), who called for political pressure from the international community, including ASEAN and the UN: "Indonesia should not stand still. A country that ratified the UN Convention on Human Rights and the initiator of the ASEAN Charter, the government should condemn this as a crime against humanity and push for a human rights-oriented solution."[148] Echoing Sundari's statement, representatives of the Prosperous Justice Party (PKS) demanded that "the suffering from Myanmar's Rohingya Muslims should immediately receive serious attention from the president."[149] The same day, DPR chairman Marzuki Ali issued a particularly strong critique. Considering the violence against Muslims in Myanmar as a gross violation of human rights and a crime against humanity, he stated that "Indonesia, which upholds human rights and is also the leader of ASEAN, must be proactive to rebuke Myanmar and urge the country to respect human rights."[150]

In an attempt to reduce domestic legitimacy costs as a result of Indonesia's muted response to the crisis, Foreign Minister Marty Natalegawa challenged the claim that Indonesia was not concerned about the situation in Rakhine State. He argued that though the issue had not been raised publicly, it had been brought up behind closed doors in multilateral and bilateral discussions with Myanmar in the past: "Our silence doesn't mean we don't care."[151] But when asked what the government would do about the situation, spokesperson Julian Aldrin Pasha responded that "the administration had taken all possible measures, but for the time being, Indonesia could only use diplomacy."[152] Referring to this statement, the *Jakarta Post* wrote that this effectively meant that "the government of Indonesia, the world's largest predominantly Muslim country, has not appeared to be actively engaged in resolving the problem."[153] The author described the Rohingya massacre as a "dilemma" for Indonesia. Interfering on behalf of the Rohingya "could backfire since Indonesia has many ongoing perceived human rights violations in relation to minorities."[154] In other words, supporting the Rohingya could create a precedent for interference in Indonesia's own internal conflicts with religious and ethnic minorities and related separatist movements. Accordingly, former politician Rizal Ramli argued that in order to fully represent its democratic credentials internationally, Indonesia first and foremost had to tackle its own shortcomings on the domestic front. Only then could it realistically draw on its experience in handling ethnic conflicts to assist Myanmar in resolving the riots.[155] *Jakarta Post* senior editor Endy Bayuni agreed that it was against the backdrop of Indonesia's own domestic situation that the government's response had to be measured: "If it pushed further Indonesia would risk other countries pointing fingers at Papua, Ahmadiyah, Shia, saying that Indonesia is treating all these people just as bad[ly] as they were. In the Rohingya case they [the government] will be very careful because this has to do with ethnic issues, which almost every country in ASEAN has a problem with. And Indonesia shares this problem."[156]

But despite Foreign Minister Natalegawa's statement, Indonesian legislators continued to complain that "diplomacy" was not enough. Pramono Anung, vice chairman of the House of Representatives, mentioned to the Indonesian newspaper *Kompas* that "a firm stance is required, not because the majority of Indonesians are Muslims, but because discrimination must not occur."[157] In addition, calls for an Indonesian initiative to end the violence against the Rohingya were voiced by lawmakers from both Islamic and Nationalist parties within the Parliament.[158] In tandem with Indonesian human rights groups, they appealed for prompt international attention to the disaster and asked the Indonesian government to officially file a protest against the government of Myanmar after it was reported that security forces had committed killings, rapes, and mass arrests of the Rohingya:[159] "We sent a letter to the president regarding the Rohingya and all the other problems within Burma. We asked the Indonesian government to take a role. The government always says it wants to take the lead, since unlike other ASEAN countries it has experience in building democracy and promoting human rights. So we told the government, OK, if you want to take the lead—this is the chance."[160] Emphasizing that it was Indonesia's "duty as a democracy" to respect human rights, House of Representatives Speaker Marzuki Ali suggested that given the government's inaction, the House could send a delegation to Myanmar to look into the alleged human rights violations against the Rohingya community in the country.[161]

In the meantime, the problem of setting a precedent by interfering in Rakhine State became even more pronounced for the Indonesian government when, on 13 August, Rohingya representatives directly appealed to the Indonesian government and parliament for humanitarian assistance. They requested that the Indonesian government intervene in Myanmar in order to enable humanitarian aid to enter the region and to advocate for the Rohingya to be accepted as citizens.[162] By supporting the Rohingya, who in the past had asked for independence from Myanmar, Indonesia could have been accused of assisting a separatist group and thereby directly supporting secessionism in an ASEAN member state. Explaining the Indonesian decision not to interfere despite strong domestic expectations for compliance with human rights protection, former Indonesian ambassador Wiryono

Sastrohandoyo said shortly after the outbreak of violence in Rakhine: "The people are eager, . . . there are lots of people collecting money and sending doctors. But the government is trying to be respectful, because if we had that kind of situation in Papua we wouldn't want interference."[163]

Indonesia's own stance, which prioritized noninterference, also reflected the collective ASEAN position in the crisis. Accordingly, on the regional level, compliance with noninterference did not create reputation costs for the Indonesian government. As the situation intensified in August 2012, ASEAN secretary-general Surin Pitsuwan sent a letter to all ASEAN foreign ministers urging them to meet and address the Rohingya issue. Pitsuwan said that the bloc should be "part of a solution to the problem."[164] The government in Myanmar, however, rejected such a meeting and said the situation was under control.[165] The ASEAN foreign ministers eventually issued a four-point statement on 17 August saying that they were closely following the developments and were ready to lend humanitarian assistance "upon the request of the Government of Myanmar."[166] However, the Myanmarese government rejected the offer, arguing that the conflict was an internal affair, and ASEAN governments were not willing to push the government on the matter.[167] In response to this claim, Surin cautioned that the atrocities being committed, if not ended, could radicalize the Rohingya Muslims and destabilize the entire region. Reiterating his call for a more "proactive ASEAN,"[168] he added that "ASEAN cannot be perceived to be standing by without taking any action on such a big scale of humanitarian difficulty."[169] Surin called the ethnic violence a "disturbing trend" and reminded the ASEAN governments that "if all of us fail, that will create an impression that we don't care."[170] But with a general lack of political will among Western governments and ASEAN states to pressure the Myanmarese government, this danger did not arise.

More problematic for the Indonesian government were the continued domestic demands for compliance with human rights protection and action on behalf of the Rohingya. Throughout August more radical Indonesian Muslims demanded the expulsion of Myanmar's ambassador for his country's treatment of the Rohingya and called on the president to withdraw support for Myanmar chairing ASEAN in 2014.[171] Addressing the public support for the Rohingya, on 13 August members of Komisi I asked the government to bring the Rohingya issue to the international level at the next emergency session of the Organization of Islamic Cooperation

(OIC).[172] In line with this, interreligious intellectuals urged Indonesia and ASEAN to intensify their diplomacy "to have the Myanmar rulers end the ethnic cleansing and pay a higher price to pluralism."[173] The domestic calls for action via the OIC were echoed in an unprecedented act of solidarity within the Muslim world. Muslim nations such as Iran, Turkey, and Saudi Arabia spoke with one voice, which favored the protection of human rights.[174] The Iranian government had already started in July to urge the United Nations to take action in order to protect the Rohingya. In a letter to UN secretary-general Ban Ki-Moon, Iran's UN ambassador, Mohammad Khazaee, wrote: "We believe that ethnic and religious cleansing against Muslims under whatever pretext is unjustifiable and inexcusable under international law, and the United Nations must take urgent measures to protect the Rohingya by calling on Myanmar's government to end its 'crackdown.'"[175] Leading to widespread international media coverage, Turkey's first lady, Emine Erdogan, together with Turkish foreign minister Ahmet Davutoglu, visited Rakhine in August, calling upon the Islamic world to pay attention to the conflict.[176] Thereupon, the king of Saudi Arabia, Abdullah, decided to grant US$50 million to the Rohingya, describing them as the victims of "several rights violations, including ethnic cleansing, murder, rape and forced displacement."[177] In an attempt to appease the growing domestic demand for action as well as the concerns of Indonesia's Muslim international audience, in mid-August the Indonesian government brought the case to the OIC.[178] Working through the OIC ensured that the matter was addressed without Indonesia directly interfering on its own. Recalling the dilemma the Indonesian government faced, former foreign minister Hassan Wirajuda highlighted that his successor had little room to maneuver: "Without Myanmar's consent to assist there was not much else Indonesia could do to help," he said.

> The problems in Rakhine are not just a case of human rights violations, but there is an ethnic and religious dimension involved, which must be handled with care, and outsiders, particularly countries like Indonesia that have and still are experiencing similar problems, need to take an inclusive approach. By saying this I am not endorsing what is happening in Rakhine, but we need to understand that addressing a conflict like the one in Rakhine is a process, and we in ASEAN should understand this. This means we

have to address the problem in all its dimensions, not only as a case of human rights violations, but also as an ethnic conflict.[179]

As a consequence, direct interference by the government could not occur. But working through the OIC as an alternative channel turned out to be difficult as well. "The problem with the OIC was that as a Muslim organization it was perceived as partial, which inhibited good communication between the organization and the Myanmarese government," Wirajuda said.[180] "This is why we were delighted when former Indonesian vice president Jusuf Kalla stepped forward in his function as the chairman of the Indonesian Red Cross." Kalla offered to share with the Myanmarese government lessons learned from handling similar ethnic conflict in Indonesia in order to address the Rohingya crisis.[181] Traveling to Myanmar, Kalla emphasized that the Indonesian Red Cross would be nonpartisan in its assistance and aid would be "purely from the PMI itself without government interference," thereby trying to make sure that the initiative was not perceived as government interference by the Myanmarese government and regional peers.[182]

In sum, from the Indonesian government's perspective, the prioritization of noninterference over human rights protection in a crisis that involved ethnic conflict and a group that had previously asked for independence was perceived as necessary in order to maintain the validity of the noninterference norm in cases of secessionism and territorial disintegration. The government thereby tried to minimize the potential for interference in Indonesia's own internal affairs. Judging from past experiences of domestic outrage in cases of international involvement in Indonesia's restive regions, or international scrutiny over its military approach to Papua, government decision-makers believed compliance with the noninterference norm would be less costly in the long term. While Indonesia's noninterference stance caused little reputational cost in relation to its Western international audience, given the lack of expectations toward action, the government tried to appease strong conflicting domestic expectations regarding human rights protection by working through the OIC and supporting the Indonesian Red Cross mission in Rakhine. These initiatives also spoke to international expectations for action on behalf of the Muslim Rohingya, articulated by representatives of Islamic nations such as Iran, Turkey, and Saudi Arabia.

WHY INDONESIA OPTED FOR NORM RECONCILIATION

The analysis of the Indonesian response to norm conflict in Myanmar has shown that even though Indonesia did not consistently prioritize one norm over the other, the response pattern nevertheless followed a clear logic: The Indonesian government generally complied with the human rights protection norm, unless the case in question involved a secessionist dimension or risk of territorial disintegration, as seen in the later stages of the Saffron Revolution and the Rakhine Riots. In such instances, the Indonesian government remained silent and prioritized the noninterference norm. The mixed response pattern together with the conflicting expectations for norm compliance suggest that this is not a case of norm prioritization or general norm replacement. As a response strategy to norm conflict, Indonesia's behavior can be best described as an attempt to reconcile the two norms and thereby shape conflicting expectations and state behavior within the region to be more in line with Indonesia's normative preferences. In doing so, the government acted strategically to minimize the social costs of noncompliance with one of the two norms in relation to its relevant audiences at the domestic, regional, and international levels.

As a response strategy to norm conflict, norm reconciliation assumes that both norms remain within a state's normative framework but in a slightly modified way. One of the two conflicting norms is assigned to be the "general" and the other one the "specific" norm. Under the presidency of Susilo Bambang Yudhoyono, human rights protection became Indonesia's "general" norm. As a democratizing country and as a relatively weak coalition government, Indonesia wanted to be seen at home and abroad as a "good democracy" and promoter of human rights within the region. This meant that in cases of choice between the conflicting norms, the government would generally comply with human rights protection. From a consequentialist perspective this made sense for the Indonesian government, as acting on behalf of human rights more often than not avoided domestic legitimacy and international reputation costs. Indonesia's domestic as well as international Western audiences both held strong preferences in favor of human rights protection. The second norm was limited to instances of secessionism or territorial disintegration. In those cases that involved a risk of territorial disintegration, the specific norm of noninterference would apply and supersede the general norm of human rights protection.

The derogation of noninterference and its simultaneous superiority over the general norm in the particular instances it regulates reflects the presence of a second strong domestic expectation for the maintenance of the territorial integrity of the Indonesian state. Among Indonesians the experience of disintegrative forces ever since their independence and the loss of East Timor has produced a fierce determination and expectation that their government would prohibit any further territorial losses and external interference that could facilitate such an outcome. Neither the domestic support for human rights protection nor the desire to safeguard the country's territorial integrity were likely to be entirely removed through arguments and persuasion without far-reaching contextual change in the contested territories. While the former expectation flowed directly from Indonesian self-identification as a democracy, the latter expectation, which made compliance with noninterference necessary in some cases, was a more existential concern about the survival of the state. Faced with two sets of conflicting domestic expectations that were both relevant for its response during the later stages of the Saffron Revolution and the Rakhine Riots, the government perceived the expectations for compliance with noninterference, as stronger and ultimately more relevant for its domestic legitimacy. As an internally relatively weak coalition government, it lacked the necessary persuasive and soft power to remove the underlying causes for the continuing domestic concern for state survival, which made a strategy of general norm replacement unlikely to succeed.

In order to minimize the anticipated legitimacy and reputation costs in the cases in which it applied noninterference as the specific norm, the government tried to highlight to its audiences the link between noninterference as a standard of behavior in the region and secessionism. Where possible, the Indonesian government additionally tried to appease conflicting expectations, as seen during the Rakhine Riots. In order to limit the domestic legitimacy costs and address international expectations of the Muslim community to protect the Rohingya, the government worked through the OIC and supported a humanitarian mission by the Indonesian Red Cross to Myanmar. With respect to its regional audience, the Indonesian government tried to encourage action on behalf of human rights protection in cases without a secessionist dimension as a legitimate response that should not be seen as an act of interference. It thereby employed three main arguments: it referred to the wider international normative environment;

provided precedents from Indonesia's own openness to external involvement in similar instances in the past; and highlighted the reputational damage to ASEAN as a consequence of Myanmar's behavior. As the largest member state within the regional organization, it had the means to get its arguments out there in order to exercise persuasive power. With their nation having successfully transitioned from an authoritarian to a democratic form of governance, Indonesian decision-makers furthermore had credibility and thus soft power within the region, which is necessary to influence the behavior of others in accordance with the norms' newly framed meaning.

4

Strategic Norm Replacement in Thailand

Following the analysis of Indonesia's response to norm conflict, this chapter assesses the response of successive Thai governments to situations of norm conflict in neighboring Myanmar. In doing so, it illustrates strategic norm replacement as a response category to norm conflict. The chapter demonstrates that in the three cases of human rights violation in Myanmar, successive Thai governments consistently prioritized the noninterference norm over human rights protection. It shows that in view of strong conflicting expectations toward action articulated at the domestic and international levels, the government justified its response by framing noninterference as the only appropriate norm to regulate interstate relations between Thailand and Malaysia. To do so, it highlighted the special geopolitical context, defined by the long and porous border between the two states.

NORM FOLLOWING IN THAILAND: THE GOVERNMENT'S RESPONSE PATTERN

Prioritizing Noninterference during the Saffron Revolution

Following a month of large-scale pro-democracy demonstrations throughout Myanmar, in September 2007 the junta brutally suppressed the peaceful protests. The response of the Thai government following the Saffron Revolution was minimal, clearly prioritizing the noninterference norm over human rights protection. The country's interim government under Gen. Surayud Chulanont, which had come to power after a military coup in 2006, only condemned the violence following the collective ASEAN statement and swiftly returned to a policy of noninterference in the aftermath.

On 25 September, at the sidelines of the UN General Assembly debate in New York, Prime Minister Surayud told reporters that he was "not unaware of the situation in the neighboring country."[1] A statement published later that day on the Foreign Ministry's website said: "The government is monitoring the situation in Myanmar closely. As a fellow ASEAN member country and a close neighbor of Myanmar we sincerely hope that peace and national reconciliation will take place there."[2] While acknowledging the conflict, the Thai government abstained from criticizing the junta or condemning the violence it used against the protesting civilians and monks. It was not until the collective ASEAN statement had been issued on 27 September that Prime Minister Surayud joined the grouping in directly condemning the junta's crackdown during his speech at the UN General Assembly: "We strongly urge Myanmar to exercise utmost restraint and seek a political solution and resume its efforts at national reconciliation with all parties concerned and work towards a peaceful transition to democracy."[3] He further stated that, as a country believing in nonviolence and tolerance, "Thailand therefore finds as unacceptable the commission of violence and bodily harm to Buddhist monks and other demonstrators."[4] According to information available to the Thai newspaper *The Nation*, the prime minister's speech was only at the last minute amended to include new paragraphs on Myanmar after a "long, drawn-out wrangling between Surayud's advisors and top Foreign Ministry officials."[5] Three out of the four added paragraphs were taken directly from the ASEAN joint statement.[6] Surayud's speech at the UN was followed by a statement given by Gen. Sonthi Boonyaratglin that highlighted Thailand's preferred noninterference stance toward the junta. The army chief, who led the Thai military coup in 2006, said that Thailand should stay engaged with Myanmar. "There are many friendly nations who help Myanmar like China and Korea, because Myanmar is a country with plenty of natural resources that the powerful nations want to obtain," he said.[7] Opposing the junta would imply losing out on natural resources like gas. Defending the Myanmarese authorities, he went on to state that the demonstrators had tried to incite the military junta.[8]

Only as international pressure mounted did Thai foreign minister Nitya Pibulsonggram announce that the prime minister would soon write a letter to Myanmar's leader, Gen. Than Shwe, to express Thailand's concerns.[9] However, *The Nation* subsequently described the letter as a "shameful gesture from a leader who claims to be democratic."[10] According to the newspaper's information, Prime Minister Surayud used the letter to Gen. Than Shwe to express "solidarity with him" and stressed "that he was speaking as one soldier to another."[11] Similarly, a high-ranking military general, Charan Kullavanijaya, expressed understanding for the junta in an interview and condemned the protesting monks for their interference in politics: "We are neighbours. We know the difficulty in Myanmar. Are we able to help with solving their internal affairs? No. We can only give advice. As I mentioned earlier, when monks come on the street, there will be difficulties. It is wrong because monks should stay away from politics."[12]

In the meantime, the Thai foreign minister, who was still in the US, on 6 October met with UN special envoy Ibrahim Gambari, who had just returned to the UN headquarters from a four-day visit to Myanmar.[13] The envoy delivered a message from UN secretary-general Ban Ki-Moon to Prime Minister Surayud urging Thailand to help facilitate Gambari's stay in Myanmar by engaging all concerned parties. Surayud responded to the UN request by stating that he would address the matter in another letter, asking the Myanmarese leaders to extend Gambari's stay to facilitate a political dialogue between the generals and opposition leader Aung San Suu Kyi. However, "there should not be any preconditions or any conditions before that. Just try to start the dialogue," Surayud added.[14]

The Thai government continued its stance of interfering as little as possible during the ASEAN summit in November 2007. Thai foreign minister Nitya Pibulsonggram responded defensively to questions asking about a possible suspension of Myanmar's ASEAN membership. "ASEAN is the master of its own house. ASEAN comprises 10 members. No one is leaving. There is no reason why anyone is going to be discussing the question of anybody exiting ASEAN," Nitja told the reporters. He added that punishment or suspension of Myanmar for human rights violations was not an option.[15] Similarly, Prime Minister Surayud stated that ASEAN respected Myanmar's wish to deal directly with the UN. "If Burma needs help, ASEAN is available but at this stage we respect their decision," he said.[16] In a show of support for the generals, the Thai government invited Myanmar's prime minister, Thein Sein, on a state visit to Bangkok, to take place after the Thai general elections in December 2007.[17]

In sum, Thailand prioritized the noninterference norm in response to the Saffron Revolution. The government tried to interfere as little as possible, and any negative statement was quickly followed by apologetic remarks that expressed understanding for the actions of the junta and blamed the protestors for interfering in politics.

Noninterference Continues in Response to Cyclone Nargis

The situation on the ground in Myanmar following Cyclone Nargis started as a humanitarian crisis, but in the view of international observers quickly evolved into a case of large-scale human rights violation as the junta denied international aid workers access to the affected areas. In responding to the crisis, the Thai government again prioritized noninterference. While taking on the role of a logistic hub for the international relief effort, the government ensured that it did not directly pressure or criticize the junta for its handling of the humanitarian fallout of Cyclone Nargis.

Following the cyclone, on 6 May 2008 Prime Minister Samak Sundaravej sent a letter to Yangon expressing his condolences for the tragic losses and offered assistance to help Myanmar recover.[18] He stated that "if Myanmar gives the green light allowing us to help, our Air Force will provide a C-130 aircraft to carry our teams there."[19] He emphasized that "this should not be precipitately carried out" but needed to "have the permission of their government."[20] In waiting for an invitation, Samak complied with the noninterference norm. Samak's offer was welcomed on the same day by Myanmar's foreign minister Nyan Win, who stated that his country appreciated the humanitarian aid. Following an invitation from Myanmar, Thai foreign minister Noppadon Pattama announced that Thailand would send US$100,000 in aid together with medicine and food to Myanmar.[21] However, strictly adhering to the Myanmarese protocol, nineteen Thai medical teams were left on standby in Bangkok to be dispatched only upon the junta's request, as the junta insisted on distributing the aid on its own.[22] The junta later asked its four neighbors, China, Bangladesh, Thailand, and India, to send humanitarian relief teams to join the distribution effort.[23]

At the same time, international criticism of the junta's handling of the crisis magnified, prominently expressed, for example, by US First Lady Laura Bush, who blamed the generals for having failed to warn their citizens of the impending storm.[24] Asked about the junta's prior knowledge of the cyclone, Thai authorities confirmed that an alert had come from the US Navy's Joint Typhoon Warning Center as early as 27 April, but they refused to comment specifically about what Myanmar knew.[25] Even on the third day after the disaster, international relief agencies—especially those from Western nations—were still waiting for permission to enter Myanmar, as the junta had not responded to a request to waive visa requirements for relief agencies.[26] In view of the restrictions, the US desperately sought Thailand's help to gain access to cyclone-ravaged Myanmar and deliver humanitarian assistance to the millions of storm victims. On 8 May, US ambassador Eric John met with Prime Minister Samak, asking him to facilitate the granting of permission from the Myanmarese leaders for the US emergency relief team to enter the country. According to Ambassador John, the prime minister gave "some assurance" that his government would work closely with the US.[27] The following day the *Bangkok Post* reported that Prime Minister Samak had agreed to negotiate on Washington's behalf to persuade the junta to accept aid from the West. He also promised to go to Myanmar, if need be, to coordinate response with the junta leaders.[28] However, the plan to go to Myanmar was abruptly canceled. Samak had failed to get through to junta leader Than Shwe and his deputy Muang Aye, due to "poor communication," according to Thai spokesperson Wichianchot Sukchotrat. The generals had subsequently informed the Thai side that they would be "too busy" with the people affected by the deadly cyclone to welcome Samak.[29] Honoring the junta's wishes, the prime minister instead dispatched his special envoy, Lt. Gen. Niphat Thonglek, to Myanmar to deliver a letter to Prime Minister Thein Sein.[30] Special Envoy Niphat declined to reveal details of the letter to the press, such as whether it asked for permission from the junta for Western relief teams to enter the country.[31]

In response to mounting international pressure, on 10 May Myanmar's government issued a statement saying that Myanmar was not in a position to receive rescue and information teams from foreign countries. Instead, priority was given to receiving relief aid and distributing it to the storm-hit regions with its own resources. The junta also announced that some aid workers had been deported.[32] Following the statement, Prime Minister Samak said, "With such a statement, there is no need for me to travel to Burma."[33] Despite his earlier promise to the US, on 11 May he called off his plan to travel to the country in order to negotiate access to the affected areas. In defense of the junta, Samak went on arguing that "he fully supported Burma as Thailand was a neighbor and he would not mind if his stance causes the West to isolate Thailand."[34] He further expressed his admiration for the junta, given that Supreme Commander Boonsang Niampradit had arranged for "swift assistance to Burma."³⁵ Given Samak's change of plans, UN secretary-general Ban Ki-Moon himself called the Thai prime minister on 12 May, asking Thailand again to convince the junta to allow international relief agencies to enter the country. The UN message was passed on to the Myanmarese authorities by Thailand's special envoy Niphat.³⁶ The following day Foreign Minister Noppadon announced that upon the direct request of UN secretary-general Ban Ki-Moon, Prime Minister Samak was going to travel to Myanmar after all on 14 May.³⁷ Noppadon told reporters that it was unclear whether Samak would be able to meet the top leadership on his visit,³⁸ but he suggested that countries wanting to assist the cyclone victims should adopt a "sympathetic and friendly approach" toward the junta.³⁹

On 14 May Samak finally left for the capital, Naypyidaw, to talk to his Myanmarese counterpart, Thein Sein.⁴⁰ The prime minister, however, failed to persuade the junta to allow foreign aid workers into the country. The government in Myanmar only agreed to the dispatch of a thirty-member Thai medical team to help the victims of Cyclone Nargis.⁴¹ Upon his return from Myanmar, Samak forcefully defended the generals. Amid reports of theft of aid supplies, restrictions on movement, and general official neglect, Samak praised the junta's relief efforts. "From what I have seen, I am impressed with their management," he said. Samak, who had met with Prime Minister Thein Sein for two and a half hours, said he had been taken to shelter centers and had seen donations, especially those items donated by the Thai royal family. Moreover, the generals had given him a "guarantee" that there had been no outbreaks of disease or starvation among cyclone survivors.⁴² Samak went on, emphasizing that the prime minister had expressed gratitude to Thailand for its assistance and had asked him to relay to the international community what he had seen. "They told me they are confident that they can deal with the problems. There is no outbreak of diseases and no shortage of food. They do not want anyone to intervene or teach them [what to do]," Samak said.⁴³

At the ASEAN emergency meeting on 19 May 2008 in Singapore, it was determined that as part of the ASEAN-led mechanism, both UN secretary-general Ban Ki-Moon and ASEAN secretary-general Surin Pitsuwan would travel to Myanmar to assess the damage caused by the cyclone. But when asked for a concrete schedule, Foreign Minister Noppadon only told the reporters that "we [ASEAN] have to listen to Burma's opinion first."[44] Following a meeting with UN under-secretary for humanitarian affairs John Holmes, the Thai foreign minister agreed that in light of the huge destruction, Thailand wanted Myanmar's officials to see the necessity of having more foreign aid workers in their country but reiterated that his government would not "force Myanmar, because we are Myanmar's friend."[45] Despite the junta's agreement to the ASEAN-led mechanism, the Myanmarese administration kept delaying access for international aid workers. While UN agencies continued to press the junta to allow in more foreign workers, Foreign Minister Noppadon only observed, "They have opened more, at least granting permission for foreign media and some international aid workers to see the devastated areas, but it is not unhindered access."[46]

To sum up, the Thai government would have been in a position to exercise much more pressure on the junta, given the level of communication it enjoyed with the generals. But at no point did the Thai government choose to openly criticize the Myanmarese government for its failure to provide adequate help to its people. Prime Minister Samak instead repeatedly publicly defended the junta leaders, thereby prioritizing a policy of noninterference over human rights protection.

Reinforcing Noninterference during the Rakhine Riots

The Thai response to the riots in Rakhine State in western Myanmar and the subsequent violence against the Muslim Rohingya in 2012 was one of absolute silence. The government under Prime Minister Yingluck Shinawatra, which had come to power after the general elections in August 2011, chose to prioritize the noninterference norm over human rights protection. During the entire period of the crisis not a single official government statement was issued by the Thai administration, which instead strengthened its bilateral relations with the government in Myanmar during an official state visit.

The signals Thailand sent by welcoming President Thein Sein for his first official state visit to Thailand on 22 July 2012 were far from indicating disapproval of his government's handling of the crisis in Rakhine.[47] Although the two governments discussed the possibility of elections in Myanmar, "the Rohingya were not a topic of the meeting," as the foreign minister of Thailand at the time, Surapong Tovichakchaikul, admitted. This statement shows that despite Thailand's direct access to the junta leaders, Prime Minister Yingluck Shinawatra chose not to touch upon the topic. On the contrary, she instead agreed with her Myanmarese counterpart to "strengthen cooperation."[48] After a ninety-minute discussion, the respective ministers signed several Memoranda of Understanding on technical cooperation, economic development cooperation, and energy security.[49] Thailand further pledged to support Myanmar in areas of human resource development, capacity building for its upcoming ASEAN chairmanship, and infrastructure development, according to a joint press statement issued by Prime Minister Yingluck.[50]

The Thai government maintained its mute response to the crisis in October as fighting between the Muslim and Buddhist groups in Myanmar recommenced, and violence against the Rohingya was reported to have become much more systematic. Instead of addressing the situation in Rakhine, the government used the ASEAN summit in Phnom Penh in November 2012 to formally announce the two countries' cooperation on the Dawei deep-sea port development in the Thai-Myanmar border area.[51]

Once again, therefore, the Thai government prioritized the norm of noninterference over human rights protection by choosing not to comment on the riots in Rakhine State. Indeed, it went even further, at least symbolically, in backing the Myanmarese government by welcoming President Thein Sein in Bangkok and intensifying cooperation.

EXPLAINING THAILAND'S RESPONSE TO NORM CONFLICT

As the above analysis has shown, the respective Thai governments chose to prioritize the noninterference norm over human rights protection in all three situations of norm conflict. They tried to interfere as little as possible and only momentarily deviated from their chosen path of action in response to direct regional or international pressure. Thailand's behavior in these instances of norm conflict therefore manifested as a relatively uniform response pattern in favor of compliance with noninterference, despite various changes in government that were both civilian and military in nature. In the following, I will explain the Thai government's norm following as a case of strategic norm replacement in response to conflicting expectations for norm following. Unlike norm reconciliation, this response strategy manifests as uniform response pattern. It does not aim to undermine the general validity of the violated norm, so is thereby in contrast to general norm replacement accounting for Thailand's generally supportive stance toward human rights protection at the regional level. In making a case for strategic norm replacement, Thailand aimed to minimize its own social costs within a specific context without impacting the behavior of others.

The Need to Please: Thailand's Special Relationship with Myanmar

Despite the mounting international pressure on the junta, applied by UN secretary-general Ban Ki-Moon and Western powers at the annual UN General Assembly debate as early as 25 September 2007, the Thai interim government of Gen. Surayud Chulanont refrained from criticizing Myanmar. Its reluctance to act on behalf of human rights protection in line with the expectations articulated by the international community reflected a strong domestic expectation that the Thai government would maintain friendly relations with the neighboring regime. This expectation was primarily articulated by the rural Thai population and the country's powerful business class, who hoped that by applying a policy of noninterference, Thailand's border trade with Myanmar and access to the country's natural resources would remain unaffected. In light of these domestic preferences, the Thai government considered domestic expectations set by the shared commitment to noninterference to be stronger than international expectations for compliance with human rights protection. Violating the noninterference norm might not only have entailed reputation costs in relation to those member states within the region that only embraced the noninterference norm, but, more importantly, it would have risked legitimacy costs at home if trade was affected by a deterioration in relation with Thailand's neighbor Myanmar.

Ever since the Asian financial crisis in 1997, the "uneasy alliance" between the liberal urban middle class and the rural population, which had facilitated democratic reform in Thailand since the 1980s, and a human rights–centered foreign policy in relation to Myanmar, had been broken.[52] The rural population's tacit consent to the democratization process had been based on the premise of simultaneous economic growth, which had led to unequaled prosperity and an enhanced quality of life for all Thais.[53] While benefiting least from the democratic reforms, the rural population was hit hardest during the Asian financial crisis, causing a high unemployment rate and a widening income gap between the city and countryside.⁵⁴ But the effects of the crisis not only undermined and ultimately destroyed the coalition between urban and rural forces. They also caused a social rift within the middle class itself, which was split between an emerging class of entrepreneurs and the traditional bureaucracy. The latter believed that the financial crisis had been caused by cronyism, nepotism, and corruption in the financial sector and wanted these deficiencies to be corrected by developing the country's democratic structures. Thai businesses, in contrast, were primarily interested in pursuing their economic interests at home and abroad, which importantly included access to Myanmar's vast natural resources. This endeavor had been hindered in the past by the Democrat-led government's human rights–centered stance toward Myanmar. Bilateral relations under Prime Minister Chuan Leekpai had thus been described as "somewhat strained over democracy and human rights."⁵⁵ The rural population in particular perceived the Democrat Party's foreign policy as a threat to flourishing border trade with the neighboring regime, upon which many of them depended to earn a living.⁵⁶ In response to acts of interference by Thailand on behalf of human rights protection, the Myanmarese junta had repeatedly closed the border and, in November 1999, imposed economic sanctions on Thailand, which hit Thai businesses hard.⁵⁷

Voting the Democrat-led government out of office in the elections of 2001, the rural population instead entrusted business mogul Thaksin Shinawatra with governing the country.⁵⁸ Outnumbering the urban middle class at the polls, the rural population redefined the parameters of the government's legitimacy, which was no longer primarily gained by pursuing democratic goals domestically and abroad but by speaking to the economic interests of the rural population and Thailand's rising business class. A commitment to development thus became the new domestic paradigm. Reflecting this change, Thaksin immediately announced a return to a noninterference policy in relation to Myanmar and other neighboring states after coming to power.⁵⁹ His foreign minister, Surakiart Sathirathai, told *The Nation* that Thailand's policy vis-à-vis its neighbors would be one of "forward engagement," guided by a business-driven rather than ideological agenda. "We must identify key relationships and focus on dimensions where we can cooperate. Our foreign policy must correspond with the economic needs of Thailand," he said.⁶⁰ Whereas former prime minister Chuan had not visited Myanmar once during his time in office, Thaksin promised to make Yangon one of his first official destinations.[61] Smooth relations with the junta facilitated access to Myanmar's market, and in what followed Thai investment in Myanmar was enthusiastically encouraged.[62] Not least due to Thaksin's "cosy relationship with the Myanmar generals," the economy recovered during his premiership.[63] By 2005 Myanmar had become Thailand's largest trading partner and major energy supplier. Since Myanmar was remade into a "lucrative market for hungry Thai businesses," public concerns over democracy, human rights, and justice diminished noticeably in designing and implementing Thai foreign policy in relation to the neighbor.[64]

Even though Thaksin was ousted in the 2006 military coup d'état, the interim military government maintained his policy of noninterference in Myanmar due to Thailand's acute economic dependence on Myanmar and the rural population's strength in numbers at the polls. In speaking to the domestic development paradigm set during the Thaksin administration, the new government tried to appease Thaksin supporters after his forced removal as prime minister. In addition, the close relations between the Thai and Myanmarese military leadership further facilitated a choice in favor of noninterference during the Saffron Revolution. Vivid public displays of their close relations had been released earlier that year during Gen. Sonthi Boonyaratglin's two-day visit to Myanmar. The general had been a leading figure behind the military coup d'état in 2006. A photograph published in the *Bangkok Post* on 29 August 2007 showed the general politely bowing his head while shaking hands with junta leader Gen. Than Shwe.[65] Taken together, the dominant domestic expectation for noninterference and the close military ties between the two countries explain why General Surayud refused to join the rest of the world in condemning the junta's crackdown.

Demonstrating the split across Thai society, Surayud's half-hearted statement on 25 September 2007 in which he failed to condemn the violence almost instantly caused resistance within the Thai urban middle class. As a consequence, the domestic expectations for legitimate action by the Thai government during the Saffron Revolution were far from uniform. As the main mouthpieces of this constituency, the liberal English-language newspapers *Bangkok Post* and *The Nation* immediately criticized General Surayud's slow response. *Bangkok Post* editor Achara Ashayagachat argued that the government was neglecting the crisis, "despite the lead set by others in the international community."[66] Concerned about Thailand's international reputation, she commented: "Prime Minister Surayud Chulanont . . . is too preoccupied with prepared messages to the world about Thailand's efforts to return to democracy that he has had little time to address the Burma problem."[67] For the Thai middle class, a tough stance toward the neighboring authoritarian regime had always served as an expression of Thailand's democratic credentials. Representing the most politicized sector of Thai society, it had grown increasingly committed to democratic values and procedures, which in the 1992 elections led to the victory of the Democrat Party with Chuan Leekpai as the new prime minister. Economic growth not only swelled the urban middle class but also increased its influence on policymaking, until the 2001 general elections and Thaksin's political victory.[68]

Politically, Surayud's lack of attention to the crisis caused relatively little opposition, reflecting a general awareness among politicians that good relations with Myanmar were essential for domestic support, especially in view of the scheduled general elections in December 2007. Accordingly, only a few outspoken Thai legislators addressed the topic.[69] On 26 September 2007, Jon Ungphakorn, a member of the Thai Senate, criticized the government for reacting too slowly to the crisis unfolding in the neighboring state.[70] He called upon the government to "relinquish its wimpish 'non-interference' position on the Burmese domestic situation and tell the Burmese regime in no uncertain terms that any use of violence to crackdown on the peaceful mass demonstrations for democracy and social justice . . . will be completely unacceptable to Thailand."[71] As a member of the ASEAN Inter-Parliamentary Myanmar Caucus, he further stated that the group believed that ASEAN countries could not realistically adhere to the current policy of "non-interference," as events in one country often affected its neighbors and sometimes the whole region. "No one can really argue with the fact that the domestic situation in Burma had immense impact on the ASEAN community as a whole, and particularly Thailand," he concluded. In view of an expected wave of Myanmarese refugees entering Thailand, which had long served as a safe haven for dissidents from the neighboring country, Ungphakorn appealed to the Thai government to directly speak out against the junta.[72] A similar call came a few days later on 19 September from Democrat Party member Kraisak Choonhavan, who openly lashed out at the Thai military for being too soft on the junta. He argued that "as a neighbour, the government's stance on the issue is shameful. The government fails to show support for the Burmese public or call on the junta to show morality towards its people."[73]

Although it is often argued that respect for human rights and their prioritization in Thailand's foreign policy is a reflection of whether the military or civilians are in power, the muted response of the Democrat Party in particular and legislators in general during the Saffron Revolution suggests otherwise. The Democrat Party's position did not differ widely from the official government stance, which tried to preserve the status quo in the country's relations with Myanmar by prioritizing noninterference over human rights protection. The liberal newspaper *Bangkok Post*, therefore, wrote indignantly during the Saffron Revolution, "What is also frustrating is the negligence of the Democrat party."[74] According to surveys at the time of the Saffron Revolution, the Democrats could still hope to win the December 2007 general elections.[75] Their silence during the crisis thus reflects the general awareness that a prioritization of human rights protection in Thailand's relations with Myanmar involved the risk of severe legitimacy costs at home. In order to win the upcoming elections, the Democrats also needed to mop up votes from the rural population and the Thai business class. As a consequence, no political party represented the views of the urban middle class during the Saffron Revolution.

In assessing the expectations articulated by its relevant audiences, the Thai government only came around to condemning the junta's violent crackdown as Western pressure mounted during the annual UN General Assembly debate and a collective ASEAN statement was issued on 27 September. "It had to be clear that the incident affected the sentiments of the people in the world and the UN had taken the lead, before Thailand would follow," Achara Ashayagachat, editor at the *Bangkok Post*, wrote, explaining Thailand's momentary deviation from its policy of noninterference.[76] Recalling the episode, Surapong Jayanama, who served as the deputy secretary-general of the Foreign Ministry at the time, elaborated on the Foreign Ministry's motivation to change the prime minister's speech in a last-minute act: "The Saffron Revolution was not the first time that they killed their own people. That has happened so many times before. We regard that as their own internal affair, as do other ASEAN states. But if it destabilizes the region or if it affects or tarnishes the credibility or reputation of ASEAN, then we can no longer stay mute or pretend nothing has happened. ASEAN had taken the lead and we had to follow."[77]

For the Thai government, the collective ASEAN position in favor of human rights protection intensified the costs of noncompliance with the human rights protection norm by adding additional reputation costs in relation to its democratic peers in the region, which had lobbied for the statement. But ASEAN pressure for a joint position on the crackdown was not the only reason why Prime Minister Surayud agreed to change his speech. "Another reason why he made this statement was to turn the tables on the Western countries," Surapong recalled.[78] The rationale was as follows: "We had to show the world that even though General Surayud was an unelected prime minister who had come to power via a coup, he was of course a democrat (small d)."[79] The domestic liberal media, however, dismissed the statement issued by the prime minister. *The Nation* indignantly wrote: "It is sad but true that the Thai delegation did not have the courage to say something of its own. They did not even bother rewording or rephrasing those sentences" taken from the joint ASEAN statement.[80] In view of the continuing violence against the protestors, an editorial in *The Nation* called upon the international community to "cut all support for the evil regime." It demanded in particular that those countries with close military and economic ties to the junta—especially Thailand—tell the generals "in no uncertain terms" that they cannot "butcher pro-democracy protesters the way they did in the past and expect the world to sit idly by."[81]

Apparently unmoved by domestic pressure from liberal Thai forces, however, the government in tandem with Thai businesses focused instead on addressing public fears of an economic downturn as a result of the crisis. The Thai government repeatedly assured its domestic audience that it was carefully monitoring the situation across Thailand's western border. Thai traders had warned that border trade with Myanmar, worth almost US$800 million per year, could be significantly hit if the ongoing protests turned violent. Apriradi Tantraporn, director-general of the Foreign Trade Department, thereupon emphasized that the border checkpoints would remain open and trade was unlikely to be affected.[82] Vice president of the Charoen Pakphand Group (one of the world's largest conglomerates) Sarasin Viraphol similarly announced that the protests would not affect the group's investments. "We will perceive Burma as a country of investment potential. The unrest involves domestic problems that should not make a negative impact on the economy," he said.[83] At the same time domestic expectations articulated by Thai Buddhist and human rights agencies in Thailand, which had called on the

Supreme Sangha Council of Thailand to take a stance against the killing of Burmese monks and civilians that were demonstrating peacefully, remained unaddressed. The joint statement of seventeen agencies argued that it would be an appropriate obligation for Thai Buddhists to help stop the violence in neighboring Myanmar. Although Thai Buddhism should not interfere in politics, nonviolent solidarity should be encouraged.[84] But in line with Prime Minister Surayud's stance, the Thai Sangha, which has long been under the tight supervision of the government, remained silent.

Domestically, the government's noninterference stance reflected the military's preferences and avoided legitimacy costs among its numerically strongest domestic audience, the rural population and Thai business class. Internationally, however, the government's noninterference policy proved problematic, as it threatened to incur reputation costs in light of the international community's emphasis on human rights protection during the crisis. Among Southeast Asian nations, Thailand—next to the Philippines—has the longest-standing ties to the Western world. Unlike most of its regional peers, it was not nonaligned during the Cold War but, rather, formally cooperated with the West and the US in particular. Therefore, in order to reduce the reputation fallout from its noninterference policy in relation to its Western international audience, Foreign Minister Nitya Pibulsonggram argued that as an immediate neighbor with 2,401 kilometers of shared border, Thailand could not push too hard without jeopardizing relations. "If they had not been bothered about their international image, they would not have defended themselves. But they did, so of course they cared," wrote Achara Ashayagachat in explaining the government's justification.[85] Following a meeting with British foreign secretary David Miliband, Foreign Minister Nitya added that "what Thailand can do best is to support ASEAN and United Nations special envoy Ibrahim Gambari."[86] Thereupon, Miliband expressed understanding for Thailand's "unique circumstances" in relation to Myanmar, as the kingdom was the first place where displaced persons from Myanmar arrived.[87] "As always, the government used its long border with Myanmar as the big excuse for doing nothing, arguing that if they say things, they would get in trouble with Myanmar," reflected Phil Robertson of HRW, who at the time worked as an independent consultant in Bangkok.[88] "And people accepted it."[89] Domestically, however, Foreign Minister Nitya's argument was judged more critically, as commentators turned the foreign minister's argument on its head:

As a Buddhist, frontline state, the government should come out with statements that are more fruitful and stronger, not wishy-washy. As a frontline state to Burma, Thailand has utterly failed to show leadership for the grouping. Since it shares a 2401-kilometer border with Burma, Thailand should have more say in ASEAN policies toward the country. The Foreign Ministry has instead preferred a passive approach. Just look at the problems caused by the Burmese junta's intransigence against its people that Thailand has to deal with. Through inept attitudes and policies, the Thais have failed to respond to Burmese people's request for basic rights and freedoms.[90]

Finally, joining in on the domestic criticism, on 2 October US chargé d'affaires in Yangon Shari Villarosa stressed that more international help was needed, especially from neighboring Thailand: "I think the Thai government should speak out critically about what's happening. I think they should reconsider business arrangements that they have with the Burmese generals."[91] She thereby hinted at the fact that though China and India had large-scale energy projects planned or under construction in Myanmar, the revenue from these investments had not yet materialized. Until the respective oil and gas taps were turned on, ASEAN countries remained the top source of Myanmar's foreign exchange revenue. Between 2005 and 2007, Thailand and Singapore had provided over 98 percent of new foreign direct investment in Myanmar. At the time, revenue from natural gas supplies to Thailand earned the Myanmarese junta approximately US$160 million per month in sales, equal to 43 percent of Myanmar's overseas revenue.[92] By stopping their investments, Thailand and Singapore could have starved the regime.[93]

The expectations toward Thailand articulated by the US were particularly important as at that time a Thai government delegation had stopped in the US on its tour to seek international recognition from world leaders after the 2006 military coup d'état.[94] To explain the political developments in Thailand and assure their counterparts that the kingdom was moving back to a democratic path, Foreign Minister Nitya met with several US senators and congressmen during his stay in the US.[95] For the Thai government, US recognition mattered in particular, as the country was its main Western ally. Since the Second World War, the United States has been the primary security and political guarantor for the Thai state. The US-Thai relationship, which has been based on robust military-to-military cooperation, solidified during the Cold War with Thailand serving as a reliable anti-Communist ally in the region.[96] In 2003, Thailand was accorded the status of a major non-NATO ally, following a brief but intense round of counterterrorism cooperation with the US during the first Thaksin administration.[97]

Given the perceived importance of US support, it was with some indignation that Foreign Minister Nitya noted that US lawmakers were actually far more interested in discussing the situation in Myanmar than Thai affairs. Following pressure from the US, Nitya finally announced that Prime Minister Surayud would soon write a letter to Myanmar's leader, Gen. Than Shwe, to express Thailand's concerns.[98] "The Thai military is receptive. They care about their image, so when the international community speaks they always listen," Laurent Meillan, head of the regional UN Office for the High Commissioner for Human Rights, stated as an explanation for Surayud's consent to contact the junta on the matter.[99] But Surayud's willingness to cooperate internationally also reflected, and was meant to counteract, a growing domestic concern, summarized by the Thai Chamber of Commerce. It worried that if the international community continued to intensify pressure on trading partners to impose sanctions on Myanmar, Thai businesses could be severely affected.[100] Although concern for the country's reputation in the Western world did not tip the balance in favor of a general prioritization of human rights protection during the crisis, Western expectations nevertheless forced the Thai government to make concessions in favor of the norm. As requested by US lawmakers, this involved writing a letter to the Myanmarese junta on the matter of the Saffron Revolution. Justifying the letter, Prime Minister Surayud apologetically stated that Thailand also had "to look at the international community, the UN and ASEAN."[101]

The Thai government's sensitivity to international expectations was evidenced again upon Foreign Minister Nitya's return to New York on 6 October, where UN secretary-general Ban Ki-Moon directly urged Thailand to help facilitate UN special envoy Ibrahim Gambari's stay in Myanmar.[102] Ban Ki-Moon's call was backed by several European governments. In an opinion piece published the following day in *The Nation,* French foreign minister Kouchner and British foreign secretary Miliband addressed ASEAN in general and Thailand in particular. They called upon Myanmar's neighbors to "play a vital role in helping to build a better future for the people of Burma."[103] Kouchner and Miliband went on, stating that for ASEAN, "turning a blind eye would jeopardize the whole process of democratization and development of this region and damages its credibility."[104] Confronted with direct international pressure articulated by the UN and Western governments, General Surayud again conceded and agreed to address the matter in another letter to Myanmar. At the same time, Surayud clarified that any dialogue with the junta had to come without preconditions, thereby trying to take the edge off his initiative, which could have been perceived as an act of interference by the Myanmarese government.

Following the momentary concession to Western expectations, the Thai government swiftly returned to its position of noninterference in relation to Myanmar. At the ASEAN summit in November 2007, when the Myanmarese junta forcefully reiterated its stance according to which the protests constituted an internal affair, the government backed the junta and ruled out any form of sanctions. *The Nation* described the government's performance at the ASEAN summit in Singapore as "two digits below par" and concluded that Thai leaders were seen "failing to appreciate the democratic aspirations inside Burma."[105] The Thai government, however, underlined its position when, "in the most obvious show of support for the generals," it invited Prime Minister Thein Sein for a state visit to Bangkok.[106]

Overall, it can be said that in view of conflicting expectations for compliance with the two norms during the Saffron Revolution, the government aligned its stance with the expectations of the numerically strongest domestic groups, the rural population and the Thai business class. These constituencies expected the government to maintain friendly relations with Myanmar and thereby guarantee continued access to the market next door. In addressing this expectation, the government avoided legitimacy costs at home. In contrast, conflicting domestic expectations in favor of interference on the basis of human rights protection expressed by the liberal urban middle class did not weigh heavily in the government's considerations. It neither showed a willingness to make concessions with respect to the expectations of its human rights advocating domestic audience, nor did it justify its actions to them. Internationally, the government justified its policy of noninterference by highlighting Thailand's special geopolitical position as a direct neighbor of Myanmar. In doing so, it hoped to reduce conflicting international expectations for compliance with human rights protection and thus minimize the reputation costs of norm violation. Despite Thailand's excuses, direct expectations were articulated by its long-term international partners, the US and the UN. The government was therefore willing to make some concessions and momentarily divert from its noninterference policy. However, in each case the government justified its position regarding the junta and swiftly returned to a stance of noninterference.

Justifying Noninterference and Making Concessions after the Cyclone

When Myanmar was hit by Cyclone Nargis in May 2008, less than a year after the Saffron Revolution, and the junta shut the country to international aid workers, the Thai government, now headed by Prime Minister Samak Sundaravej, again opted for a noninterference policy in response to the crisis. A crony of ousted Prime Minister Thaksin Shinawatra, Samak had come to power following the general elections in December 2007.

On the domestic level, the government's prioritization of noninterference over human rights protection once again reflected a domestic expectation for friendly relations between the two states. In safeguarding close relations with Myanmar, Prime Minister Samak tried to please his main voter base, the rural population and the business class, who were dependent on continued access to Myanmar and the flourishing border trade. The government's prioritization of noninterference over human rights protection was further facilitated by the fact that even the urban middle class initially articulated few expectations for an alternative approach. "Domestically the crisis was primarily seen as a humanitarian disaster," Achara Ashayagachat from the *Bangkok Post* explained.[107] Against that backdrop, Thailand was believed to have done its bit in delivering humanitarian aid to Myanmar.

However, justifying the government's noninterference stance on the international level proved more difficult in light of direct international expectations for action on behalf of human rights protection. These expectations caused the Thai government to make repeated concessions to its international audience, though it rarely followed through with its promises in a constructive way. After the cyclone hit Myanmar, UN agencies and international aid organizations immediately gathered in Bangkok, where many had their regional headquarters, to make preparations for a major disaster relief effort. "The UN support system is not sufficient inside Myanmar," said Terje Skavdal, regional director of the UN Office for Coordination of Humanitarian Affairs, hoping for fast access to the closed-off country.[108] The junta had previously appealed for international assistance.[109] But while asking international donors for material goods such as food, medicine, and roofing material, plastic sheets, temporary tents, fresh water, and mosquito nets, the generals refused to issue visas to international aid workers to coordinate the distribution of aid within the country, thereby risking the lives of more civilians.[110] As a consequence, the West and the United Nations shifted the frame of the crisis from a humanitarian disaster to a case of human rights violations. Highlighting the extent of human suffering, US ambassador Eric John urged the junta to make a quick decision in order to let the US disaster team in as soon as possible.[111] Similarly, French foreign minister Bernard Kouchner and British foreign secretary of state David Miliband asked the generals to "lift all restrictions on the distribution of aid."[112] The UN also reiterated its call on the government to let aid and aid workers in, arguing that it was "imperative at this point that they do open up and allow a major international relief effort to get under way."[113] Increasingly desperate, it was the US government that first appealed directly to the Thai authorities, asking them to facilitate access to Myanmar by negotiating with the junta on behalf of the West and the UN. Samak's response to Ambassador Eric John's request on 8 May reflects the ambiguous relationship that had been cultivated between the People's Power Party (a successor organization to Thaksin's Thai Rak Thai Party) and the West (the US in particular). As a longtime ally, Thailand would always listen to requests made by the US, no matter who was in power, noted Sunai Phasuk of HRW. But substantive action would often be delayed, in particular when sentiment toward the US or the West was not good among the leadership. "At the time of the cyclone Prime Minister Samak was in charge, who did not like the US at all. Samak is known as one of the most conservative politicians in Thailand," Phasuk elaborated.[114]

Samak's stance toward the US reflected a general deterioration in relations between Thaksin supporters, the so-called Red Shirts, and the US following the ousting of the prime minister in the 2006 military coup. Thaksin's supporters saw the coup as an illegal and illegitimate act of forced regime change instigated by the military against the will of the majority of the Thai people.[115] The overall Western response to the coup-makers, however, was muted, and Thailand continued to be considered a key ally of the US and Western democracies within the region.[116] Thus, although US expectations were noted during the crisis in Myanmar following the cyclone and were symbolically addressed, US pressure proved insufficient to get Prime Minister Samak to take actual substantive action. "Prime Minister Samak relied on the existence of large conservative forces in Thai society to back him up. It was not just him versus international requests, but him plus millions of Thais thinking the same," noted Sunai Phasuk of HRW.[117] As a result, Samak only reluctantly acted on the US' behalf during Cyclone Nargis and immediately called off his visit to Yangon when the junta resisted. Having to choose between action in accordance with human rights protection and noninterference, Samak prioritized Myanmar's expectations over Western calls. "They did not want us to come in," said former ambassador and advisor to the Foreign Ministry Surapong Jayanama. "And frankly we thought the international community was already doing enough," he added.[118]

It was only after Samak canceled his visit to Myanmar that Thai media started to critically comment on the crisis, which had previously been framed as a humanitarian disaster. The *Bangkok Post* now urged the junta to admit that it did not "have the capacity to tackle this gigantic task by itself."[119] Myanmar could no longer solemnly rely on the assistance of a few "trusted neighbours" like Thailand, India, and China, the paper wrote.[120] The situation worsened when, on 10 May, the Myanmarese government seized two planeloads of critical aid sent by the UN, forcing the body to suspend further help. Tony Banbury, regional director of the World Food Programme (WFP), desperately appealed to the junta to release the aid. "Please, this food is going to people who need it very much.... Those victims who need this assistance are not part of a political dialogue. They need this humanitarian assistance," he pleaded.[121] Paul Risley, coordinating the relief effort of the WFP, added: "The frustration caused by what appears to be a paperwork delay is unprecedented in modern humanitarian relief efforts."[122] UN relief coordinator Richard Horsey reiterated the UN call to suspend visas when stating that it was urgent that the authorities in Myanmar open up. "There aren't enough boats, trucks, helicopter in the country to run the relief effort of the scale we need," he emphasized.[123] However, impervious to the pressure, Myanmar's generals insisted that visas would be considered on a case-by-case basis.¹²⁴ In view of the deadlock, on 12 May UN secretary-general Ban Ki-Moon contacted Prime Minister Samak directly, asking him again to go to Myanmar and speak with the generals. Foreign Minister Noppadon Pattama said that Thailand had also been contacted by telephone by the foreign ministers of the UK, Canada, Norway, and the EU, seeking their mediation with Myanmar's rulers to facilitate the international access to the cyclone-hit areas.¹²⁵ But despite the increasingly critical reception of the junta's handling of the crisis, domestically the international pressure exerted on the Thai government was received negatively. Even the liberally minded journalists of the *Bangkok Post* defended the Thai authorities, arguing that so far Thailand had done its best by offering its condolences as well as delivering token but much-needed aid to Myanmar.¹²⁶ They ascribed the fact that Thai aid had entered the country to Samak's "junta-appeasing policy and the junta's recognition of an admirable reception during a visit to Thailand by Burmese Prime Minister Thein Sein."¹²⁷ The visit ended only two days prior to the natural disaster in the neighboring state. The paper further argued that, "by doing too much too soon," Thailand could create a bad impression and affect the warm relations between Thailand and its neighbor.¹²⁸ Therefore, the kingdom should not be pressured by the international community, or even UN secretary-general Ban Ki-Moon, to lobby the military government in Myanmar to open up its doors to foreign assistance.¹²⁹ The paper pointed out that Thailand had to protect its own interests in responding to the crisis. In pushing the generals too hard, the kingdom could be considered by Myanmar as a proxy of the Western world.¹³⁰

Following a familiar pattern, Prime Minister Samak acknowledged the expectations articulated by UN secretary-general Ban Ki-Moon and renewed his promise to travel to Myanmar. However, once in the country he did little to convince the junta to open up. His mission did not lead to an improvement of access. "We did not want to pressure them," said Surayud Jayanama:

> The Myanmarese government was quite understandably very concerned about whether to accept humanitarian aid from outsiders and let them into the country. It would have been a difficult situation to control. For a military regime with more than fifty years in power that was a very natural reaction. They were very suspicious of destabilizing policies designed by Western countries and

disguised as humanitarian aid. This is why they kept their narrative alive, saying "we are in control of the situation, no worries, this is our internal matter and we take care of our own problems."[131]

As head of the Thai Red Cross, which was part of the Thai relief effort, former Thai ambassador and foreign minister Tej Bunnag closely followed the events. "Prime Minister Samak was of the same mind as the generals, rather anti-Western, pro-Thai and very nationalistic. He agreed with the attitude of the Burmese government," Bunnag said, adding: "I doubt he had a serious conversation with the junta. When Samak came back he made some very embarrassing statements."[132] Upon his return, the prime minister praised the relief work of the junta, arguing that the situation was under control. The episode once again highlighted that while receptive to international expectations, especially if articulated by long-term partners such as the US and the UN, the Thai government was not willing to sacrifice its good relations with the neighboring regime and thereby risk potential domestic legitimacy costs if trade with and access to Myanmar were affected. By praising the junta's response to the cyclone, the government tried to revoke any reputational damage its concession to the UN expectation of traveling to Myanmar might have caused.

The tone of the domestic liberal media drastically sharpened following Samak's statements. The *Bangkok Post* accused Samak of acting as if he were "a spokesman for the Burmese junta," telling the world that no foreigners including the UN should worry or interfere.[133] Editor Sanitsuda Ekachai, moreover, expressed frustration with Thailand's "half-baked democracy," accusing the government of having "blood on its hands for helping to maintain the bloody paths strewn with dead bodies of the Burmese."[134] The government would allow the junta to continue killing its own people because top politicians and businesses in Thailand did not want to lose lucrative opportunities to exploit Myanmar's timber, natural gas, gems, and hydroelectric dams, she argued.[135] In light of Samak's statements, *The Nation* branded Thailand as "the strongest supporter of the regime" and urged the international community to continue to press for admittance to the country.[136] Juxtaposing Samak's stance with former Thai foreign minister and now ASEAN secretary-general Surin Pitsuwan's efforts during the crisis, the newspapers lauded Surin and urged the UN to work together with ASEAN instead of Thailand.

In response to the disaster, the ASEAN foreign ministers convened an emergency meeting for 19 May in Singapore.[137] Whereas some ASEAN foreign ministers, most notably Indonesian foreign minister Hassan Wirajuda, used the special meeting to pressure the junta, Samak's government, in contrast, used the special summit as an opportunity to finalize a memorandum of understanding (MoU) with the military regime for the construction of the Tavoy port and a separate road-link project in Myanmar. The MoU was signed on 19 May by Thai foreign minister Noppadon and his counterpart from Myanmar, Nyan Win.[138] Bowing to pressure from its ASEAN neighbors, the Myanmarese generals ultimately agreed to an ASEAN-led mechanism to distribute aid in the country. "They thought since there is no other choice, instead of being submissive to the international pressure, why not have ASEAN come in, instead of the international community—that was a face-saving formula for them," former Thai ambassador Surapong Jayanama said.[139] In light of the junta's consent to ASEAN involvement, Foreign Minister Noppadon announced that following a direct request from UN secretary-general Ban Ki-Moon, Thailand had agreed to offer Don Mueang Airport as a logistical hub for the relief effort.[140] Ban Ki-Moon had approached the Thai government two days earlier, on 17 May. Both calling and writing to the authorities, he had urged Thailand to act as the regional relief center for shipments of essential supplies to Myanmar. More directly, the UN secretary-general had asked whether the WFP could use the empty cargo hangars of Don Mueang Airport as a base to distribute aid.[141]

To summarize, by prioritizing noninterference and only delivering humanitarian aid upon Myanmar's request, the Thai government avoided domestic legitimacy costs and reputation costs as a reliable neighbor of Myanmar. The two objectives were closely intertwined in that a positive reputation among the Myanmarese generals was perceived as a crucial precondition for the Thai government to address the domestic development paradigm and thereby avoid domestic legitimacy costs. It was only after mounting international pressure, most directly articulated by the US and the UN, that Prime Minister Samak agreed to negotiate with the generals on behalf of the Western world. In responding to the strong international expectations for action, the government tried to avoid reputation costs as a "good democracy" and ally. At the same time, substantive action in line with the expectations rarely followed. While making concessions to its international audience, the Thai government worked hard to ensure that Myanmar did not perceive these concessions as acts of interference.

A Lack of Expectations and Silence during the Rakhine Riots

Thailand's response to the Rakhine Riots and the subsequent violence against the Rohingya Muslims was one of complete silence. The prioritization of noninterference reflected the continuing expectations of the Thai rural population and businesses to maintain good relations with Myanmar and was further facilitated by a relative lack of both regional and international expectations to act in accordance with the country's commitment to human rights protection.

Domestically, the plight of the Rohingya initially garnered a fair bit of attention in the press, although expectations for action on behalf of the minority group were primarily expressed in relation to the international community and the UN and less so the Thai government. After the state of emergency was declared in Rakhine on 10 June, half a dozen international and local human rights organizations based in Bangkok issued an open letter to UN secretary-general Ban Ki-Moon. Concerned about the crisis in Rakhine State, they urged the UN to "intervene and protect a million Rohingya people of Arakan from a planned genocide."[142] Rohingya organizations and Thai NGOs such as the People's Empowerment Foundation argued that paramilitary and racist Rakhine were burning houses and shooting people, with some being burned alive. They called on the UN for "immediate action to stop this serious genocide and ethnic cleansing by sending a UN peacekeeping force to Arakan to protect innocent people."[143] The group added that international and ASEAN intervention was urgently needed to save people's lives in the state.[144] The *Bangkok Post* subsequently commented that "terrible events" were underway in western Myanmar, which would "bear careful watch from its neighbours, especially Thailand."[145] The paper argued that the Myanmarese president, Thein Sein, and his supporters had given little sign that they were able to handle the crisis.[146] This was particularly troubling, the *Bangkok Post* added, as the world seemed concerned about the nascent democracy in Myanmar but less so about the actual fate of the Rohingya. It concluded: "Unless the world applies pressure on Myanmar to review its inhumane treatment of the Rohingya . . . the tragedies of the Rohingya boat people will never end."[147]

At the same time human rights activists in Bangkok organized a seminar to address the crisis. The activists reiterated the call for the UN and ASEAN to "quickly intervene in the spiraling sectarian conflict" as the government in Myanmar was not doing enough to control the situation, costing lives.[148] Debbie Stothard, deputy secretary-general of the International Federation for Human Rights (IFHR), urged the international community and UN representatives inside Myanmar to "no longer sit by and wait for the violence to subside." Instead, they needed to intervene before the hatred could spread throughout the country.[149] The following day, at the Bangkok-based Foreign Correspondents' Club, she accused ASEAN of simply ignoring the situation and having "closed their eyes and ears to the genocide."[150]

Whereas human rights groups in Thailand and liberal forces within Thai civil society were concerned by the crisis unfolding in Myanmar, the majority of the Thai population appeared less sympathetic. Ever since 2009, when the Rohingya had first arrived in large refugee groups in Thailand, the government had counteracted the initial sympathy the wider public had shown toward the plight of the Rohingya with a comprehensive propaganda campaign. "There was a lot of propaganda by the military and the conservative politicians saying that the Rohingya would join the Muslim insurgents in the Deep South and therefore could not be trusted," Sunai Phasuk from HRW recalled.[151] "Because of our own problems with Muslim Malays in the South, there is a misperception amongst Thai policymakers, most civilians and the military, who see Muslims as a threat," Phasuk added: "They see the Rohingya as troublemakers in Myanmar, because they are in conflict with the Burmese and the Buddhist Rakhine, and for that reason they have been expelled from their land. If they are not welcome back at home, then why should Thailand welcome them? That is the rationale of most people."[152] The government used the fear of the arrival of thousands of stateless Muslims, which had the potential to further destabilize the situation in Thailand's Deep South, to diffuse domestic expectations for action on behalf of the Rohingya.[153]

In view of the relative lack of expectations among the wider public that the government comply with human rights protection during the Rakhine Riots, there was absolutely no response by the Thai government "at a time when you would have hoped to see a lot, given the situation in Rakhine," according to Phil Robertson from HRW.[154] Instead of addressing the crisis, Prime Minister Yingluck Shinawatra, who had become head of government in the 2011 general elections, was busy trying to assure her domestic audience that nothing was wrong in the countries' neighborly relations, after President Thein Sein had repeatedly delayed a long-planned first official visit to Bangkok. There had been intense speculation that the welcome given to opposition leader Aung San Suu Kyi in Thailand earlier that month was the reason.[155] The Nobel laureate had been released from house arrest in 2010 and in a historic by-election in 2012 won a seat in parliament. Evidently concerned about upsetting Myanmar, Sihasak Phungketkeow, permanent secretary of the Thai Foreign Ministry, recalled that instructions had been given to allow Suu Kyi to visit the places she wanted, but not at the cost of possibly hurting relations with Myanmar. "The Foreign Ministry asked us to keep it low-key. They didn't want it to become news," the governor of Tak province, Suriya Prasatbuntitya, added. Thai officials imposed curbs on her inspection of a refugee camp by prohibiting her from giving a public address and declined her request to meet with exiled leaders of ethnic minority groups.[156] It was finally confirmed that President Thein Sein's visit to Bangkok would take place on 22 July 2012.

In advance of the leaders' meeting, the *Bangkok Post* urged the Thai government that "the existence and problem of Rohingya should be raised during Thein Sein's visit," as Thailand and other neighbors were all too aware of the plight of these people.[157] Thein Sein had previously told the UN that the Rohingya people in Rakhine were simply not welcome in Myanmar and that the "only solution" was to hand them over to the UN high commissioner for refugees to resettle them in third countries. "These are not only tough words but unacceptable ones," the *Bangkok Post* commented, stressing that the Rohingya had rights that needed to be respected.[158] "Thein Sein must be disabused of the notion that he will find sympathy, let alone help as he seeks a solution to his problem with Myanmar people," the editorial went on.[159] Calling his Rohingya statement "racist, malicious and threatening," the *Bangkok Post* demanded that his words "must not stand unchallenged."[160] On the day prior to Thein Sein's visit, the plight of the Rohingya again came to the forefront when Amnesty International circulated information according to which the Rohingya were increasingly suffering targeted attacks including killings, rape, and physical abuse. The NGO also accused both security forces and ethnic Rakhine Buddhists living in the region of carrying out fresh attacks against Rohingyas. "Some of this is by the security forces' own hands, some by Rakhine

Buddhists with the security forces turning a blind eye in some cases," Amnesty researcher Benjamin Zawacki said.[161]

But despite some domestic pressure and new evidence of the severity of the situation in Rakhine, "the Rohingya were not a topic of the meeting," as Surapong Tovichakchaikul, Thai foreign minister at the time, confirmed.[162] Instead the focus was on the countries' respective economic interests: "We talked a lot about the Dawei deep-sea port. To convince President Thein Sein of the port project, we took him to our eastern seaport, to show him how we develop our industry. We also discussed how Thailand could support Myanmar in terms of education and access to medication along the border, as we want to develop that border area on both sides."[163]

This shows that despite Thailand's exceptional access to the junta leaders, Prime Minister Yingluck Shinawatra chose not to touch upon the topic. Putting the events into perspective, Sunai Phasuk of HRW recalled: "The Thai government thought that the Myanmarese military would continue to control the country and even the NLD was not very pro-Rohingya. So the Thai rationale was that if concerns for the Rohingya were voiced too actively, they would risk bilateral relations with Burma."[164] Looking back at the meeting, former foreign minister Surapong Tovichakchaikul added that from the government's perspective the main concern was to facilitate Myanmar's reintegration into the international community, as opposed to emphasizing human rights problems inside the country:

> At the time some European countries and the US started to lift sanctions. We were all really happy about this and the developments in Myanmar. As foreign minister, when I had the chance to meet my counterparts from other countries, we would ask them to ease the sanctions on Myanmar. It seemed to me that at the time all our friends in the world agreed and responded to this, thereby improving the situation in Myanmar considerably. Myanmar and Thailand are very close. The border between our countries is long, and our own stability depends on what happens in Myanmar. As a friend we were happy to provide support if Myanmar requested help from Thailand. But we did not want to interfere.[165]

Unsurprisingly, Bangkok-based human rights activists expressed their disappointment that Myanmar's human rights abuses were not addressed during the talks. As Khin Ohmar of the Burma Partnership argued, "The issue of human rights should have been a focal point since Thailand has long sheltered a large number of displaced persons."[166] Amnesty International researcher Benjamin Zawacki added that the internal problems in Myanmar constituted the root causes of displacement, which led to the "boat-people" on Thai shores, and that Prime Minister Yingluck should have raised these issues in her discussion with Thein Sein.[167] The meeting of the two leaders also provoked several small-scale protests in front of the Government House in Bangkok as well as the embassy of Myanmar. A group of Muslim students from Thammasat University called on the Myanmarese government to "stop the massacre of Rohingya."[168] Muang Kyaw Nu, president of the Rohingya Society of Thailand, who was among the protestors, described the events: "During that time the Burmese government officials were always warmly welcome in Bangkok." He added that as far as government relations were concerned, Thai officials did not want to anger the Burmese generals for the sake of Thai business in Myanmar.[169]

Following Thein Sein's state visit, the Rohingya crisis essentially disappeared from Thai news coverage until Aung San Suu Kyi left on 16 September for a landmark visit to the US. Her visit overlapped with President Thein Sein's trip to the US, which was due later that month in order for him to attend the UN General Assembly debate.[170] According to the *Bangkok Post* their visits to the US had been marked by tough questions, albeit primarily regarding the future path of reform and less so the Rohingya.[171] In light of the overlap of the visits, US officials insisted that Thein Sein receive the same warm welcome as Suu Kyi, as he deserved to be recognized for pushing through such speedy reforms in the Southeast Asian nation.[172] Both President Thein Sein and opposition leader Aung San Suu Kyi were honored in the US for their roles in reforming the country. After the relative lack of Western condemnation of Myanmar's failure to address the crisis, the reception of Thein Sein in the US again signaled that engagement and cooperation with the regime were internationally acceptable. As a consequence, the risk of suffering international reputation costs by prioritizing noninterference was absent, further reducing the chance that Thailand's government would make concessions in favor of human rights protection during the Rakhine Riots.

As fighting recommenced in Rakhine on 23 October, human rights groups again raised concerns in Thailand. They stated that the Rohingya were becoming increasingly desperate as "a campaign to force them out of the country intensified, with Buddhist monks taking a lead role in whipping up sentiment against them." Chris Lewa from the Arakan Project said: "Tensions are rising, the attacks have started again . . . they are losing all hope. They are now in an unacceptable position."[173] A few days later, on 27 October, HRW released satellite images showing "extensive destruction of homes and other property in a predominantly Rohingya Muslim area." The group thereupon urged the Myanmarese government to protect the Rohingya, who it said were under "vicious attack."[174] Chris Lewa added that "Rakhine state has now spiraled into complete lawlessness" as violence was spreading to the south with the "clear purpose of expelling all Muslims, not just Rohingya."[175] The UN was equally alarmed and expressed grave concern over reports of deaths and thousands displaced following a fresh wave of communal violence.[176] The organization warned that Myanmar's reforms were under threat from the continued unrest between ethnic Rakhine and the Rohingya.[177] "The vigilante attacks, targeted threats and extremist rhetoric must be stopped," a spokesperson for UN secretary-general Ban Ki-Moon stated.[178] However, the UN concerns were directed at the junta and included no expectations for action from the Thai government to address the human rights violations.

In view of the silence on the side of the Thai government, the domestic liberal forces in the country instead praised the initiative of former Thai foreign minister and outgoing ASEAN secretary-general Surin Pitsuwan. As "one of the first rational voices," he had called for a more proactive ASEAN, asking the group to intervene to help calm the violence in western Myanmar.[179] In an editorial, the *Bangkok Post* condemned the "heartless and wrong-headed thinking" of Myanmar's government. "The idea that the Rohingya born in Myanmar are somehow inferior human beings is not just heartless but legally wrong," it wrote.[180] However, despite Surin Pitsuwan's personal activism, through which he had warned about a radicalization of the Rohingya and appealed to ASEAN's image in the world, the organization collectively respected Myanmar's call for noninterference. Together with a lack of international expectations for Thailand to comply with the norm of human rights protection, the regional consensus to respect Myanmar's wishes meant that in prioritizing the noninterference norm over human rights protection, no reputation costs were involved for the Thai government. The positions taken by Thailand's regional and international audiences were compatible with the domestic preference for noninterference, articulated by the numerically strongest groups, namely the rural population and the Thai business class.

Overall, the Thai government again opted for a policy of noninterference during the Rakhine Riots, thereby avoiding legitimacy costs, as bilateral relations with the neighboring regime remained intact. Given the relative absence of international expectations, it neither had to justify itself internationally nor fear reputation costs from prioritizing noninterference. In portraying the Rohingya as reinforcements for the Muslim insurgents in Thailand's Deep South, the government had diffused domestic sympathy with the plight of the Rohingya that had arisen when groups of refugees first arrived on Thailand's shores in 2009.

WHY THAILAND OPTED FOR STRATEGIC NORM REPLACEMENT

The analysis of Thailand's response to norm conflict revealed a uniform response pattern. In all three situations of norm conflict, the government prioritized the noninterference norm over extraterritorial human rights protection and promotion. It did so despite conflicting expectations regarding norm compliance articulated by its relevant international and, at times, regional audiences. In choosing which norm to prioritize, the dominant domestic expectation in the crises and the related concern over legitimacy costs were decisive. Following the Asian financial crisis, the largest domestic groups—the rural population in tandem with the Thai business class—had redefined the basis for the government's legitimacy, which was no longer primarily earned and defended by promoting democratic values in Thailand and abroad but rather through a prioritization of economic development. This new domestic paradigm fundamentally affected Thailand's relations with Myanmar as a major market for Thai businesses and a provider of income for the urban population through border trade. In order to avoid legitimacy costs in the three analyzed cases of human rights violations in Myanmar, the respective Thai governments therefore largely abstained from interference, which could have put the friendly relations between the neighboring countries at risk and thereby created legitimacy costs. As this approach was backed by a large conservative force within Thailand, conflicting domestic expectations articulated by a liberal urban middle class were mostly ignored. As a result, no major differences were visible between the interim military government of General Surayud and his elected civilian successors Samak Sundaravej and Yingluck Shinawatra. Similarly, with the exception of a few voices, the Democrat Party was largely mute during the crises, underlying the striking continuity of noninterference in Thailand's relations with Myanmar ever since the general elections of 2001.

The domestic expectation for compliance with noninterference in relation to Myanmar was first and foremost a reflection of the extreme economic interdependence of the two countries. In order to address the dominant domestic expectation, and thereby protect their domestic legitimacy, Thai policymakers in practice had to prioritize noninterference over human rights protection *in relation to Myanmar*. Its prioritization of noninterference was therefore strategic and context-specific rather than general. The government did not desire a general weakening of the human rights protection and promotion norm within the region. Accordingly, it did not intend to alter the behavior of others. Its response strategy was exclusively driven by the desire to influence the expectations of its dissenting audiences within one particular context, thereby illustrating a case of strategic norm replacement.

In order to pursue a policy of noninterference in relation to Myanmar, while minimizing international reputation costs, Thailand's close proximity to Myanmar was crucial. The government argued that because of its geostrategic position as a direct neighbor of Myanmar with an extremely long and porous shared border, Thailand would not be in a position to push the neighboring regime. In doing so, the government tried to invalidate current and future international expectations that Thailand would embrace a more human rights–centered approach in relation to Myanmar and achieve acceptance of its policy of noninterference. Given its leading position in ASEAN, its long-standing relations with UN officials, and its access to US decision makers as one of two regional allies, Thailand was in a favorable position to get its message out there. Previous cross-border issues with Myanmar supported the credibility of the argument put forward. The government thus had the necessary persuasive power for trying to influence future expectations of its relevant audiences and thereby minimize the social costs of violating one of the two conflicting norms.

The evidence suggests that the government had some success with its argument, generating understanding for Thailand's special position in relation to Myanmar with its international audience. Thailand's international audience nevertheless articulated some direct expectations regarding action in accordance with human rights protection. It was primarily the US and the UN that pressured the Thai government to take a more active role during the Saffron Revolution and Cyclone Nargis. In view of their expectations, Thai governments made some concessions, but substantive action was often delayed or its impact diffused by their simultaneously defending the Myanmarese generals. This shows that although consecutive Thai governments evidently tried to avoid international reputation costs, at the same time they did their best to ensure that Myanmar did not perceive their actions as a violation of the noninterference norm.

5

From Norm Reconciliation to Conflict Denial in Malaysia

Having looked at the response to the norm conflict in Indonesia and Thailand, this chapter assesses the Malaysian response pattern and its strategy for addressing the norm conflict. Confronted with large-scale human rights violations in Myanmar, the respective Malaysian administrations had to choose between compliance with the noninterference and the human rights protection and promotion norms. This chapter shows that the government's compliance with the two conflicting norms alternated. At times it applied the noninterference norm; at others it complied with human rights protection. I demonstrate that given a shift in domestic expectations, Malaysia switched from an attempted strategy of norm reconciliation to a strategy of conflict denial. The Malaysian case study therefore not only illustrates two categories of response to norm conflict but also provides important insights into the determining factors that lead to a change in expectations, thereby incentivizing a government to adjust its strategy. Of the three Southeast Asian states, the dual processes of democratization and liberalization set in latest in Malaysia. Serious domestic engagement with human rights protection across party lines only came about following the commencement of Abdullah Badawi's premiership in 2003. As a consequence, the human rights protection norm was more nascent in Malaysia and internalized to a lesser degree than in Indonesia and Malaysia. The level of internalization facilitated the shift in domestic expectations, which was ultimately triggered by a major national crisis.

NORM FOLLOWING IN MALAYSIA: THE GOVERNMENT'S RESPONSE PATTERN

Alternating Compliance during the Saffron Revolution

The Malaysian response to the gross human rights violations committed by the military regime during the Saffron Revolution was swift and forceful, clearly prioritizing human rights protection over the noninterference norm. The Malaysian government openly requested that ASEAN rethink its policy of constructive engagement with Myanmar in favor of a more intrusive mechanism and, if necessary, take action against the junta's will.

As the situation in Myanmar escalated, Malaysia was in fact among the first ASEAN countries to address the crisis. Even prior to the collective ASEAN statement at the sidelines of the UN General Assembly debate on 27 September, Malaysian foreign minister Syed Hamid Albar said on 25 September that the junta had to take "appropriate measures" to bring about change.[1] Addressing Myanmar's military rulers directly, he stated that they "should take steps towards reconciliation before pro-democracy protests potentially blow up into turmoil" and thereby affect the neighboring Southeast Asian nations.[2] Albar went on to state that in light of the protests, the military junta "must now take notice of the aspirations of the people."[3] In doing so, the foreign minister not only clearly commented on Myanmar's internal affairs but also made unrequested policy recommendations.[4] In addition, Albar encouraged Myanmar to be open and called upon all parties to resolve the turbulence.[5]

When, a day later, the foreign minister was asked to comment on reports according to which the military rulers in Myanmar threatened to take stern measures against the protestors in Yangon, Albar urged the junta to avoid taking such action. To find a solution leading toward democracy, he instead called upon the junta to "get back to the negotiation table,"[6] and fully engage with the UN secretary-general's special envoy to Myanmar, Ibrahim Gambari. "Now there is no going backward, there is a need for political process, they should not deal with the demonstrations by using force," Albar told reporters after the ASEAN meeting of 27 September in New York.[7] In addition, he set tangible expectations for action by the generals: "We want to see the tangible side of political reconciliation, and that Aung San Suu Kyi is released."[8]

Malaysian pressure on the junta intensified when Malaysian prime minister Abdullah Amad Badawi addressed the situation in Myanmar in his speech at the UN General Assembly on 28 September: "It would be remiss for Malaysia as a member of ASEAN to ignore the situation in Myanmar. ASEAN has done everything possible to encourage Myanmar towards reconciliation and democracy. Their failure to do so has brought upon them the current situation. Let me express my country's disapproval together with other ASEAN countries on the use of excessive force by the Myanmar government to put down justifiable civilian protest."[9] Openly condemning the junta's use of force, Badawi went on to call on Myanmar's government to give its fullest cooperation to enable UN special envoy Gambari to fulfill his mission on behalf of the international community. He urged the junta to both engage in dialogue and to release Aung San Suu Kyi.[10] In a meeting with journalists, the prime minister justified his decision to include remarks on Myanmar during his address at the UN General Assembly.[11] Badawi stated that in view of the latest developments in Yangon, where lives were lost when soldiers opened fire on demonstrators, it was necessary for the Malaysian government to make known its displeasure.[12] The deteriorating situation in Myanmar warranted a strong collective statement from ASEAN, the prime minister continued, and a collective stance by governments in the region to reflect their concern over the political turmoil in Myanmar. Badawi acknowledged that the ASEAN statement was "unprecedented" because of its bluntness and "can be seen as a climax, a result of the sentiments of ASEAN foreign ministers."[13] It thus demonstrated ASEAN's commitment to restoring democracy in the country, he said.[14]

In view of the violent crackdown, Badawi not only condemned the junta's actions but also critically reflected on ASEAN's role. He admitted that the policy of constructive engagement adopted by ASEAN had failed, as Myanmar's progress to democracy had been too slow: "It has been the formula used when we deal with Myanmar, but up to this stage, it has not been successful although it has been many years already."[15] As a result, he suggested, ASEAN had to change its approach vis-à-vis Myanmar, and this time ASEAN members would ensure that Myanmar adhered to and fulfilled the regional group's requests. Like his foreign minister, Badawi formulated a clear set of expectations for the generals by calling upon them to immediately stop the violence against protestors, get back to the negotiating table, restore democracy in the country, and release all detained political leaders including Aung San Suu Kyi.[16] Even though Badawi did not elaborate on the means by which ASEAN would ensure that Myanmar fulfilled these requests, his statement raised the possibility of enforcement.[17]

To coordinate efforts in solving the crisis, on 16 October Foreign Minister Albar and Prime Minister Badawi both met with UN special envoy Ibrahim Gambari. In the course of these talks, they reassured Gambari of Malaysia's support but ruled out the suspension of Myanmar's ASEAN membership as a possible response to the violent crackdown. Yet Albar agreed that "more needed to be done."[18] Instead of suspending Myanmar, the foreign minister said that ASEAN would "coax Myanmar to engage with the United Nations through the special envoy, Ibrahim Gambari."[19] He went on to state that it was important for ASEAN to back the UN's efforts: "We can request Myanmar to work closely with the UN. It is the best way and best channel for Myanmar."[20] Albar further guaranteed that ASEAN would persuade the generals to allow Gambari to visit the country again soon and continue negotiations to achieve a lasting democratic process.[21]

As the talks with Myanmar continued, showing few results, the Malaysian government became increasingly impatient. Najib Razak, deputy prime minister at the time, stated in late October that Malaysia and ASEAN had almost reached the point of exasperation in finding a solution to the Myanmar problem.[22] "There is a need for an immediate end to the violence suffered by its citizens," he said. "ASEAN, in my view, has an obligation to do whatever it takes to facilitate peace and transition there."[23] In stating this, Najib essentially issued a Malaysian blank check to ASEAN in dealing with the recalcitrant regime.[24]

Interestingly, however, Malaysia's strong tone changed quite drastically at the ASEAN summit in November 2007. Prior to the meeting Malaysian policymakers had stated that while they hoped the situation in Myanmar would not be the focus of the meeting, they believed it inevitable that the problem would be discussed among the ASEAN heads of state. After all, the world's attention was on the summit, at which the new ASEAN Charter would be adopted.[25] The Charter was also supposed to include a clause committing the member states and ASEAN as an organization to democracy, good governance, and human rights. But instead of further pressing the Myanmarese regime to respect the rights of its citizens, Badawi assured his Myanmese counterpart that as long as Myanmar continued negotiations with the UN, Malaysia would not interfere independently.[26]

To sum up, Malaysia's response to the Saffron Revolution was among the strongest within ASEAN. It displayed a resoluteness and rights-based argumentation that was unusual for most of the organization's member states. Malaysia thus clearly distinguished itself by expressing its disapproval and by urging Myanmar to adhere to international human rights standards. However, by the time of the ASEAN summit in Singapore, the Malaysian stance had shifted from a prioritization of human rights protection to a policy of noninterference.

Prioritizing Noninterference during Cyclone Nargis

The humanitarian crisis that unfolded in Myanmar following Cyclone Nargis in 2008 quickly evolved into a case of large-scale human rights violations as the junta denied international aid workers access to the affected areas. However, Malaysia's response to Cyclone Nargis exclusively focused on providing humanitarian relief and only with the explicit consent of Myanmar as the host state. Thereby, the Malaysian government framed the crisis as a humanitarian problem as opposed to a case of human rights violation. The government, which was still led by Prime Minister Abdullah Badawi, repeatedly stated that it would comply with the noninterference norm.

On 7 May, five days after Cyclone Nargis made landfall in Myanmar, the Malaysian government declared that it was prepared to send aid to Myanmar, but only if requested by the military junta.[27] On 8 May, the Malaysian Foreign Ministry issued a statement saying that the government was saddened and surprised by the tragedy and reported that it was in the process of finalizing the details of delivering aid, based on Myanmar's appeal for help to the UN.[28] Deputy Prime Minister Najib Razak explained that at that moment the government was considering the best way of assisting the victims of the disaster and that, if requested by Myanmar, this could include dispatching the Malaysian Armed Forces Medical Team.[29]

After the junta had given its consent, on 11 May, the Malaysian government announced that Malaysia would send humanitarian relief aid totaling US$1 million in cash and another RM500,000 worth of basic necessities to help the victims of Cyclone Nargis.[30] Deputy Prime Minister Najib said that the aid would be brought to Myanmar on the following day, including five thousand blankets, clothing, biscuits, instant noodles, thirty tents, and medicine.[31] Two days later Malaysia's National Security Council secretary, Muhammad Hatta Abd Aziz, confirmed that an eighteen-member mission had handed over the aid to Myanmar's government through Malaysia's ambassador in Yangon. The mission comprised officers from Wisma Putra, the Health Ministry, the Malaysian Armed Forces, and the Malaysian Red Crescent.[32] According to information published by the Malay-language newspaper *Berita Harian*, the Malaysian delegation was "well received" by the junta leaders.[33] A senior military official from Myanmar expressed the country's appreciation and welcomed the humanitarian effort from Malaysia, which was always one of the first countries to provide assistance when disaster hit, according to the official.[34] In line with its exclusively humanitarian response to the crisis, the Malaysian government took a low profile during the Special ASEAN Ministerial Meeting in Singapore on 19 May 2008. Following the meeting, which had been scheduled to convince Myanmar to open up and welcome international assistance, Malaysian media merely reported that the new foreign minister of Malaysia, Rais Yatim, had used the gathering to hand over the allocated US$1 million of humanitarian aid to his Myanmarese counterpart, Nyan Win, on behalf of the Malaysian government.[35]

Despite Myanmar's consent to the ASEAN-led initiative, the continued slow pace of granting visas was widely criticized. Taking a critical stance vis-à-vis the junta for the first time, Deputy Prime Minister Najib Razak said in a panel discussion at a security conference on 1 June (which was also attended by Myanmar's deputy defense minister, Aye Myint) that given ASEAN's willingness to provide more relief, Myanmar should facilitate the relief efforts from the regional organization. "At the risk of offending my colleague here, I would certainly speak on behalf of ASEAN countries, [when saying that] we would like to play a bigger role in the context of the tragedy of Myanmar," Najib said.[36] He went on to state that "a human tragedy of the highest proportions might fall on the people of Myanmar, if the government of Myanmar does not allow greater participation of ASEAN countries and the world."[37] Najib thereby admitted that the human suffering was not caused by the cyclone alone but was also generated by the inaction of the junta. Nevertheless, instead of further pressing the junta for greater cooperation, Najib passed the responsibility to ASEAN: "We respect its sovereignty and resort to ASEAN-led initiatives to deliver humanitarian aid and assistance."[38] Referring to the ASEAN-led mission, the deputy prime minister stated that Malaysia welcomed "Myanmar's trust and confidence in ASEAN's role in coordinating the international response."[39] He encouraged the generals to cooperate with the organization in stressing ASEAN's track record, which according to Najib had "neither been a destabilizing force in the region nor interfered in the internal affairs of member states."[40]

By relying primarily on ASEAN's responsibility to pressure Myanmar into opening up to international aid workers, Malaysia's own response to Cyclone Nargis prioritized noninterference and framed the crisis as a humanitarian disaster as opposed to a case of human rights violations. Upon receiving Yangon's consent, the government focused on providing humanitarian assistance and only once commented critically on the situation in Myanmar after the regime had already consented to an ASEAN relief effort. It otherwise focused on emphasizing its respect for Myanmar's sovereignty.

Prioritizing Noninterference during the Rakhine Riots

Although Malaysia was the first ASEAN country to comment on the violent riots between the Muslim and Buddhist communities in Rakhine State in Myanmar, the government at no point criticized the junta for standing by or for the involvement of its security forces in the atrocities. Moreover, when Malaysia did act by providing humanitarian aid, it always insisted on gaining official consent from the authorities in Myanmar and proactively reassured the generals of its commitment to noninterference.

As early as 12 June, two days after the state of emergency was declared in Rakhine, the Malaysian government—now headed by Prime Minister Najib Razak—stated its willingness to provide assistance to Myanmar in the country's effort to settle the conflict between the Buddhist and Muslim communities in Rakhine State. In communicating this position, Foreign Minister Anifah Aman highlighted Malaysia's concern that the conflict might spread to other areas in Myanmar.[41] The Foreign Ministry and the Malaysian embassy in Yangon stressed that they would continue to monitor the situation in Rakhine but at the same time emphasized that "Malaysia is confident [that] Myanmar can find a settlement to the tension and bring those responsible to justice."[42] Malaysia went on to express its "deepest sympathy to the government and the people of Myanmar over the ethnic conflict in Rakhine."[43] Following the Malaysian offer to assist Myanmar, Malaysian media reported that the junta had turned down the offer to provide humanitarian aid, arguing that "the situation in Rakhine has been brought under control and therefore the need for assistance from other ASEAN member states did not arise at the moment."⁴⁴ In light of this rebuff, the Malaysian government apparently saw the need to justify itself for having offered assistance:⁴⁵

> Malaysia always maintains a policy of non-interference in any country's internal affairs. However, Malaysia believes that no country, especially ASEAN member states, should be left alone in difficult times without any offer of assistance. In this connection, I have also conveyed the warm wishes and a message from the Honorable Dato' Sri Najib Tun Hj Abdul Razak, the Prime Minister of Malaysia to President Thein Sein that Malaysia's offer of assistance to Myanmar is borne out of a sense of responsibility and spirit of neighbourliness as a member of the ASEAN family.⁴⁶

Malaysian foreign minister Anifah Aman, moreover, emphasized that his Myanmese counterpart, Wunna Maung Lawin, had expressed appreciation of the Malaysian offer apparently determined to establish that Malaysia's offer had not been perceived by Myanmar as interference. He further highlighted Myanmar's confirmation that should assistance be needed, they would approach Malaysia.⁴⁷

It was not until the end of August that Myanmar requested Malaysian help. During a meeting on 31 August between the two foreign ministers at the 16th Summit of the Non-Aligned Movement in Teheran, the decision was made that a Malaysian humanitarian mission would leave for Rakhine on 9 September to deliver essential items and logistics support.⁴⁸ In line with the Malaysian noninterference stance in the crisis, the mission was to be implemented purely by nongovernmental bodies, most importantly the Putra 1Malaysia Club. A team of forty-five volunteers was to go to the Bangladeshi border, where more than one hundred thousand Rohingya had sought refuge.⁴⁹ Putra 1Malaysia president Abdul Azeez emphasized again, "This mission is a 100 percent humanitarian project and we do not interfere in the country's internal affairs and political problems involved."⁵⁰ The Foreign Ministry of Malaysia welcomed the government of Myanmar's decision to accept the assistance provided by Putra 1Malaysia to the residents of Rakhine State. According to a statement issued by the Malaysian Foreign Ministry, the government of Myanmar had expressed its appreciation for the friendship and constant support shown by the Malaysian government and its concern for the people of Myanmar.[51]

Despite the agreement, however, Myanmar's junta did not provide official permission until 17 September. "I received a letter of authorization signed by Myanmar's foreign minister, yesterday," Foreign Minister Aman finally announced.[52] In the letter the junta made the mission conditional on aid being delivered by ordinary vessels instead of military ones.[53] According to the Malaysian newspaper *Berita Harian*, the delay to the mission was prompted by the junta's concern that if assistance were delivered by a Malaysian organization, it would be perceived as exclusively benefiting the Muslim population of Rakhine. It was only following a guarantee by the Putra 1Malaysia Club that help would be delivered regardless of race and religion that Myanmar accepted a Malaysian presence in Rakhine. The multiracial and multireligious composition of the relief team, which also included five Buddhist monks from Malaysia, supported the offer.[54] With permission granted, the Myanmarese junta finally approved fifty-seven visas for Malaysian volunteers to embark on the relief mission.[55]

After weeks of delay, the first group of volunteers left for Myanmar on 19 September to prepare for the arrival of the relief mission and aid.[56] A special trading vessel, carrying approximately five hundred tons of relief items, left on 25 September for Myanmar.[57] Following the departure of the relief mission, Deputy Prime Minister Muhyiddin Yassin reiterated that Putra 1Malaysia did not intend to interfere in the internal problems of Myanmar but hoped to alleviate the suffering of the people in the neighboring country. "This assistance mission is meant to carry out our responsibility as a neighbour and is in the spirit of ASEAN," he said.[58] The Putra 1Malaysia mission was the first run by a major organization to be allowed to enter the Rakhine region.[59] "Given the good relationship between Prime Minister Datuk Seri Najib Razak and President Thein Sein, we are highly respected and were given the space to conduct the mission, despite the many obstacles we faced," Putra 1Malaysia president Abdul Azeez reported.[60]

Following the well-received relief mission, the government of Myanmar also invited the organization Mercy Malaysia to repair and upgrade a hospital in Rakhine to increase access to healthcare for more than sixty thousand people.[61] After the renewed fighting in October 2012, Foreign Minister Aman expressed Malaysia's willingness to extend further humanitarian assistance while guaranteeing that there would be no action without

Myanmar's consent.[62] When Myanmar did not ask for further help, Malaysia kept its word and sent no further volunteers. At the annual ASEAN summit in November 2012, Malaysian representatives expressed some concern over the growing humanitarian crisis in the region. They argued that ASEAN member states needed to agree on a strategy to address conflicts in the Rakhine region involving the ethnic Rohingya and Buddhists of Myanmar. Foreign Minister Aman, however, quickly shut down the debate by simply stating that Malaysia welcomed Myanmar's move to restore peace and order in the Rakhine region.[63]

Overall, it can be said that the Malaysian government complied with the noninterference norm in this third instance of norm conflict. In framing the crisis solely as a humanitarian disaster, it focused on providing humanitarian assistance with the official consent of Myanmar's authorities. Even then it felt the need to justify its offer of assistance by stressing its commitment to noninterference.

EXPLAINING MALAYSIA'S RESPONSE TO NORM CONFLICT

The empirical analysis of the Malaysian response pattern in the three situations of norm conflict has shown that over time the respective governments did not consistently prioritize one norm over the other. Instead, compliance alternated between the two norms. In what follows, Malaysia's response to norm conflict is explained in light of the structure of expectations set by its commitment to the norms of noninterference and human rights protection and promotion. Given the shift in compliance, we would expect to see a shift in the strength of expectations to act in accordance with the norms by at least one of the government's relevant audiences. In light of new expectations, a government that wishes its actions to be perceived as legitimate by its relevant audiences might find itself urged to reevaluate its response.

Prioritizing Human Rights Protection during the Saffron Revolution

When the peaceful pro-democracy protests in Myanmar began, Malaysian parliamentarians across the ruling and opposition parties immediately voiced strong expectations that the government should interfere on behalf of human rights protection. The Malaysian members of the ASEAN Inter-

Parliamentary Myanmar Caucus harshly condemned the violence. Caucus president and party member of the United Malays National Organisation (UMNO) Zaid Ibrahim stated that the reaction of Myanmar's authorities toward the peaceful protestors was totally unacceptable.[64] He called upon ASEAN leaders, singling out Malaysia, to immediately intervene: "Malaysia and ASEAN must come into the very forefront in regional and international efforts to support a peaceful resolution of the monk-led mass protest marches in Rangoon and Mandalay... especially as ASEAN had given the Myanmar military junta a new legitimacy and fresh lease of life by admitting Myanmar into ASEAN ten years ago."[65] Malaysian parliamentarians emphasized the greater moral appropriateness of human rights protection in the particular situation by characterizing the junta's behavior as "unacceptable."[66] They also accused Malaysia and ASEAN of complicity in having brought about the current crisis, by accepting Myanmar as a member state of the regional organization. Malaysia in particular, under former prime minister Mohamad Mahathir, had been a proponent of Myanmar's accession to ASEAN.[67]

In weighing the costs and benefits of compliance with either norm, addressing expectations at the domestic level was particularly important for Prime Minister Badawi. With Badawi coming to office after twenty-two years of semi-authoritarian rule under Mahathir, the legitimacy of his administration had become closely intertwined with allowing for greater political participation through consultation and accommodation.[68] Badawi's more inclusive approach to policymaking had especially empowered civil society and minority groups beyond the numerically dominant ethnic Malays.[69] Moreover, he had encouraged participation of parliamentarians and civil society not only in domestic debates but also at the regional level, and with the Press Act had given rights to the media.[70] In the specific case of Myanmar, this greater openness had led to a high level of legislative engagement in foreign policy, formerly unseen in Malaysia. In 2004, this resulted in the formation of ASEAN's first Parliamentary Caucus on democracy in Myanmar. Its purpose was to monitor the situation in the country and ensure genuine democratization in Myanmar.[71] In order to avoid domestic legitimacy costs in view of a widely shared expectation to act in accordance with the government's commitment to human rights protection, it was necessary for Prime Minister Badawi to at least condemn the violence against the protestors and express Malaysia's opposition. In speaking up and prioritizing human rights protection, Badawi also distanced himself from the loathed domestic heritage of his predecessor, Mahathir Mohamad. The long-term prime minister had been one of the staunchest supporters within the region of Myanmar's admission to ASEAN. Hence the government's perception of the weight of domestic expectations tilted the balance in favor of interference.

In considering Malaysia's response to the Saffron Revolution, domestic expectations in favor of human rights protection were supported and reinforced by strong international pressure on ASEAN collectively to take a role in checking the regime in Myanmar (as discussed in chapter 3). The international expectations placed upon the heads of state within ASEAN were particularly direct as the crisis in Myanmar peaked at the time of the annual meeting of the UN General Assembly in September 2007 and was condemned by almost all Western governments in their speeches and direct meetings with ASEAN representatives. Upon arriving at the UN headquarters in New York, US assistant secretary of state Kirsten Silverberg immediately announced that among other things, US secretary of state Condoleezza Rice would press for ASEAN leverage to end the crackdown in Myanmar and to initiate genuine democratic reforms. The ASEAN ministers were scheduled to meet Secretary of State Rice on the sidelines of the UN General Assembly debate on 27 September.[72]

In view of the international reaction to the Saffron Revolution, which clearly framed the events as a case of large-scale human rights violations and called for the expression of disapproval of any state committed to human rights protection, ASEAN's reputation and the reputations of its individual member states were put on the line. As one of the founding members of ASEAN, Malaysia had a particular motivation to maintain a strong reputation for the organization. But in addition, as a relatively small state in the region, Malaysia was also dependent on ASEAN's combined force to have a relevant voice not only in the wider Asia-Pacific area but also globally in international forums.[73] In committing the region to democratic values and human rights protection alongside noninterference as codified in the legally binding ASEAN Charter, the regional dimension of the norm conflict strengthened the costs of noncompliance with the human rights protection norm for individual ASEAN member states. It allowed international audiences to pressure member states not only directly, based on their individual commitment to the norm, but also via the organization's reputation.

Beyond a concern for ASEAN's reputation, Malaysia also had aspirations for its own international posture. After decades of Mahathir's confrontational and often openly anti-Western stance internationally,[74] Badawi moved away from projecting the country as a leader in the developing world and instead tried to establish Malaysia internationally as a cooperative and moderate Islamic state that could interact more productively with the West.[75] In pursuing international recognition for Malaysia's moderate Islamic identity, Badawi emphasized that the country aimed to respect democracy, good governance, and human rights, both at home and abroad, and was keen to participate actively in global politics and institutions.[76] He simultaneously sought closer relations between the Western and Islamic worlds.[77] "Before becoming prime minister, Badawi had served as a professional diplomat and foreign minister," Syed Hamid Albar, who had served as foreign minister under Badawi, said, continuing: "He was sensitive to the international context and believed that as the world had changed, we as a nation also had to start acting differently. We tried to find our place in a world shaped by a majority of democracies. In such an environment we could no longer allow blatant abuses of human rights."[78]

In promoting Malaysia's moderate Islamic identity in relation to the Western and Islamic worlds, Badawi stressed the concept of "Islam Hadhari," which described a moderate and progressive view of Islamic civilization.[79] Although originally introduced by Mahathir, it was primarily during Badawi's administration that the concept of moderate Islam was stipulated and put into practice internationally.[80] Consisting of nine core principles, Islam Hadhari called for, inter alia: good governance; free and liberated people; protection of the rights of minorities, women, and children; as well as general human rights.[81] Internationally, Badawi and his administration used the concept to emphasize that the ideas of good governance, democracy, and accountability to God and the people were not antithetical to Islam but instead were "clearly embodied in the Holy Qur'an and the traditions of Prophet Mohammad."[82] In line with the internationally stipulated identity and role conception of Malaysia as a moderate Islamic model state, Badawi repeatedly stated that it was Malaysia's duty "to demonstrate, by word and by action, that a Muslim country can be modern, democratic, tolerant and economically competitive."[83] In order to gain international recognition for the country's stipulated identity, condemning human rights violations and promoting respect for human rights were viewed as more beneficial than remaining silent. Taken together, domestic and international expectations in favor of human rights protection during the Saffron Revolution made a strong case for compliance with the norm, which would avoid both domestic legitimacy and international reputation costs.

However, Malaysia's response to the Saffron Revolution also warranted an assessment of the expectations articulated at the regional level. This was particularly difficult during the Saffron Revolution as a collective ASEAN statement coexisted next to individual member states' responses to the crisis. While the former condemned the violent crackdown, individually the majority of ASEAN member states respected Myanmar's call for noninterference and abstained from commenting on the events. Looking back at the period, former foreign minister Syed Hamid Albar explained Badawi's motivation for aligning his policy with the collective ASEAN statement by pointing out the domestic and regional context at the time: "Malaysia was surrounded by very vocal newly democratized peers and in view of the domestic changes in Malaysia, [and] Badawi wanted to come up with a foreign policy that was worthy of a democratic leader."[84] In order to be seen as equally committed to human rights protection and promotion in the region by its democratic peers, support for the collective ASEAN stance was crucial and reinforced domestic and international expectations regarding human rights protection.

In justifying his motivation to condemn the junta's violence during his address at the UN General Assembly debate on 28 September, Badawi therefore echoed the rights-based expectations articulated by his various audiences. He said that Malaysia, along with other ASEAN countries, disapproved of the excessive use of force by Myanmar's government to quell a civilian protest.[85] In view of the latest developments in Yangon, where lives were lost when soldiers opened fire on demonstrators, Malaysia could not remain silent.[86] Looking back at Malaysia's motivation to support the collective ASEAN statement and align its individual stance, Foreign Minister Albar emphasized that consequentialist considerations based on the objective of reducing the social costs of compliance coincided with notions of appropriateness: "The statement was ASEAN diplomacy at its best; we came up with a statement, so there was less pressure on ASEAN as a whole and on the individual member states—from the world and our people. It might have come as a surprise to the world, but for us it was not surprising. We did not have another choice. It was necessary, but it was also very right."[87]

Malaysia's own statement at the UN was subsequently lauded by the government's domestic as well as international audiences. From the perspective of minimizing legitimacy costs at home and maximizing reputation internationally, Malaysia's decision to interfere had thus been successful. The largest Malay-language newspaper, *Berita Harian,* excitedly wrote that it was unprecedented that Malaysia, a country that in the past had been known for its staunch support of Myanmar, strongly urged the junta to free pro-democracy leader Aung San Suu Kyi and other prisoners, as well as accelerate the process of restoring democracy.[88] Malaysian parliamentarians also expressed approval. The president of the People's Justice Party (PKR) and deputy chair of the Malaysian Parliamentary Caucus on Democracy in Myanmar, Wan Azizah Wan Ismail, for example, welcomed Prime Minister Badawi's condemnation of the Myanmarese junta in New York. She recognized with satisfaction that the "Malaysian government had long last acknowledged PKR's basic assertion that ASEAN's policy of constructive engagement had failed to bring peace and freedom in Burma."[89] As neighbors, Malaysians could empathize with the despair of the Myanmarese people, she argued.[90]

Malaysia's swift and clear response in favor of human rights protection was also internationally recognized. British foreign secretary David Miliband, for example, applauded Malaysia for its clear stance, arguing that in a globalized, interdependent world, individual countries could not isolate themselves from the lives of others, as internal crises had potential effects on other countries: "I also welcome the very forthright statements by Prime Minister Datuk Seri Abdullah Badawi and Foreign Minister Datuk Seri Syed Hamid Albar since the ASEAN statement, as well as the leading role Malaysia is playing in the region in support of the people of Myanmar and Gambari's mission."[91] At the same time, however, the Malaysian government recognized that despite the collective ASEAN statement, individually the majority of ASEAN member states did not share Malaysia's stance. The Badawi administration therefore made its strong statement very consciously. As Foreign Minister Albar explained, in interfering in the crisis on behalf of human rights protection, the prime minister had meant to send a clear message to the world and to ASEAN: "Badawi felt that ASEAN, almost five decades after its formation, needed to change," he said, adding: "Badawi and I believed that noninterference had to be tempered with justice and compassion. I do believe in sovereignty, noninterference and trust, but I felt and still feel that when there are external dynamics, we should be willing to sit down to discuss and cooperate in order to find a solution instead of denying the presence of the problem."[92]

Along with accommodating immediate domestic and international expectations, Badawi therefore also acted in the hope of changing the long-term trajectory of the noninterference norm in ASEAN. In short, he viewed himself as initiating a process of norm reconciliation. Instead of framing Malaysian interference in this case as a singular exception, Badawi's government attempted to establish certain forms of interference in general as justifiable exceptions to the norm. More specifically, the prime minister argued that interference should be considered legitimate when a situation inside a country has a tangible impact on other neighboring member states or the ASEAN region as a whole. With the help of a regionally more acceptable "justificatory detour," via spillover effects on neighbors or an impact on the region as a whole, the norms of noninterference and human rights protection would then be reconciled. By attempting to solve the norm conflict at the regional level and institutionalizing the modification of the norms, ASEAN's normative framework could once again serve as an action-guiding device for the organization's member states. In addressing the crisis, the Malaysian foreign minister therefore also emphasized the regional dimension of the Saffron Revolution. In his comments on 26 September, he stated that nothing less than ASEAN's credibility and reputation were on the line. Foreign Minister Albar characterized the unrest in Myanmar as worrisome and an embarrassment for ASEAN. "Although it is an internal situation, you cannot isolate your internal crisis from affecting ASEAN," he said, adding: "We do not want to interfere, yet, we want them to resolve the problem."[93] The military junta had to show that it was heading toward democratization; otherwise ASEAN would be seen as a joke, not capable of resolving the issue.[94]

In justifying its chosen stance during the Saffron Revolution to its regional peers, the majority of which individually still prioritized noninterference, the Malaysian government tried to minimize regional reputation costs. But it also attempted to change regional behavior in accordance with its own preferences by modifying the meaning of the noninterference norm. Regional acceptance of a relaxed version of the norm would have permitted the Malaysian government to respond in accordance with anticipated expectations for compliance with human rights protection in future situations of human rights violations without violating regional expectations for compliance with noninterference. Badawi's initiative to reconcile the norms reflected a domestic consensus for extraterritorial human rights protection at the time and an international environment that more often than not condemned violations of human rights across the globe.

But Malaysia's response to this crisis also demonstrated the limits of what its government considered legitimate means of interference, even where gross human rights violations were taking place. Despite expectations both at the domestic and international levels that called on the Malaysian government to go beyond verbal interference, Badawi's administration refused to do so. When Myanmar made no progress in meeting any of the demands made by ASEAN and the UN, namely releasing political prisoners and restoring democracy, domestic expectations in Malaysia moved away from just condemning the junta toward singling out political consequences for the regime. Malaysian opposition politician Soorian Arjuan from the Democratic Action Party (DAP) urged ASEAN to take "immediate and cogent steps . . . to isolate the regime."[95] The regional organization could not and must not accommodate this embarrassment any longer and should move to expel Myanmar from its ranks.[96] Similarly, PKR member Wan Azizah Wan Ismail said: "Should there be no improvement . . . we believe that Burma should not only be barred from attending the ASEAN summit in Singapore this November, but that the Malaysian government should lead the rest of the region by tabling a resolution to expel Burma from ASEAN immediately, and in addition to apply trade sanctions on the recalcitrant junta."[97]

Malaysian lawyers from the Bar Council also urged ASEAN to expel Myanmar, arguing that evidently ASEAN's efforts of constructive engagement had failed and a clear message had to be sent to the regime.[98] The topic of sanctions also became a point of contention in discussions with the UN. Prior to a meeting between Foreign Minister Albar, Prime Minister Badawi, and UN special envoy Ibrahim Gambari, it was leaked that Gambari expected commitment to "real action" from ASEAN and its member states. He was quoted as saying that it was not enough for ASEAN countries to make statements expressing concern.[99] Although Gambari publicly remained vague as to what "real action" entailed, the Malaysian government interpreted this as a request for the suspension of Myanmar from ASEAN, which was then forcefully ruled out by the Malaysian foreign minister.

Under pressure both at home and internationally, Albar justified this decision by arguing that not only did the body have no mechanism to suspend or impose sanctions but that such actions would simply force Naypyidaw to turn inward and look to China for support.[100] Rastam Mohd Isa, secretary-general at the Foreign Ministry at the time, elaborated: "Our view was, yes, there was a severe problem in Myanmar, which we had to address. This required some form of interference. But did we want to deal with them by using the big stick, something the Europeans were very keen to do, or take a different approach? Malaysia felt that there needed to be a balance."[101]

In order to understand what "balance" means in this context, recall that traditionally ASEAN's interpretation of noninterference not only entailed a strict prohibition of the use and threat of force but also ruled out means such as "naming and shaming." Accordingly, a reconciliation of the norms of noninterference and human rights protection also meant finding ways of interference that did not endanger the sensitive structure of trust among ASEAN member states that, with the help of the noninterference norm, had been painstakingly built in the formerly conflict-ridden region. Malaysia was therefore willing to openly comment, condemn, and make unrequested recommendations, but it ruled out political or economic sanctions. In shaping the type of actions considered legitimate to demonstrate commitment to human rights protection and implement the norm in practice, the regional context influenced the government's response to norm conflict. For governments willing to act upon human rights protection, this implied the use of light (verbal) as opposed to heavy (material) actions. At the same time, the region's embeddedness in the "East Asian" cultural context, with its emphasis on publicly "saving face," meant that shaming was considered far more harmful by Southeast Asian policymakers than their Western counterparts.

To sum up, Malaysia's response to the Saffron Revolution in Myanmar prioritized human rights protection over noninterference. It did so based on a comparison of the costs and benefits of compliance with either norm for its domestic legitimacy as well as regional and international reputation. In order to address conflicting regional expectations for noninterference, Malaysia justified its actions by emphasizing the regional implications of the crisis and adopted a strategy of norm reconciliation. Although noninterference continued to be the default norm, interference would be justified where domestic crises involving human rights violations had an impact on other member states or the region as a whole. Interestingly, by the time of the ASEAN summit in November 2007, the Malaysian government had moved away from its stance of human rights protection in Myanmar and accepted the junta's call for noninterference within the region. In the following section, the change to noninterference will be explained by again drawing on the structure of normative expectations.

A Return to Noninterference: Saffron and Cyclone Nargis

By the time of the ASEAN summit in November 2007, Badawi was no longer pressuring the Myanmarese leaders to initiate reforms and reconciliation in Myanmar. Accepting the junta's call for noninterference from within the region, he now addressed their expectations and prioritized the noninterference norm over human rights protection and promotion. The government's change in response has to be seen in light of a shift in the perceived strength of domestic expectations in favor of human rights protection, especially among the government's dominant domestic audience, the Malays.

In the run-up to the ASEAN meeting, Badawi's administration was facing a major domestic legitimacy crisis. The prime minister had come under siege within his own party, UMNO, when previously embarking on a series of economic and administrative reforms. These measures were supposed to address corruption and diminish bureaucratic processes that slowed down foreign investment in Malaysia.[102] Yet even without touching upon Malaysia's affirmative action laws, which gave constitutional privileges to ethnic Malays and indigenous peoples (the so-called Bumiputra), resistance to Badawi's reform plans instantly formed within the party and the Malay community at large. They objected to his attack on "money politics," from which they had benefited in the past.[103] Moreover, Malay elites saw in Badawi's leadership style of participation, accommodation, and consensus an attempt to undermine their dominance in Malaysian society. The party insisted on embedding the Malay agenda in the Ninth Malaysia Plan, which extended the New Economic Policy and affirmative action for another fifteen years to 2020, until the 30 percent goal of Malay equity ownership would have been met.[104] In order to keep the party united and to reduce resistance within UMNO, Badawi gave in to the demands. As a consequence, public funds continued to be redistributed primarily to the Malay community, which led to tensions with the Indian and Chinese minorities.[105] When the Centre for Public Policy publicized a report in 2006 that claimed that Malay equity ownership was actually already close to 45 percent, and therefore the affirmative action goals had been achieved, an ethnically divisive dispute erupted.[106]

Public resentment found expression in two large-scale antigovernment rallies that took place in November 2007. They were precipitated by allegations of continued corruption and discrepancies in the electoral system that favored the ruling coalition and dominant political party, UMNO. In Kuala Lumpur, forty thousand people attended the Bersih rally, a movement initiated by the opposition parties to campaign for electoral reform.[107] Another rally was held on 25 November 2007 in the Malaysian capital, led by the Hindu Rights Action Force (Hindraf). The organizers had called the protest over discriminatory policies favoring ethnic Malays. In a country that had not seen large-scale demonstrations since the days of Reformasi following the Asian financial crisis of 1997 and where protest was generally not considered a part of public culture, this constituted a major domestic crisis for the government. Among the ruling elites and the Malay community at large, the protests were perceived as a threat to the status quo and the system of Malay domination.

The two rallies occurred at the same time as the ASEAN summit following the Saffron Revolution in November 2007. Moving away from support for extraterritorial human rights protection in Myanmar, the main expectation of the Malay domestic audience toward the Malaysian government was now to contain the protests in Malaysia and maintain regime stability. This swift shift in the strength of domestic expectations reflects the fact that engagement with human rights was still a rather recent development within Malaysian society. Compared to most of its democratic peers within ASEAN, internalization of the norm was still weaker, which made it easier for the pressure of the domestic audience to change. The shift in expectations disrupted the domestic consensus in favor of human rights protection that the Malaysian government had been faced with during the earlier stages of the Saffron Revolution. With its domestic legitimacy under attack primarily by the minority groups, the government tried to maintain support from its main electoral base, the Malays, by addressing their primary domestic concerns. To contain the protests and maintain regime stability, it also employed coercive means. The government called the protests illegal and attempted to suppress them by using excessive force. Hundreds of people were arrested, and five Hindraf leaders were detained under the Internal Security Act (ISA) on the basis that they posed a threat to national security.[108]

The domestic events in Malaysia, and the steps taken by the government to address them, had implications for Malaysia's stance in cases of human rights violations at the regional level. "After the rallies there was no more criticism," said Suaram activist Chew Cy. "If Malaysia had continued to criticize Myanmar over its crackdown on protesting people, Myanmar would just have turned around and said, 'You are cracking down on your own protestors. What right do you have to judge or lecture us?'"[109] Accordingly, Malaysia rejected Singapore's invitation to UN special envoy Ibrahim Gambari to brief the nations on the situation in Myanmar, after the junta leaders had objected. Talking to the press, Foreign Minister Syed Hamid said pointedly: "The host country invited Gambari—it was not something that was done by ASEAN."[110] Moreover, Prime Minister Badawi accepted that Myanmar did not want interference from ASEAN but preferred to deal with Gambari directly. To achieve the stated objectives, it would be better for ASEAN to support Gambari and work through the UN, Badawi said.[111]

By moving away from interference and handing over responsibility to the UN, Badawi could concentrate on the domestic situation in Malaysia. But more importantly, with the domestic consensus in favor of regional human rights protection subsiding, the government no longer had an incentive to question the strict interpretation of the noninterference norm within the region. To the contrary, in continuing to violate the noninterference norm, the government would have contributed to a normative regional environment that could facilitate interference in its own now strained internal affairs. In addition, it would have exposed Badawi and his administration to charges of hypocrisy from its ASEAN peers. Accordingly, a prioritization of human rights protection over noninterference had become unsustainable for the Malaysian government following the November protests in Kuala Lumpur.

Badawi's policy change in response to the Saffron Revolution was facilitated by the regional and international context. Collectively, ASEAN moved away from its human rights–centered stance during the summit. Following the meeting, Singaporean prime minister and ASEAN chair Lee Hsien Loong announced that ASEAN accepted Myanmar's demand for regional noninterference in what the junta considered to be an internal crisis. Similarly, by the time of the summit, international pressure no longer targeted ASEAN directly. The change in Malaysia's stance toward noninterference was, therefore, possible without having to offer its democratic ASEAN peers or international audience a justification of its actions.

The weakened domestic expectations for compliance with human rights protection also explain the government's policy of noninterference in the aftermath of Cyclone Nargis in Myanmar. The legitimacy crisis of the ruling coalition in Malaysia, Barisan Nasional (BN), had become even more pronounced after the general elections in March 2008, which were a political disaster for the prime minister and his party. UMNO and the BN had suffered one of the worst defeats in their history with a loss of their two-thirds majority of seats in Parliament.[112] BN only won 51.2 percent of the popular vote as opposed to 64 percent in the 2004 election, while the main opposition parties improved their performance from 9 percent to a shocking 37 percent. As a consequence, the ruling coalition lost its mandates to govern in four federal states and henceforth controlled only eight of the thirteen federal states.[113] Whereas the ethnic minorities, primarily represented by the opposition, greeted the establishment of opposition-led state governments and the formation of a significantly different Malaysian central government with enthusiasm, the political uncertainty of the election results further exacerbated Malay fears that their societal privileges might be forfeited. With BN's political hegemony eroded, the government continued to rely on coercive means to maintain control and was focused on meeting the expectations of its dominant domestic audience. This included further restrictions of press freedoms and the freedom of expression, as Malaysia dropped to an all-time low in international rankings for press freedom (132 of 195 ranked countries). While tolerating some public assemblies, the government oppressed those held to oppose its claim to power.[114]

In such a domestic environment, expectations for action in Myanmar in accordance with Malaysia's commitment to human rights protection during the aftermath of Cyclone Nargis were almost exclusively articulated by the parliamentary opposition and human rights activists within the country. As visas continued to be delayed in Myanmar, the activist and Peace Malaysia coordinator Mukhriz Mahathir criticized the junta, saying it "should do the right thing and let in international aid teams."[115] The Malaysian Parliamentary Myanmar Caucus reiterated his call on the following day, which urged Myanmar's government to postpone its planned constitutional referendum in view of the crisis caused by Cyclone Nargis.[116] AIPMC vice president and Malaysian opposition leader Wan Azizah Wan Ismail sent a letter to Myanmar's ambassador in Malaysia stating that the junta's decision to continue with the referendum seemed to show that it was not giving due concern to its citizens' plight.[117] Further emphasizing the Myanmarese junta's neglect of its humanitarian responsibilities, she submitted a motion to the Malaysian Parliamentary Speaker's office that requested that Myanmar postpone the planned constitutional referendum following the devastating cyclone and instead focus on the relief effort. The motion also called upon the regime to provide the necessary space for aid workers who were still on standby, waiting for visas to get into the country to assist the cyclone victims.[118] She urged the Malaysian government to use its political and diplomatic influence in the region to have the vote postponed and get the generals to focus on the people who had suffered from the impact of the cyclone.[119] For its part, the Malaysian government decided not to comment on the motion, which was later rejected by the Speaker of the House, Pandikar Amin Mulia. The Speaker argued that passing the motion in parliament would violate Malaysia's practice of neutrality and noninterference in the internal affairs of other states.[120]

But Malaysian opposition parliamentarians kept inquiring. A member of the DAP asked Foreign Minister Abdul Rahim Bakri whether, in light of the contemporary crisis, the Malaysian government regretted having supported Myanmar's accession to ASEAN in 1997. The foreign minister responded in the negative, saying that Myanmar was a country "close to us" and without ASEAN "it would have to depend on the big powers which would eventually have usurped its sovereignty."[121] He went on to stress that although the referendum on a new constitution was not well received by the international community, "as a sovereign state, Malaysia respects the decision and hopes that democracy will quickly return to Myanmar."[122] It would not be for Malaysia to determine whether "the move" (referring to the referendum) was sincere or not.[123] Opposition politician Lim Kit Siang, who was also part of the ASEAN Inter-Parliamentary Myanmar Caucus, commented that such an attitude reflected "dismally" on all ASEAN leaders and governments, who could "definitely do more."[124]

While the opposition referred to the junta's role in aggravating the human suffering by concentrating on the constitutional referendum and banning international aid workers from the country, the government framed the crisis as a humanitarian disaster. In line with its stance taken at the ASEAN summit in November 2007, the Malaysian government emphasized its commitment to noninterference. It thereby respected Myanmar's demand for compliance with the noninterference norm and, by focusing on the humanitarian response to the disaster, mirrored the framing of the majority of ASEAN member states during the crisis. By addressing the regional expectation for noninterference and upholding the validity of the noninterference norm, the Malaysian government tried to protect itself from regional pressure in response to its own handling of its domestic crisis and its use of coercive means to maintain its own regime stability. "Among ASEAN states it is quite common that issues are thrown back at you," argued former foreign minister Syed Hamid Albar when explaining Malaysia's policy of noninterference in response to Cyclone Nargis. "At that time we went through a difficult domestic period and we were worried about regional 'throwback,' so we remained silent."[125] In maintaining a policy of noninterference during Cyclone Nargis, the government thus attempted to shield itself from "rhetorical entrapment" at home and allegations of hypocrisy in light of its demand for respect for human rights regionally but simultaneous failure to uphold them domestically.[126] In line with the policy change on the regional level ever since the protests in November 2007, Malaysia's rhetoric also changed. Internationally, the Malaysian government no longer emphasized Malaysia's model character in successfully managing peaceful relations across ethnically and religiously distinct domestic groups but instead stressed a shared commitment to Westphalian values and the need for compliance with nonintervention. At the 2008 General Assembly address, Malaysian foreign minister Rais Yatim stated: "Malaysia is concerned over recent attempts by certain powerful member states to question the national laws of countries and the administration of justice under those laws. It needs to be restated—we have no right to meddle, in any form of manifestation or under any pretext or circumstances, in the conduct of the internal affairs of other countries."[127]

The Malaysian policy of noninterference during Cyclone Nargis avoided domestic legitimacy costs among its main audience, the Malay community. Given that the majority of nondemocratic ASEAN members individually abstained from interference during the crisis, it also addressed regional expectations. However, Malaysia's policy of noninterference was in conflict with international expectations articulated in the aftermath of the cyclone. Although no explicit expectations were addressed to the Malaysian government, ASEAN as an organization was called to act on behalf of human rights protection. International pressure on ASEAN peaked during Cyclone Nargis, as some Western governments circulated the idea of humanitarian intervention in Myanmar on the basis of RtoP. Malaysian media instantly dismissed the notion, arguing that, as a natural disaster, Cyclone Nargis was not a case for RtoP and the United Nations could not legitimately intervene by force without Myanmar's permission.[128] The Malaysian government did not officially comment on French foreign minister Kouchner's call for intervention on the basis of RtoP, but in framing the crisis as a humanitarian disaster it refrained from recognizing Cyclone Nargis as a case of human rights violation. Explaining Malaysia's rationale, former foreign minister Syed Hamid Albar said: "We did not see it as a human rights issue. Treating it as such would have further politicized the situation. For us it was a humanitarian problem, and the question was how do we get aid into Myanmar? It was clear that there would be no messing with Myanmar's sovereignty in the handling of the crisis."[129]

While supporting the ASEAN-led relief mechanism and thereby reducing reputation costs for the organization, the Malaysian government, in line with its own noninterference stance, took a low profile during the ASEAN emergency meeting in Singapore on 19 May. It did not pressure the junta into opening up and primarily used the meeting to deliver Malaysia's promised US$1 million aid to Myanmar.[130] Acting more assertively during the meeting in order to diminish reputation costs for ASEAN was unnecessary for the Malaysian government as Indonesia, upon direct appeal from the UN, took the lead in persuading the generals in Myanmar to cooperate with ASEAN and the international community.

In conclusion, it can be said that Malaysian compliance with the two norms changed from human rights protection to noninterference as a consequence of a shift in domestic expectations following the protests in November 2007 and the general elections in March 2008. In prioritizing noninterference during the later stages of the Saffron Revolution and Cyclone Nargis, the government not only avoided further domestic legitimacy costs but also addressed regional expectations in favor of noninterference. In order to invalidate international expectations during Cyclone Nargis, the Malaysian government rejected the framing of the crisis as a case of human rights violation and treated it instead as a humanitarian disaster. Concerned about reputation costs for ASEAN as an organization, which was the primary target of international expectations, Malaysia supported the ASEAN-led mechanism but abstained from pressuring the junta on its own.

Maintaining Noninterference during the Rakhine Riots

After the disastrous elections of 2008, Badawi tried to stay in office but ultimately ceded to mounting party pressure and resigned. In April 2009, he handed party leadership over to his deputy, Najib Razak, who then became head of government. During the Rakhine Riots of 2012 Najib continued to comply with the noninterference norm, despite the presence of influential Muslim voices in the country that called on the government to take a more prominent role in defending the Rohingya. Similar requests were also made internationally by other Islamic states, who lobbied for an intervention by the OIC and support for the Rohingya by the Muslim community.

Early on in the crisis, the violence against the Rohingya Muslims in Myanmar became a matter of domestic concern in Malaysia. In this context, calls for interference based on a commitment to general human rights protection were combined with arguments about the need for solidarity with fellow Muslims. The Muslim Lawyers Association of Malaysia stated that given Malaysia's "vociferous" support for Myanmar's admission to ASEAN in 1997, it was now up to Malaysia to "boldly remind the Myanmar ambassador of the very ideals of ASEAN mutual respect and humanitarian solidarity which were offered to Myanmar along with its invitation into ASEAN several years ago."[131] Expressing a clear expectation for compliance with human rights protection from the Malaysian government, he went on to argue that the "Malaysian government must offer every human resource at its command to organize and defend the Rohingya people."[132]

The case of the Rakhine Riots was also addressed in parliament. Similar to Malaysian lawyers, politicians across party lines primarily relied on arguments based on general human rights protection to frame their call for interference. The opposition Malaysian Islamic Party (PAS) called upon the Malaysian government to intervene in Myanmar to stop the violence against the Rohingya community. "We want the government to play an active role against this, as what is happening in Burma is unacceptable to the international community, especially the ASEAN countries," he said.[133]

Mujahid Yusuk Rawa, also from the PAS Party, warned that inaction could turn the Southeast Asian region into "killing fields" based on religious hatred, conflict, and ethnic cleansing. He argued that the "slaughter" of thousands of Rohingya had "shattered" the hope of peaceful coexistence among the different faiths in the Southeast Asian region. The PAS legislator not only framed the crisis as a case of human rights protection but also highlighted the regional dimension of the violence in Rakhine, thereby providing an additional justification for interference within ASEAN. When reminded of the ASEAN practice of noninterference, he replied that they were facing a case of severe human rights violations and as a universal principle, "leaders cannot keep silent about it."[134]

Support for a more active stance in the Rohingya crisis also came from former prime minister Mahathir Mohamad and his political rival Anwar Ibrahim. As the de facto opposition leader, Anwar said that the Pakatan Rakyat (People's Pact)[135] wanted the Malaysian government to file an official protest against the violence in Rakhine.[136] Similarly, Mahathir vocally condemned the violence against the Rohingya.[137] During his time as head of government, Mahathir had been one of the staunchest supporters of noninterference but now called upon Prime Minister Najib to highlight the plight of the Rohingya community on the international stage.[138] He argued that Myanmar's laws and actions had created problems for other countries, such as Thailand, Bangladesh, and Malaysia, where many Rohingya had been forced to take refuge.[139] In highlighting the regional consequences of the crisis, Mahathir provided a justification for interference based on the spillover effects of the violence. By grounding his argument in the impact on others instead of the human suffering in Rakhine, he tried to increase the likelihood of acceptance within the region. Prime Minister Badawi had used similar reasoning during the Saffron Revolution in order to justify his interference in Myanmar's domestic affairs.

Framing the Rohingya crisis more in terms of Muslim solidarity, the Malaysian Consultative Council for the Islamic Organization (MAPIM) urged Prime Minister Najib Razak to defend the Rohingya Muslims, who had increasingly become victims of persecution.[140] MAPIM secretary-general Mohd Azmi Abdul Hamid said that his office had sent a letter to the Malaysian prime minister to inform him about the situation in Rakhine. According to Hamid, Najib had strong influence within ASEAN, which he hoped could be used for an intervention to solve the crisis. In specifically calling upon the Muslim world to act, he argued that the situation in Rakhine transcended political boundaries and needed attention from all stakeholders within the Muslim community.[141] He added: "I hope the next parliamentary session will take the initiative to voice this view at the ASEAN level, for it to be discussed regionally and globally."[142] Similarly, treating the fate of the Rohingya as a problem of the Muslim world, the Secretariat of the Regional Asia Ulama Association sent a resolution to the president of the World Ulama Association, Yusuf Al-Qaradawi, asking him to hold an emergency conference on how to defend the Muslim Rohingya.[143] The Malaysian Institute of International Islamic Cooperation (IKIAM) equally highlighted the special responsibility of the Islamic world in the crisis. "It is time for the world to intervene, especially the Islamic states, to find a solution to the upheavals involving Muslim Rohingya and Buddhist Rakhines in Rakhine State," IKIAM chairman Zahidi Zainul Abidin said.[144]

The above discussion shows that the framing of the call for interference in the Rakhine Riots differed among various actors in the government's domestic audience. Those more readily socialized to universal human rights due to their professions, for example lawyers and politicians, primarily provided rights-based justifications for interference. In addition, they often emphasized the spillover effects of the crisis on the region, thereby trying to circumvent regional expectations for noninterference. In contrast, representatives of Malaysian Muslim organizations more often than not emphasized the religious dimension of the conflict in Rakhine. In responding to the crisis, they ascribed a special responsibility to Muslim bodies and Islamic states. Irrespective of the framing of the crisis, what is striking is that almost all support for interference within the country came from Muslim-Malay voices. Among those, many—most prominently Mahathir Mohamad—had in the past not been at the forefront of human rights protection within the region. This suggests that religion had a catalytic effect on their willingness to assist others. At least among parts of Muslim-Malay society, the internalization of human rights, therefore, seemed to be quite particular. Instead of displaying a universal understanding of human rights, internalization of the norm reflected a more particularist notion of Muslim solidarity during the Rakhine Riots. Assistance was offered not just to any stranger but preferentially to non-nationals of a shared religious affiliation. This partial understanding of human rights once again mirrors the fact that engagement with human rights within the country only really became permissible during the premiership of Abdullah Badawi. The Malay community especially had little previous exposure to human rights discourse.

Domestic voices calling for interference on behalf of the Rohingya were reinforced at the global stage. While Western countries largely refrained from interfering in the crisis for fears of jeopardizing the reform process in Myanmar, several Islamic countries, including Iran, Turkey, and Saudi Arabia, harshly condemned the violence against the Rohingya and called the UN, OIC, and Islamic states to action. But despite the domestic and international pressure for interference, the Malaysian government remained silent. Independently and within the ASEAN framework it was unwilling to interfere. When Foreign Minister Anifah Aman was asked in parliament about the role played by the Malaysian government as a member of the OIC in addressing the "Rohingya Muslim Genocide," he simply referred to the regional stance of noninterference.[145] "The non-interference practice is our way of recognizing a country's sovereignty. It is consistent with our policy against ethnic conflict in the Rakhine state of Myanmar," he said.[146] The government's policy of noninterference reflected that, at the time, rebuilding its domestic legitimacy among the key ethnic minorities, just one year ahead of the 2013 general elections, was more important to the government than addressing Muslim-Malay expectations for action on behalf of the Rohingya. In contrast to their fellow Malay countrymen, the minority groups were far less enthusiastic about government involvement in the Rakhine Riots. Several factors contributed to the shift in their expectations after Cyclone Nargis and explain why there were fewer voices calling for Malaysian interference based on human rights concerns independent from religious affiliation.

The first factor was a noticeable decline in the protection and enforcement of their own rights within Malaysia. After the 2007 riots and 2008 general elections, the country was more divided than ever. In order to restore UMNO's power, Prime Minister Najib embarked on a dual strategy that contained coercive as well as legitimacy-based elements. In order to portray the new government as inclusive and open, responding equally to the growing socioeconomic needs and demands of its people of *all* ethnic descents, he launched "1Malaysia" as the new domestic paradigm. It aimed to forge a Malaysian identity that transcended ethnic and religious divides. At the same time, Najib continued to curtail the freedom of the press, restricted the role of the legislature, and straightjacketed the judiciary by filling "bottleneck positions" such as the attorney general's office with party cronies. Power was increasingly transferred back to the executive. Whereas the first element of Najib's domestic strategy aimed at winning legitimacy across the ethnic groups, the second, more coercive, element had the objective of avoiding another legitimacy crisis by increasing the executive's control over the party, policymaking, and public opinion. It also led to a decline in respect for and protection of human rights in Malaysia. The deteriorating human rights situation at home affected domestic belief in the appropriateness of human rights protection as part of Malaysia's foreign policy. "People see human rights violations elsewhere and think discrimination exists here, too. Not as bad obviously, as nobody is shot and houses aren't burned. But if we cannot fix what happens here, why would we be concerned about something similar happening elsewhere?" human rights activist Chew Cy asked.[147] Political activists and opposition parliamentarians expressed similar views, stressing that it would be hypocritical to lobby their government to get involved in foreign cases if Malaysia could not solve its own democratic issues: "We think that our own government is not much better. In Indonesia the NGOs and civil society face a different domestic situation. They believe their government could do more, but is not doing enough, so they pressure it. Here we think that our government does not have the credibility anymore to knock at the door of Myanmar and say, 'I think you are violating human rights.'"[148]

In short, the strength of domestic expectations for the government to conform with the norm of human rights protection and promotion internationally had declined by the time of the Rakhine Riots in 2012. The deteriorating human rights situation at home following Najib's accession to power again reflects that the internalization of human rights protection has been weaker in Malaysia than in ASEAN's "liberal" democracies. Checks and balances within the political process were less well institutionalized, allowing the government to use limitations within the constitutional guarantees of certain rights, such as freedom of expression and assembly, to oppress domestic protest and opposition.

While the increased restriction of rights at home led to a general decline in the expectations of minority groups regarding the potential for Malaysia to engage in extraterritorial human rights protection, a second element has to be considered, which actually led to pronounced resistance against interference in the crisis. The religious dimension of the Rakhine Riots and the fear of a Muslim Rohingya refugee wave hitting Malaysia meant that, during the crisis, large sections of the Indian and Chinese minorities openly opposed Malaysian involvement in the Rakhine Riots. Especially in the opposition-led state of Penang, with a large Chinese voter base, calls were loud to prevent further Rohingya migration to Malaysia. As a more economically affluent and Islamic nation, Malaysia already hosted a large community of Rohingya. Bordering Thailand and facing the Andaman Sea, Penang had in the past been the place of first arrival for many Rohingya refugees coming to Malaysia. "When the Rohingya were left out on the sea as a result of the border closure in Thailand, some people suggested that they should land in Penang," opposition parliamentarian Kian Ming Ong recalled: "But Penang voters pressured the chief minister in Penang, who is the secretary-general of my party, not to allow the Rohingya to land there. They were afraid of being overrun by Muslims and feared that the presence of large numbers of Muslim migrants could further affect their space in Malaysian society. These are people that would otherwise be very progressive on a lot of human rights issues, but showed little compassion regarding Muslim foreign migrants coming to their country."[149]

Although the religious dimension of the Rakhine Riots had a reinforcing effect on expectations regarding human rights protection among the Malay community, it led to the opposite reaction among the ethnic minorities. Afraid of the spillover effects of Muslim migration to Malaysia, the strength of their expectations for government compliance with extraterritorial human rights protection diminished. In comparing the costs and benefits of compliance with the two norms, the Malaysian government had to choose between addressing the conflicting expectations of the Muslim-Malay community and the ethnic minorities. In order to enhance its legitimacy among the ethnic minorities prior to the upcoming 2013 general elections, the government opted to address the expectations of the latter. "The Malaysian authorities feared that by getting involved in the crisis, they would become a magnet and more Rohingya refugees would come to Malaysia," former special envoy to Myanmar Razali Ismail explained, adding: "We already have tensions between the communities here. So if you add more people, you intensify that conflict. The opposition would have accused the government of trying to buy Muslim votes. So in staying out of the conflict, the multi-ethnic composition of Malaysia really was the main problem. Even though we want the Rohingya to have justice in Myanmar, this does not mean that we can have them all here."[150] In short, the government worried that the arrival of more Muslim migrants could be perceived by the minorities as an attempt to further increase the influence of Islam in Malaysia. This would not only have risked undermining the "1Malaysia" policy but would also have alienated Indian and Chinese voters less than a year ahead of the general elections in May 2013.

On the regional level Malaysia's noninterference policy did not risk reputation costs as the majority of member states, as well as ASEAN collectively, had maintained compliance with the noninterference norm during the Rakhine Riots. On the domestic and international level, however, a policy of noninterference threatened to cause legitimacy and reputation costs with the Muslim-Malays and Islamic nations. In order to manage the conflicting expectations, which had remained unaddressed by the government's choice of noninterference in the crisis, Najib pursued two strategies. To begin with, his administration tried to undermine the foundation of domestic calls for human rights protection by framing the Rakhine Riots as a humanitarian disaster as opposed to a case of human rights violations. As the crisis progressed and calls for interference continued, the government made concessions to its Malay and international Islamic audiences by supporting the work of the OIC in Rakhine. Although not taking a prominent role in the deliberations on the topic, Malaysia participated in the extraordinary OIC meeting in August 2012.[151] Following the meeting, Prime Minister Najib said that he considered it a positive signal that Myanmar was inviting the OIC secretary-general to find a good solution to the Rohingya problem. "Myanmar's President Thein Sein called me to explain what happened and expressed his willingness to cooperate with the OIC representatives," he stated.[152]

Overall, by complying with the noninterference norm, the Malaysian government tried to enhance its domestic legitimacy among the ethnic minorities in line with its "1Malaysia" paradigm prior to the 2013 general elections. In framing the crisis in Rakhine as a humanitarian disaster as opposed to a case of human rights violation, the government tried to invalidate domestic expectations in favor of human rights protection that conflicted with the government's noninterference stance. It later made concessions to appease domestic and international calls for interference on behalf of the Rohingya by supporting the work of the OIC.

MALAYSIA'S RESPONSE STRATEGIES AND WHY THEY CHANGED

The mixed response pattern displayed in Malaysia can be explained as the result of a shift in the government's estimation of the strength of domestic expectations and its perception of the legitimacy costs of complying with human rights protection as opposed to noninterference. In order to best address changing domestic as well as conflicting international expectations for norm compliance, the government over time adapted its response strategy from attempted norm reconciliation to conflict denial. In adjusting its response strategy the government tried to minimize the social costs of norm compliance as domestic expectations changed.

During the Saffron Revolution the Malaysian government initially acted upon the human rights norm in view of strong pressure at the domestic and international level, as well as pressure from its democratically advanced ASEAN peers. To justify its interference to the majority of ASEAN member states that had individually remained silent during the crisis, the government tried to reconcile noninterference with human rights protection. It argued that in cases that had a significant impact on neighboring states or the region as a whole, interference should not be considered illegitimate. In order to avoid future reputation costs at the regional level by prioritizing human rights protection, the Malaysian government suggested an official modification of the norm within ASEAN's normative framework. A modified noninterference norm would allow interference by neighbors and regional peers if a domestic crisis affected their jurisdictions or the region as a whole. Being confronted with conflicting expectations for norm compliance, as a majority of regional peers continued to abide to noninterference, norm reconciliation represented a compromise between the two norms that both continued to coexist in the region's normative environment. To generate acceptance for its own behavior, the Malaysian government needed persuasive power. It used the various ASEAN meetings to justify its own actions. But more than that, it also advocated for a new interpretation of the noninterference norm within the region, thereby trying to influence future expectations and the behavior of others. It did so, via arguments and soft power, as it led by example. Norm reconciliation was the best outcome Malaysia could hope to achieve in order to minimize its social costs. With its relatively short history of democratization and human rights protection, it lacked the credibility as a normative leader in the region to aim for general norm replacement.

In line with a shift in the perceived strength of domestic expectations for compliance with human rights protection, the administration of Prime Minister Abdullah Badawi changed its policy toward noninterference at the ASEAN summit in 2007. The new expectations primarily articulated by the government's main domestic audience, the Malays, reflected the domestic situation in Malaysia. In the wake of the Bersih and Hindraf mass protests in November 2007, which questioned the domestic system of Malay domination, the dominant Malay expectations now revolved around containment of the protests and maintenance of regime stability. In addressing these expectations, Badawi also employed coercive means, which at the regional level required a return to noninterference in order to shield the regime from interference in its own now-strained domestic affairs. It maintained a prioritization of the noninterference norm during Cyclone Nargis. In order to invalidate pressure in favor of interference from its international audience during the cyclone, and thereby avoid reputation costs, the government opted for a strategy of conflict denial. It rejected the framing of the crisis as a case of human rights protection. Instead, it portrayed the aftermath of the cyclone as a humanitarian disaster.

The new government headed by Prime Minister Najib Razak employed a similar strategy of conflict denial during the Rakhine Riots. Facing conflicting domestic expectations, he aligned his stance with the preferences of the ethnic minorities that were against Malaysian involvement in the crisis based on a fear of attracting further Muslim migration to the country. In addressing their concerns instead of Muslim-Malay expectations for compliance with human rights protection, Najib hoped to enhance his legitimacy among the ethnic minorities prior to the upcoming general elections. In order to minimize legitimacy costs among the Malay majority, the government again framed the crisis as a case of humanitarian disaster, denying the presence of human rights violations in Rakhine. In addition, it worked through the OIC to address the crisis, without, however, taking a major role.

The various shifts in the expectations of the domestic audience reflect the fact that compared to other ASEAN democracies, internalization of human rights protection was still relatively weak in Malaysia, as well as the presence of a major domestic crisis, which in addition affected the strength of expectations for human rights protection. The dominant societal group, the Malays, had only recently been exposed to universal human rights standards following Badawi's accession to power. The relatively fresh engagement with human rights is also reflected in the framing of the Rakhine Riots, whereby justifications for interference on the basis of general human rights protection and Muslim solidarity merged. Each shift in the relevant domestic expectations was triggered by national crises that threatened to alter the respective group's domestic status. The Bersih and Hindraf mass protests in November 2007 questioned the domestic system of Malay domination and Muslim migration threatened to alter the ethnic makeup in the minority-ruled states.

Conclusion

This book began with the following two questions: How do states and their governments respond to norm conflict in practice? And why do they respond the way they do? In addressing these questions, it sought to fill a knowledge gap in the discipline of international relations, which has so far given little theoretical or empirical attention to norm conflict as a challenge to foreign policy decision-making. With the help of three country case studies, I explored the proposition that governments respond to norm conflict by prioritizing one norm over the other as well as by managing domestic and international expectations for norm compliance. In doing so, governments seek to minimize the anticipated legitimacy and reputation costs of noncompliance with either norm. By adopting a consequentialist but socially embedded approach to norm following, I outlined a dynamic theoretical framework for explaining state response in situations of norm conflict. Five different responses to norm conflict were developed in the theory chapter of the book to guide the case selection and serve as a reference point for the empirical analysis of the "real-world" cases of norm conflict in Southeast Asia.

In exploring norm conflicts empirically, this book told the story of the governments of Indonesia, Thailand, and Malaysia and how they responded to the norm conflict between noninterference in the internal affairs of states and human rights protection in cases of human rights violations. It did so with reference to three instances of gross human rights violations in Myanmar, namely the Saffron Revolution in 2007, Cyclone Nargis in 2008, and the Rakhine Riots in 2012. While facing the same problem, the respective governments each experienced the norm conflict in a unique way, depending on the strength of the domestic expectations for norm compliance with either of the two norms and how they interacted with the regional and international expectations set by the governments' prior commitment to the conflicting norms.

In what follows, this conclusion reviews the findings from the case studies in light of the initial theoretical expectations. It then moves on to address the "lessons learned" and discusses the findings' implications for future research on norm conflict.

REVIEWING THE RESPONSES TO NORM CONFLICT

A consequentialist but socially embedded approach to norm following reflects that the three logics of action normally used within the discipline do not, on their own, satisfactorily explain responses to norm conflict. By emphasizing the social costs of norm violation at the domestic and international levels as motivational forces, the approach to explaining norm following adopted here offered both an explanation of *how* governments respond to norm conflict as well as *why*. Moreover, it served to narrow down expectations for when governments are likely to adopt different response strategies to norm conflict in order to manage expectations for norm compliance. As a first determining factor, it relies on whether the expectations for norm compliance articulated by the relevant audiences converge or conflict and are likely to change over time. With the help of constructivist insights from work on norm replacement and cycles of normative change at the international level, expectations regarding the likelihood of the adoption of a strategy could be further refined. Whether the choice of a strategy is likely or not further depends on a government's power resources, most notably its persuasive and soft power, its intention to impact the behavior of others as well as its (un)certainty regarding future expectations (see table 1).

Although each of the three governments chose a different response for addressing norm conflict, one element in the response was stable across all cases. Confronted with conflicting expectations for norm compliance by the different audiences, all governments shared a greater concern for domestic legitimacy than reputation costs at the regional and international levels and thus acted in accordance with domestic expectations. In choosing which of the two norms to prioritize, response to norm conflict therefore always reflected the dominant domestic expectations in order to avoid or at least minimize domestic legitimacy costs. Only then did the governments try to manage conflicting expectations by providing justifications that legitimized their behavior vis-à-vis the dissenting audiences abroad, or, if necessary, made momentary concessions. The specific empirical findings of the individual cases will be reviewed against the backdrop of the theoretical expectations in the following sections.

Norm Reconciliation in Indonesia

The Indonesian case study illustrates norm reconciliation as a response strategy to norm conflict. Theoretically, the strategy has been described as most likely in cases in which a government faces strong conflicting expectations for norm compliance at the domestic and/or international levels but has little confidence in its ability to convince the dissenting audience of general norm replacement because it lacks the persuasive power and leadership to do so. In accordance with the theoretical expectation, the empirical analysis showed that in view of strong conflicting domestic expectations for norm compliance that were both broadly shared across society, the Indonesian government adopted norm reconciliation as a response strategy to norm conflict. Confronted with strong domestic expectations in favor of a prioritization of human rights protection throughout all instances of rights violations in Myanmar, human rights promotion and protection in practice became Indonesia's "general" norm. Recall that in order for both norms to remain part of the state's normative structure, as intended by norm reconciliation, a modification of the respective norms' meanings is required. To remove the overlap between the normative directives, both norms are the subject of change: After determining a "general" norm, a gap needs to be created within that norm that allows a "special" norm to be legitimately applied in those instances that fall within the gap. Thereby, the "special" norm becomes a legitimate exception to the "general" norm and supersedes it in cases that fall within its sphere of application. More often than not, complying with human rights protection as the "general" norm avoided not only domestic legitimacy costs for the Indonesian government but also international reputation costs. In two of three instances of norm conflict, both the West and the UN as relevant international audiences supported a rights-based approach to the crises.

However, Indonesia's support of human rights protection in its foreign policy was not absolute. The government only complied with human rights protection in those cases that did not involve a notion of secessionism or the risk of territorial disintegration. In these instances, it remained silent and prioritized the noninterference norm. This reflected the presence of a

Conclusion 163

second conflicting set of expectations, which the government believed would be difficult, if not impossible, to remove without far-ranging contextual changes inside Indonesia. Maintaining noninterference as a regional standard in this "special" case mattered to the Indonesian government because of strong domestic pressure to guarantee the territorial integrity of a unitary Indonesian state. The fear of external interference in the restive regions of Indonesia, such as Papua, has been omnipresent in Indonesian society, and Indonesian governments have been very much aware of it. The fear of territorial disintegration has its origin in the very real and recurrent secessionist threats the country has had to survive ever since its independence and that reached a climax with the loss of East Timor in 2002. The pronounced Indonesian determination to prevent further secessionism thus explains the prioritization of noninterference in the later stages of the Saffron Revolution and the Rakhine Riots, which involved a risk of territorial disintegration and notions of secessionism.

Effectively, the Indonesian government defined the presence of disintegrative forces in an internal conflict as a legitimate exception to human rights protection. The Indonesian government thus created a "gap" within its "general" norm that not only allowed for but also necessitated the application of noninterference as the "special" norm. To fit within this "gap," the sphere of application of noninterference had to be reduced. In other words, the Indonesian government "stripped off" the first two dimensions of the regional noninterference norm as defined by Acharya (see table 2).[1] These dimensions ruled out *any* criticism of governments in their handling of internal affairs, most importantly state-society relations. In its practical application, the Indonesian government instead reduced the noninterference norm to its third and fourth dimensions, which explicitly refer to territorial matters: they proscribe support for rebel groups and prescribe regional support in counterinsurgencies. This derogation of the norm by the Indonesian government reflected a desire to loosen the strict interpretation of noninterference as stipulated within ASEAN, and to allow for verbal condemnations in cases of human rights violations, while at the same time upholding noninterference as a regional standard in internal cases in which the territorial integrity of a state is at risk.

In order to determine norm compliance in cases in which the domestic expectations conflicted, the Indonesian government made a judgment regarding which domestic expectation mattered more: the protection of the rights of non-nationals or the territorial integrity of the Indonesian state. The fact that few Indonesians prove willing to discuss the human rights violations that occur in the course of the secessionist conflict in Papua, where the rights of Indonesian *nationals* and not foreigners are concerned, helps to explain the government's response in favor of noninterference. The government anticipated that even though they were less tangible at the moment of choice, the potential legitimacy costs of creating a regional environment that allowed for interference in secessionist conflicts were more severe. By violating the norm of noninterference in cases with a secessionist dimension or the potential for territorial disintegration, the Indonesian government would have risked undermining the validity of noninterference as a behavioral standard for ASEAN member states in those instances. Moreover, it would have set a concrete precedent for interference in its own secessionist conflicts, most importantly in Papua. In complying with the noninterference norm, the Indonesian government thus protected itself from intrusive behavior and the anticipated domestic legitimacy costs that external interference in regions such as Papua would have entailed. As a motivational force, domestic and regional expectations therefore went hand in hand.

However, in order for norm reconciliation to succeed as a response strategy to norm conflict, the government had to generate acceptance for the application of the norms in their modified forms. As a consequence, norm reconciliation still requires persuasive power and normative leadership to influence future expectations and impact the behavior of others, but to a lesser degree than general norm replacement. The Indonesian government's justificatory effort sought to minimize the immediate domestic legitimacy and international reputation costs whenever the government applied noninterference as its "special" norm, despite the presence of domestic and international expectations in favor of human rights protection. But in repeatedly pointing out the link between noninterference and secessionism in the region, it also pursued the longer-term strategic objective of generating acceptance for the norms' new meaning and spheres of application. In relation to its regional audience, the Indonesian government tried to establish action on behalf of human rights protection in cases without a secessionist dimension as a legitimate response that should not be seen as an act of interference. It thereby employed three main arguments: it referred to the wider international normative environment; provided precedents from Indonesia's own openness to external involvement in similar instances in the past; and highlighted the reputational damage to ASEAN as a consequence of Myanmar's behavior.

In sum, the government's response to the norm conflict between human rights protection and noninterference demonstrates a clear attempt to reconcile the norms according to an a priori defined pattern. Thereby the conflicting expectations for norm compliance at the domestic level were decisive. Only following a successful resolution of conflicts in its restive regions, most importantly in Papua, would the Indonesian government have been in a position to either attempt a general replacement of noninterference with human rights protection within the region or, in transcending ASEAN as a relevant audience, to consistently prioritize human rights protection in line with the anticipated domestic and international expectations.

Strategic Norm Replacement in Thailand

Thailand was chosen to illustrate a case of strategic norm replacement in response to norm conflict. The case study showed that the Thai government tried to frame its response as a legitimate exception to the general rule in order to fulfill domestic expectations for a policy of noninterference in relation to Myanmar, while at the same time minimizing the anticipated international and, at times, regional reputation costs of noncompliance with human rights protection. In short, the Thai government sought to replace human rights protection with noninterference as a standard of behavior for Thailand specifically in its relations with Myanmar. It used its special position as a direct neighbor of Myanmar as an argument to justify its norm following vis-à-vis its dissenting audiences. In doing so the government tried to influence the expectations of others toward its behavior with respect to Myanmar. This required persuasive power to successfully put forward its arguments and have them heard, but no normative leadership and thus soft power. The Thai decision makers did not try to generally undermine the validity of the human rights protection norm within the region or influence the norm following of its peers.

Unlike Indonesia, the Thai government across all three situations of norm conflict in Myanmar faced the expectations of two distinct domestic groups that disagreed over legitimate responses to the crises. While the urban middle class called upon the government to comply with human rights protection, the rural population and Thai business class expected the government not to compromise economic relations with neighboring Myanmar as a consequence of its foreign policy. They relied on continued access to Myanmar's natural resources and border trade to earn a living. Successive Thai governments, both predominantly military and civilian in form, aligned their responses with the preferences of the rural population and business class, as they constituted the numerically stronger domestic groups, and their support was decisive for winning elections. In order to address their expectations, the government felt compelled to comply with noninterference in the crises as invoked by the Myanmarese government.

In complying with the noninterference norm, the primary objective of the Thai government was thus not to satisfy regional expectations. Instead, the government's main concern was to avoid upsetting Myanmar, whose government had invoked noninterference as the only legitimate standard of behavior. During the premiership of Chuan Leekpai, who pursued a rights-based approach towards Myanmar, Thais had learned that ignoring Myanmar's expectations could quickly lead to sanctions, such as a closing of the border. To avoid such coercive measures, the government complied with noninterference. Indeed, even without the actual threat of material punishment, the precedent of such measures provided reason enough to comply with the no-interference norm. Therefore, more than physical proximity, the decisive factor in the strategy of strategic norm replacement was actually the extreme economic interdependence between the two countries and Myanmar's special relevance for the accomplishment of development as Thailand's dominant domestic paradigm. The extreme economic interdependence with Myanmar increased the strength of the domestic expectations for compliance with the noninterference norm, which in this form might not be the case in relation to Thailand's remaining neighbors. It is therefore not clear whether Thailand would pursue the same strategy in cases of human rights violations in other neighboring states.

However, while close proximity was not a decisive factor in shaping the strength of the expectations for norm compliance, it was central to the government's argumentation legitimizing its actions. In pursuing a strategy of strategic norm replacement, the challenge for the Thai government was not to redefine the meaning of either of the two norms, as seen in Indonesia's response, but to make a case for the inappropriateness of interference specifically in Thailand's relations with Myanmar. With regard to its Western audience, which directly called upon the Thai government to act in favor of human rights protection, the Thai authorities justified the need for noninterference with reference to its special geopolitical position as a direct neighbor and its extreme vulnerability to internal events in Myanmar given the extremely long and porous border between the countries. It argued that in order to protect that border from illegal migration, human trafficking, and other cross-border crime, it was dependent on Myanmar's cooperation and stability within the neighboring country. The government thus presented its policy of noninterference as a geopolitical necessity instead of a strategic choice. By establishing noninterference as the *only* appropriate norm in Thailand's relations with Myanmar, the government hoped to reduce international expectations regarding interference in the future.

Ironically, previous Democrat-led Thai governments had used the same argument—Thailand's extreme vulnerability as a neighbor to internal events in Myanmar—as a justification to its regional peers to prioritize human rights protection over noninterference in relation to Myanmar. In 1998 Foreign Minister Surin Pitsuwan had suggested a review of the noninterference norm within ASEAN in favor of a practice that he described as "flexible engagement." Regionally, flexible engagement was presented as a way of reconciling noninterference with nontraditional, transborder security concerns, including threats to human security. Surin argued that interference should be allowed in cases in which internal events had an effect on neighboring countries or the region as a whole. For Thailand this revised interpretation, given its position as a neighbor, would have enabled it to consistently prioritize human rights protection in its relations with Myanmar. In so doing, the strong domestic and international expectations toward human rights protection at the time would have been addressed without creating reputation costs at the regional level.

In short, there were two ways in which Thailand could have used the argument of its extreme vulnerability as a neighbor to justify its choice for norm compliance in relation to its relevant audiences. It could be used as part of strategic norm replacement, as seen in Thailand's response to the more recent cases of human rights violations in Myanmar, as well as part of a strategy of norm reconciliation pursued by former foreign minister Surin Pitsuwan during a period in which domestic and international expectations for human rights protection converged, but conflicted with regional expectations for compliance with the noninterference norm. In both scenarios, the argument incorporated in a response had the potential to resolve the norm conflict for the government, as long as the dissenting audiences accepted the justification. While the Democrat-led government had to convince its regional peers of the legitimacy of prioritizing human rights protection, the governments in office during the later crises in Myanmar had to persuade their Western international audience of the legitimacy of prioritizing noninterference. The evidence presented in the case-study chapter suggests that, at least in the latter case, Thai governments were reasonably successful in generating understanding for Thailand's "special situation" among its Western audience.

Nevertheless, during the Saffron Revolution and Cyclone Nargis, some conflicting regional and international expectations toward human rights protection were articulated. Internationally, the US and the UN expressed direct expectations for action, which could have been interpreted as acts of interference by the Myanmarese junta. By prioritizing the noninterference norm in line with the dominant domestic expectations, Thailand left these international expectations unaddressed. To appease these expectations and minimize the anticipated reputation costs, the Thai government incorporated an additional element in its larger response of context-specific norm replacement. It tried to reduce the international reputation costs by making immediate concessions. Both Prime Minister Surayud and his successor, Samak, attempted to satisfy the direct expectations of the US and UN by responding to their calls for the Thai government to use its influence in Myanmar and urge the junta toward restraint and cooperation with the West. At the same time, however, Thai authorities tried to make sure that their concessions to the West were not perceived as interference by the generals in Naypyidaw. Therefore, Thailand refrained from criticizing the junta at any point during its missions to the country and strictly operated only with the junta's consent.

Regionally, Thailand's noninterference stance most of the time required little justification, given the majority of states' preferences for noninterference within the regional organization. The Saffron Revolution proved an exception when several ASEAN states, including Indonesia and Malaysia, forcefully interfered in favor of human rights protection. By highlighting the ramifications of noninterference on the organization's reputation, in tandem with Singapore as the ASEAN chair, ASEAN's more democratically advanced member states managed to bring about a collective ASEAN statement prioritizing human rights protection. As a consequence, the Thai government found itself in a situation where it had to justify its noninterference stance not only to the world but also to its key ASEAN peers that called for conformity with the collective ASEAN statement. Given its desire to be seen as one of the "good members" of ASEAN by the world and within the organization, the Thai government could not afford to ignore the regional expectation to support the statement. As a result, at the UN General Assembly meeting on 28 September 2007, the Thai government momentarily aligned its stance with the collective ASEAN position. Following the UN General Assembly meeting, the Thai government instantly returned to its stance of noninterference.

In sum, the analysis of Thailand's response to the three instances of norm conflict illustrated how strategic norm replacement as a response strategy can be adopted on the basis of a special relationship. This was necessary as the extreme economic interdependence between Myanmar and Thailand increased the strength of domestic expectations for a noninterference policy in relation to Myanmar, whereas the international and at times regional expectations were in favor of compliance with human rights protection. In addition, Thailand's general support for human rights protection at the regional level suggests that the government did not desire a *general* weakening of the norm. Strategic norm replacement as a strategy reflects that one government can adopt several response strategies to the same norm conflict depending on how the properties of the "target country" (in this case Myanmar) affect the structure of expectations that this government faces.

Changing Response Strategies in Malaysia

Over time the Malaysian government changed its response strategy. In line with changing domestic expectations, Malaysia first tried to reconcile the norms at the regional level but later adopted a strategy of conflict denial in order to minimize the domestic legitimacy and international reputation costs that flowed from conflicting expectations for norm compliance at the domestic, regional, and international levels. As a case study, Malaysia not only illustrated two response categories to conflicting expectations in a situation of norm conflict but also helped to identify factors that facilitated a change in expectations thereby leading to a change in strategy.

During the initial stages of the Saffron Revolution, the objective of avoiding domestic legitimacy and international reputation costs proved relatively easy for the Malaysian government to manage. Similar to Indonesia, it faced a strong domestic consensus calling for human rights protection in its foreign policy toward Myanmar. Accordingly, the Malaysian government forcefully condemned the junta's violence against civilian protestors. In prioritizing the human rights protection norm, the government not only addressed domestic expectations but also aligned its policy vis-à-vis Myanmar with Western international expectations that called upon ASEAN to condemn the violence. However, its compliance with the human rights protection norm raised issues with Malaysia's regional peers, which, despite the collective ASEAN statement, individually prioritized noninterference. In order to mitigate the regional reputation costs of its interference, the Malaysian government thus emphasized the crisis's impact on ASEAN's collective reputation. More generally, in order to justify its interference in a way that would be acceptable to the majority of authoritarian ASEAN member states, Malaysia tried to frame the crisis as a regional problem as opposed to an internal affair. Thus, strictly speaking, the noninterference norm would not apply.

But the Malaysian government went beyond simply justifying a one-time violation of the noninterference norm. Backed by a broad domestic coalition in favor of human rights protection, as well as Western expectations regarding interference, Malaysia suggested a regional review of the norm. Lacking the normative leadership and thus soft power within the region to attempt general norm replacement, Malaysia opted for a strategy of norm reconciliation to resolve the norm conflict between noninterference and human rights protection. Thereby noninterference was framed as the "general" and human rights protection as the "specific" norm. Malaysian foreign minister Syed Hamid Albar essentially revived Surin Pitsuwan's proposal of 1998 to reinterpret the scope of noninterference and take into account the concerns of affected neighbors or the region as a whole. Albar argued that in cases that had an impact on neighboring states or the region as a whole, noninterference should no longer be considered illegitimate. In order to legitimately engage in extraterritorial human rights protection, interfering states had to take a "justificatory detour," via spillover effects on their jurisdiction or by demonstrating an impact on ASEAN, such as its reputation. Yet, at a time when the international community more often than not condemned human rights violations, Albar's reinterpretation of the noninterference norm would have made action on behalf of human rights protection within the region considerably easier for ASEAN member states to justify.

In the end, however, Malaysia never tabled the proposal for discussion at the ASEAN summit in November 2007, as shortly before the meeting, the country experienced a major domestic crisis. As a consequence, the previous consensus in favor of human rights compliance eroded. The government now faced a new structure of expectations that no longer supported interference. Broadly, expectations regarding legitimate action within Malaysian society were divided along ethnic and religious lines and reflected the views of the Muslim-Malay majority on the one hand, and the Chinese and Indian minorities on the other. Although pressure to interfere was upheld by the opposition, primarily representing the views of the minority groups, the Malay majority, in contrast, turned their focus inward following the large-scale protests in Kuala Lumpur in November 2007 and the huge electoral losses of the governing coalition, Barisan Nasional, in the 2008 general elections. The Malay pressured the ruling coalition to do everything it could to preserve the status quo of Malay domination in politics and society at large. Although the domestic crisis most likely constituted the necessary trigger for a shift in Malay expectations for norm compliance, the swift drop in support for human rights protection also reflects the fact that engagement with human rights protection was still relatively new in Malaysia, especially among the Malays, and therefore the norm might have been less internalized than, for example, in Indonesia or Thailand.

In trying to contain the protests, the government also employed coercive measures such as the detention of the protest leaders. The domestic turmoil in the wake of the November protests and the general elections led the Malaysian government to regionally return to strict adherence to the noninterference norm. This affected both the later stages of the Saffron Revolution and Malaysia's response to the junta's lockdown of the country following Cyclone Nargis. In complying with noninterference, the Malaysian government, like the government in Indonesia, tried to reduce the risk of domestic backlash in the form of external interference in its own strained internal affairs by maintaining the validity of the norm within the region. In order to do so, it had to respect the voices within the region that urged compliance with noninterference in the two crises. The objectives of pursuing a regional reputation for compliance with noninterference and avoiding domestic legitimacy costs were therefore tightly intertwined.

Returning to a noninterference policy without having to accept major international reputation costs was relatively easy for the Malaysian government. For most of the Saffron Revolution, it was in tune with Western expectations as it forcefully condemned the junta's crackdown. By the time Malaysia had altered its stance to protect itself from charges of interference, international pressure on ASEAN had mostly subsided. During Cyclone Nargis, Malaysia individually adopted a strategy of conflict denial to address conflicting expectations. The Malaysian government did not recognize the junta's responsibility for, or even involvement in, the human suffering. In framing the crisis as a humanitarian disaster, the Malaysian government presented a counternarrative to the interpretation of the situation that contested the appropriateness of interference on behalf of human rights protection as mostly suggested by Western nations.

Unlike Thailand, it would have been much more difficult for Malaysia to establish exceptional circumstances in relation to Myanmar to justify a strategy of strategic norm replacement. In addition, domestic turmoil and uncertainty meant that it was much harder for the government to predict how domestic expectations for compliance with the conflicting norms would develop in the future. This reflects the theoretical expectation that as a strategy to deal with norm conflict, conflict denial is particularly suitable for short-term response and in contexts defined by uncertainty about future expectations for norm compliance. In only questioning the interpretation of a specific situation and not the general validity of the conflicting norms, conflict denial as a response strategy least affects the relevant audiences' expectations regarding the government's future behavior in situations regulated by the two norms. The strategy of conflict denial was facilitated by the ambiguity of the situation in Myanmar, which started as a humanitarian crisis caused by a natural disaster and the support for a humanitarian as opposed to human rights–centered framing of the crisis by the majority of ASEAN member states. In order to reduce the international pressure on ASEAN to persuade the generals to open the country, the Malaysian government supported Indonesia's suggestion of an ASEAN-led mechanism to coordinate the relief work in Myanmar.

During the Rakhine Riots, the Malaysian government, now headed by Prime Minister Najib Razak, maintained its noninterference stance, despite the fact that influential representatives of the Muslim-Malay population called for interference on behalf of the rights of the Muslim Rohingya community. In prioritizing noninterference, Najib, one year ahead of the general elections, complied with the norm that best addressed the expectations of the Chinese and Indian minorities during the crisis, thereby hoping to enhance his legitimacy among these ethnic groups. They feared that interference would trigger an influx of Muslim Rohingya refugees to Malaysia, which would further marginalize their position in the Muslim-dominated Malaysian society. While the government again justified its lack of action with the noninterference norm, in this particular instance it did not try to affect the behavior of its peers by complying with the norm. Instead, the government hoped that by remaining silent it could dissuade Rohingya refugees from heading toward Malaysia as a safe haven.

Malaysia's policy of noninterference tallied well with the regional expectations of what constituted a legitimate response to the crisis. Even states that were normally more willing to interfere, such as Indonesia, remained silent. Similarly, the West and the UN took a cautious approach to the Rakhine Riots, articulating no concrete expectations vis-à-vis ASEAN or individual member states. What proved more problematic for the Malaysian government were the anticipated legitimacy costs of having to align its stance with the minorities' expectations regarding action, instead of those of the Muslim majority. Similar calls for interference on behalf of the Rohingya were articulated at the international level within the Muslim world. To invalidate these expectations, the Malaysian government again adopted a strategy of conflict denial, framing the crisis as a humanitarian disaster as opposed to a case of human rights protection. When the expectations for interference in favor of human rights protection persisted, the government conceded to working through the OIC in order to address the situation in Rakhine.

The expectations for human rights protection at the domestic and international levels during the Rakhine Riots in themselves are interesting, as most of the arguments that were articulated in favor of interference did not center on human suffering but rather on the Rohingyas' Muslim identity. Religious solidarity appeared to have a strengthening effect on their expectations regarding interference on behalf of the rights of non-nationals. In Malaysia, the plight of the Rohingyas caused even former prime minister Mahathir Mohamad to openly call for interference on their behalf, after he had been one of the strongest defenders of an absolute noninterference policy during most of his time in office. The impact of religion on expectations regarding human rights protection among individuals and groups that otherwise did not support interference suggests that their commitment to assistance was still partial. The suffering of fellow religious believers triggered the greatest concern, rather than coming to the aid of a generic stranger. This advocacy for interference on the basis of religious affinity thus mirrors the practice of humanitarian intervention as seen in nineteenth-century Europe. At this time, European powers presented intervention as a legitimate response to the failure of foreign authorities, such as the Ottoman Empire, to fulfill their obligations to protect Christians and European nationals within their territories.[2]

To conclude, the Malaysian government over time changed its response strategy, reflecting the change in domestic expectations and variation in the government's assessment of their relevance for its domestic legitimacy. The Malaysian government strategically addressed the expectations of the different ethnic groups depending on which best served its domestic legitimacy at a given moment in time. Although it first complied with the human rights protection norm embedded in a strategy of norm reconciliation, it later prioritized noninterference and relied on a strategy of conflict denial to address conflicting expectations for norm compliance during Cyclone Nargis and the Rakhine Riots. Decisive for the strength of the domestic expectations for norm compliance was the relative "newness" of the human rights protection norm, which led to an inconsistent interpretation of situations of choice, as well as the internal crisis in Malaysia, which at least temporarily strengthened expectations for compliance with noninterference.

REFINING THE THEORETICAL FRAMEWORK

The findings from the case studies suggest some specifications and refinements to the theoretical framework. In assessing response to norm conflict in Southeast Asia, it became obvious that, in some contexts, focusing on domestic as well as international expectations is not enough, as set out in the theoretical framework chapter. Next to domestic and international expectations, in Southeast Asia voices from within the region had to be considered. While regional expectations might not be relevant everywhere and in every norm conflict, in Southeast Asia they importantly mattered in interacting with and reinforcing the anticipated legitimacy costs that governments might suffer in leaving domestic expectations unaddressed. In doing so, the impact of regional expectations went beyond an exclusive concern for reputation at the regional level. In leaving regional expectations unaddressed, governments additionally risked retaliation from their peers and an undermining of the validity of the regionally supported norm. Both aspects had the potential to negatively affect their legitimacy at home. In the cases of Indonesia and Malaysia, an important dimension of domestic legitimacy referred to the maintenance of regime stability and territorial integrity. Both could be considerably weakened if the validity of the noninterference norm deteriorated and external interference within the region became more common. In Thailand, domestic legitimacy was strongly interlinked with a development paradigm, an important part of which was access to the Myanmarese market, which Myanmar's government could restrict should its Thai counterpart not comply with its demand of noninterference in its internal affairs. Given these findings, future research should a priori factor in the possible relevance and impact of regional expectations for response to norm conflict.

One of the most central issues in dealing with expectations for norm compliance relates to the question of which audience wins when conflicting expectations are articulated across the domestic, regional, and international levels. The proposition formulated in chapter 1 suggested that most governments would prioritize domestic over international expectations for norm compliance. This reflects the intuitive notion that even though reputation costs at the international level are unpleasant and potentially complicate interstate relations, leaving domestic expectations unaddressed entails the risk of increased domestic resistance, electoral setbacks, and even loss of power. The analysis of responses to norm conflict in Southeast Asia confirmed the proposition. Moreover, it showed that domestic expectations are not only prioritized over international expectations but also win in cases in which they conflict with regional expectations for norm compliance. In confirming that domestic expectations are treated preferentially, the analysis served as an important first step in determining whether foreign policy decision-makers are guided more by the expectations of behavior addressed to them by their domestic or international (and regional) audiences. At least with respect to relatively weak governments in developing contexts, future research can now a priori expect that governments will comply with the norm favored by their dominant domestic audience.

While the theoretical framework acknowledged that audiences at any level (including "the people") are most likely not "uniform" and can articulate various expectations toward the government, chapter 1 did not further investigate this possibility. Instead, for reasons of parsimony, it spoke about domestic and international expectations as if there were just one expectation at each level. The analysis of expectations in the three case-study countries highlighted that this is not the case, especially in relation to the domestic audience. In all three states more than one relevant domestic expectation for legitimate action in response to the human rights violations in Myanmar was articulated—either because different domestic groups expressed conflicting expectations (Thailand and Malaysia), or because society at large held expectations connected to the norms that in particular situations could not both be fulfilled at the same time (Indonesia). Where different domestic groups articulate conflicting expectations, their impact at the ballot box during elections can be decisive. In cases in which one domestic group holds conflicting expectations that cannot be simultaneously addressed, the government has to make an informed choice regarding which of the underlying reasons for supporting compliance with the norm the public ultimately considers more important.

The analysis of response to norm conflict in the case-study countries also helped to further specify enabling conditions for some of the response strategies. They can relate both to the expectations themselves and to the likelihood of success of a response strategy. In assessing domestic expectations for norm compliance in Thailand, it could be shown that extreme economic interdependence between two countries can lead to a shift in the domestic expectation for norm compliance. Extreme economic interdependence therefore serves as one factor that can determine variation in domestic expectations across different contexts. The articulated domestic expectation is specific to a particular context and is not meant to affect the general validity of the norm. In cases in which a context-specific shift in domestic expectations is accompanied by conflicting regional or international expectations for norm compliance, strategic norm replacement therefore represents an attractive strategy. But in order for strategic norm replacement to have a chance of success, the responding country has to be in a position in which it can credibly establish "exceptional circumstances" in relation to the host country. The analysis of response to norm conflict in Thailand has shown that close proximity can be an enabling condition for establishing "exceptional circumstances" vis-à-vis the dissenting audience. In a scenario involving neighboring nations, the chances of making a successful argument for a legitimate exception to the general rule increase, as neighbors can always point to their special vulnerability to events in the country next door. This proved particularly effective in cases in which the responding government could refer to precedents in which past compliance with the conflicting norm had a direct negative impact on its own jurisdiction due to spillover effects. Thereby, reference to (nontraditional) security threats in particular seemed to be successful in generating international acceptance of the strategic norm replacement.

The analysis of response to norm conflict in Indonesia and Malaysia helped to further narrow down the factors that affect the governments' confidence in their ability to generate acceptance for the replacement of a conflicting norm. Instead of adopting a strategy of general norm replacement, the Indonesian government opted for norm reconciliation in all three situations of norm conflict. The Malaysian government used a strategy of norm reconciliation for most of the Saffron Revolution, before it changed its stance in the later phase of the crisis. Both governments faced strong conflicting expectations that either related to the identity of the state (human rights protection) or regime stability and state survival (noninterference). Thereby it did not matter on which level these expectations were articulated in order to make a strategy of norm reconciliation attractive, as long as the government believed that generating acceptance of general norm replacement would be difficult to achieve. Norm reconciliation is thus not likely only where constitutive norms are involved but also where norms shield states and societies from existential threats to the survival of the state.

Finally, in assessing response to norm conflict in Southeast Asia, it also became apparent that we should distinguish between long-term and short-term responses to norm conflict. The latter category includes not only conflict denial but also even more immediate "concessions" to conflicting expectations. Conflict denial can cover periods of uncertainty about future expectations for norm compliance, for example during a domestic crisis, as seen in the case of Malaysia. Concessions to conflicting expectations for norm compliance, in contrast, can be expected where the arguments that are part of the longer-term strategy do not suffice in appeasing conflicting expectations. This is most likely where conflicting expectations toward a government are directly and persistently raised. In the case of Thailand, for example, the government adopted a long-term strategy of context-specific norm replacement in relation to situations of norm conflict in Myanmar. However, to appease immediate conflicting expectations, it made concessions to its Western audience (for example, writing letters, traveling to Myanmar). Similarly, Indonesia and Malaysia tried to appease conflicting expectations for action level on behalf of the Rohingya Muslims during the Rakhine Riots at the domestic and international levels by supporting the work of the OIC.

LESSONS LEARNED AND IMPLICATIONS FOR FUTURE RESEARCH

Possibly the most important takeaway from this book is the acknowledgment that norm conflict as a serious decision-making problem for governments exists in their decision-making and sometimes in their identity commitments. Understanding how governments deal with norm conflicts is crucial because norms are not stable. They come and go. As identities evolve and contextual changes take place, norm conflicts can arise. Especially in times of far-ranging normative change, we can expect norm conflicts to be frequent. With global challenges ahead such as combating climate change, which for many states creates a conflict between the right to development and a commitment to climate protection, an improved understanding of response to norm conflict is more important than ever.

But instead of recognizing that conflicting norms often continue to coexist with each other and thereby create situations of norm conflict, most research within the constructivist tradition of IRT conceptualizes norm change as a rather superficial process that focuses as norm adoption and automatically results in norm replacement.[3] I showed that to be confident of a state's commitment to a norm, it is necessary to also assess it on a deeper level than is usually done within the discipline of IRT and to emphasize domestic measures, namely norm implementation into national law and compliance in practice and discourse. However, establishing a government's norm commitment that goes beyond formal norm adoption is not only important in demonstrating that a government is likely to experience a norm conflict in situations in which both norms apply. Its credible commitment also provides the foundation for domestic, regional, and international expectations for norm compliance. These expectations importantly impact the government's decision-making in situations of norm conflict by indicating what kind of action is considered more appropriate in their eyes. Given the special importance of domestic expectations, it is crucial to open the "black box" of the state to include and emphasize agency at the domestic level—yet again, something that the discipline, with its radical demarcation between the international and domestic spheres, has traditionally been reluctant to do. Thereby, the deep empirical work undertaken in this book helps to clarify the reasoning and rationality behind norm compliance. It shows how the same norms held by different actors play out in practice, how the interpretation of norms is susceptible to contextual factors, and how violations need to be justified to different legitimizing audiences.

Finally, the study of response to norm conflict in Southeast Asia helped to advance our understanding of how normative change takes place. The choice to comply with one norm rather than another in situations of norm conflict, coupled with the legitimation of a government's choice, constitute the microprocesses that over time can contribute to larger normative change. For actual normative change to take place, it is crucial that others accept the state's behavior and justifications, as norms by definition are shared. The findings from Southeast Asia suggest that the aspirational outcome of normative change in response to situations of norm conflict does not have to be full-fledged norm replacement. Instead, subtler normative adjustments are made that allow for both norms to remain as part of the shared normative system. In outlining a theoretical framework of response to norm conflict and exploring it empirically, the book contributed toward understanding the judgments that states make in situations of norm conflict. And yet much remains to be done in order to increase the generalizability and predictive power of the framework. Future research should apply the findings from Southeast Asia to other regional contexts. The pattern of norm reconciliation found in Indonesia, for example, might very well be generalizable beyond Southeast Asia for countries with a democratic identity and ongoing secessionist conflicts.

Given that this book specifically deals with Southeast Asia, let me end with some final words on the region and the normative conclusions this research allows to draw for this particular part of the world. The study of norm conflict showed that while prioritizing domestic expectations, Southeast Asian governments cared about their international reputation. They were particularly susceptible to international pressure, which did not only target the individual state but also ASEAN as a whole. From a normative perspective that perceives action on behalf of extraterritorial human rights protection as desirable under certain conditions, this implies two things: First and foremost, Western governments should maintain, if not increase, their pressure on ASEAN as an organization in cases of human rights violation within the region.[4] Second, in order for Western expectations to continue to have such an impact on governments' decision-making in Southeast Asia, and potentially in other regions, the democratic West needs to maintain its position as a relevant international audience to these states. Two parallel developments have been undermining this relevance of the West in Southeast Asia. On the one hand, Western influence has been steadily replaced by a Chinese presence in the region. On the other hand, Western credibility as a global advocate of liberal norms has been questioned as Western societies have undergone change in favor of populist, xenophobic, and isolationist policies. If left unchecked, these developments might further support a normative reorientation in Southeast Asia that, after a brief period of rapid democratization and improved human rights standards, is already backsliding. As a consequence, governments might no longer even perceive of a norm conflict between human rights protection and noninterference.

Acknowledgments

This book was inspired by my four-year-long journey at the European University Institute. While several years have passed since then, being able to conduct this kind of research at the EUI and in Southeast Asia was a phenomenal experience, which the Institute made possible. I am very grateful for those years and the support.

My special thanks go to Jennifer Welsh, who has been a source of inspiration and encouragement. I also want to thank Jörn Dosch, Ulrich Krotz, and Wayne Sandholtz for their feedback, along with the two unknown peer reviewers who were incredibly helpful as I worked to hone and refine this book.

Without the welcoming support of various institutions in Southeast Asia that provided me with a temporary academic home, this research would not have been possible. I am particularly grateful for the help of researchers and friends at CSIS Indonesia, the IR Department at the Chulalongkorn University in Bangkok, and ISIS Malaysia. During my various fieldwork stays in Southeast Asia I had the opportunity to meet a large number of policymakers, academics, journalists, and human rights activists who all generously shared their knowledge and experience with me. Their interviews were immensely helpful and important for the book and I'm very grateful for their time and trust in me.

At times, I slightly underestimated the amount of work that researching and writing a book entailed. I would not have been able to finish the manuscript without the help and patience of my editors and the entire University Press of Kentucky team. Thank you all for having my back during the entire process.

Finally, above all, I owe the greatest thanks to the love and support of my family and closest friends.

Notes

Introduction

1. Samuel P. Huntington, *The Third Wave: Democratization in the Late Twentieth Century* (Norman: University of Oklahoma Press, 1991).

2. Richard Price, "Reversing the Gun Sights: Transnational Civil Society Targets Land Mines," *International Organization* 52, no. 3 (1998): 613–44.

3. Antje Wiener, *The Invisible Constitution of Politics: Contested Norms and International Encounters* (Cambridge: Cambridge University Press, 2008); Antje Wiener, *Contestation and Constitution of Norms in Global International Relations* (Cambridge: Cambridge University Press, 2018), https://doi.org/10.1017/9781316718599; Amitav Acharya, "How Ideas Spread: Whose Norms Matter? Norm Localization and Institutional Change in Asian Regionalism," *International Organization* 58, no. 2 (2004): 239–75; Betcy Jose, *Norm Contestation: Insights into Non-Conformity with Armed Conflict Norms* (Cham: Springer International, 2018).

4. Anja Jetschke, *Human Rights and State Security* (Philadelphia: University of Pennsylvania Press, 2011); Thomas Risse, Stephen Ropp, and Kathryn Sikkink, *The Power of Human Rights: International Norms and Domestic Change* (Cambridge: Cambridge University Press, 1999); Jose, *Norm Contestation*.

5. Martha Finnemore and Kathryn Sikkink, "International Norm Dynamics and Political Change," *International Organization* 52, no. 4 (1998): 887–917; Kathryn Sikkink, *The Justice Cascade: How Human Rights Prosecutions Are Changing World Politics* (New York: Norton, 2011); Rosemary Foot, *Rights beyond Borders: The Global Community and the Struggle over Human Rights in China* (Oxford: Oxford University Press, 2000).

6. Ian Hurd, "The Strategic Use of Liberal Internationalism: Libya and the UN Sanctions, 1992–2003," *International Organization* 59, no. 3 (2005): 502.

7. Alexander Wendt, *Social Theory of International Politics* (Cambridge: Cambridge University Press, 1999), 230.

8. Ann Florini, "The Evolution of International Norms," *International Studies Quarterly* 40, no. 3 (1996): 373.

9. Alexander Wendt, "Anarchy Is What States Make of It: The Social Construction of Power Politics," *International Organization* 46, no. 2 (1992): 391–425; Wendt, *Social Theory of International Politics*; Finnemore and Sikkink, "International Norm

Dynamics and Political Change"; Risse, Ropp, and Sikkink, *The Power of Human Rights*.

10. The effect of transnational expectations on state behavior is demonstrated as part of the spiral model by Risse, Ropp, and Sikkink in *The Power of Human Rights*. On domestic and international expectations, see also Jetschke, *Human Rights and State Security*.

11. For a similar understanding of how norms work, see Jetschke, *Human Rights and State Security*. She argues that norms cannot predict courses of action without looking at an intervening process that explains how one norm becomes dominant. She considers discourse to be the relevant intervening process.

12. Thomas Risse, "'Let's Argue!': Communicative Action in World Politics," *International Organization* 54, no. 1 (2000): 1–39.

13. For an application of the framework-first outline (described in my 2018 dissertation) to international organizations' responses to norm conflicts, see Tom Buitelaar and Gisela Hirschmann, "Criminal Accountability at What Cost? Norm Conflict, UN Peace Operations, and the International Criminal Court," *European Journal of International Relations*, no. 27 (2021): 548–71.

14. For exceptions, see Acharya, "How Ideas Spread"; and Sikkink, *The Justice Cascade*.

15. Amitav Acharya, *Constructing a Security Community in Southeast Asia: ASEAN and the Problem of Regional Order* (London: Routledge, 2001); Amitav Acharya, *Regionalism and Multilateralism: Essays on Cooperative Security in the Asia-Pacific* (Singapore: Times Academic Press, 2002); Jürgen Haacke, *ASEAN's Diplomatic and Security Culture: Origins, Development and Prospects* (London: Routledge, 2003), http://www.routledge.com; Alex Bellamy and Mark Beeson, "The Responsibility to Protect in Southeast Asia: Can ASEAN Reconcile Humanitarianism and Sovereignty?," *Asian Security* 6, no. 3 (2010): 262–79; Shaun Narine, *Explaining ASEAN: Regionalism in Southeast Asia* (Boulder, Colo.: Lynne Rienner, 2002); Mely Caballero-Anthony, "Evolving Regional Governance in East Asia: From ASEAN to an East Asia Community," in *Governance and Regionalism in Asia*, ed. Nicholas Thomas (Abingdon, UK: Routledge, 2009), 32–65; Jürgen Rüland, "ASEAN and the Asian Crisis: Theoretical Implications and Practical Consequences for Southeast Asian Regionalism," *Pacific Review* 13, no. 3 (2000): 421–51.

16. Lilianne Fen and Hanna Krebs, "Regional Organisations and Humanitarian Action: The Case of ASEAN," HPG Working Paper, 2014, 1–19; Miki Honda, "Natural Disaster and Humanitarian Assistance in Asia: The Case of Myanmar," *GIARI Working Paper* 4 (2009): 1–14; Lee Jones, "ASEAN's Albatross: ASEAN's Burma Policy, from Constructive Engagement to Critical Disengagement," *Asian Security* 4, no. 3 (2008): 271–93; Lee Jones, *ASEAN, Sovereignty and Intervention in Southeast Asia* (Basingstoke, UK: Palgrave Macmillan, 2011).

17. Finnemore and Sikkink, "International Norm Dynamics and Political Change"; Ellen Lutz and Kathryn Sikkink, "International Human Rights Law and

Practice in Latin America," *International Organization* 54, no. 3 (2000): 633–59; Sikkink, *The Justice Cascade*, 2011; Jeffrey Checkel, "Norms, Institutions, and National Identity in Contemporary Europe," *International Studies Quarterly* 43, no. 1 (1999): 83–114; Frank Dobbin, Beth Simmons, and Geoffrey Garrett, "The Global Diffusion of Public Policies: Social Construction, Coercion, Competition, or Learning?," *Annual Review of Sociology* 33, no. 1 (2007): 449–72; Sarah Percy, "Mercenaries: Strong Norm, Weak Law," *International Organization* 61, no. 2 (April 2007): 367–97; Jeffrey Legro, "Which Norms Matter? Revisiting the 'Failure' of Internationalism," *International Organization* 51, no. 1 (1997): 31–63.

1. Theorizing and Studying Response to Norm Conflict

1. Alexander Wendt, *Social Theory of International Politics* (Cambridge: Cambridge University Press, 1999); Friedrich Kratochwil, *Rules, Norms, and Decisions: On the Conditions of Practical and Legal Reasoning in International Relations and Domestic Affairs* (Cambridge: Cambridge University Press, 1991); Annika Björkdahl, "Norms in International Relations: Some Conceptual and Methodological Reflections," *Cambridge Review of International Affairs* 15, no. 1 (2010): 9–23; Andrew Hurrell, "Norms and Ethics in International Relations," in *Handbook of International Relations*, ed. Walter Carlsnaes, Thomas Risse-Kappen, and Beth Simmons (London: SAGE, 2002); Gary Goertz and Paul Diehl, "Toward a Theory of International Norms: Some Conceptual and Measurement Issues," *Journal of Conflict Resolution* 36, no. 4 (1992): 634–64; Anja Jetschke, *Human Rights and State Security* (Philadelphia: University of Pennsylvania Press, 2011).

2. Martha Finnemore and Kathryn Sikkink, "International Norm Dynamics and Political Change," *International Organization* 52, no. 4 (1998): 887–917; Thomas Risse, Stephen Ropp and Kathryn Sikkink, *The Power of Human Rights: International Norms and Domestic Change* (Cambridge: Cambridge University Press, 1999); Jetschke, *Human Rights and State Security*; Amitav Acharya, "How Ideas Spread: Whose Norms Matter? Norm Localization and Institutional Change in Asian Regionalism," *International Organization* 58, no. 2 (2004): 239–75.

3. Kathryn Sikkink, *The Justice Cascade: How Human Rights Prosecutions Are Changing World Politics* (New York: Norton, 2011); Antje Wiener, "Contested Compliance: Interventions on the Normative Structure of World Politics," *European Journal of International Relations* 10, no. 2 (2004): 189–234; Antje Wiener, *The Invisible Constitution of Politics: Contested Norms and International Encounters* (Cambridge: Cambridge University Press, 2008); Antje Wiener, "Contested Norms in Inter-National Encounters: The 'Turbot War' as a Prelude to Fairer Fisheries Governance," *Politics and Governance* 4, no. 3 (2016): 20–36; Antje Wiener, *Contestation and Constitution of Norms in Global International Relations* (Cambridge: Cambridge University Press, 2018), doi:10.1017/9781316718599; Diana Panke and Ulrich Petersohn, "Why International Norms Disappear Sometimes," *European Journal of International Relations* 18, no. 4 (2012): 719–42; Mona Lena Krook

and Jacqui True, "Rethinking the Life Cycles of International Norms: The United Nations and the Global Promotion of Gender Equality," *European Journal of International Relations* 18, no. 1 (2012): 103–27; Wayne Sandholtz, "Explaining International Norm Change," in *International Norms and Cycles of Change*, ed. Sandholtz and Stiles Kendall (Oxford: Oxford University Press, 2009), 1–18; Wayne Sandholtz, "The Multiple Path to Norm Replacement," paper presented at the International Studies Association meeting, Atlanta, 2016, 1–27; Betcy Jose, *Norm Contestation: Insights into Non-Conformity with Armed Conflict Norms*, Cham, Switzerland: Springer International, 2018).

4. Amitav Acharya, *Constructing a Security Community in Southeast Asia: ASEAN and the Problem of Regional Order* (London: Routledge, 2001); Acharya, "How Ideas Spread"; Hiro Katsumata, "ASEAN and Human Rights: Resisting Western Pressure or Emulating the West?," *Pacific Review* 5 (2009): 619–37; S. S. Tan, "Herding Cats: The Role of Persuasion in Political Change and Continuity in the Association of Southeast Asian Nations (ASEAN)," *International Relations of the Asia-Pacific* 13, no. 2 (May 1, 2013): 233–65, doi:10.1093/irap/lcs020. See also Seng Tan, "Rescuing Constructivism from the Constructivists: A Critical Reading of Constructivist Interventions in Southeast Asian Security," *Pacific Review* 19, no. 2 (2006): 239–60; Seng Tan, "Providers Not Protectors: Institutionalizing Responsible Sovereignty in Southeast Asia," *Asian Security* 7, no. 3 (2011): 201–17; Catherine Michelle Renshaw, "Human Rights and Regionalism in Southeast Asia" (Ph.D. diss., University of Sydney, 2014); Lina Alexandra, "Indonesia and the Responsibility to Protect," *Pacific Review* 25, no. 1 (2012): 51–74; Alex Bellamy and Mark Beeson, "The Responsibility to Protect in Southeast Asia: Can ASEAN Reconcile Humanitarianism and Sovereignty?," *Asian Security* 6, no. 3 (2010): 262–79; David Capie, "Localization as Resistance: The Contested Diffusion of Small Arms Norms in Southeast Asia," *Security Dialogue* 39, no. 6 (2008): 637–58; and Mely Caballero-Anthony, "Evolving Regional Governance in East Asia: From ASEAN to an East Asia Community," in *Governance and Regionalism in Asia*, ed. Nicholas Thomas (Abingdon, UK: Routledge, 2009), 32–65.

5. Sandholtz, "Explaining International Norm Change," 1; on the dual quality of norms, see also Wiener, *The Invisible Constitution of Politics*, 38.

6. Peter Katzenstein, "Introduction: Alternative Perspectives on National Security," in *The Culture of National Security: Norms and Identity in World Politics*, ed. Katzenstein (New York: Columbia University Press, 1996), 1–32; Wiener, "Contested Compliance"; Sandholtz, "Explaining International Norm Change."

7. Hurrell, "Norms and Ethics in International Relations," 11; Janina Dill, *Legitimate Targets? Social Construction, International Law and US Bombing* (New York: Cambridge University Press, 2015), 32.

8. Krook and True, "Rethinking the Life Cycles of International Norms," 105; Björkdahl, "Norms in International Relations," 13.

9. Sandholtz, "The Multiple Path to Norm Replacement," 9.

10. Kratochwil, *Rules, Norms, and Decisions*, 10; Hurrell, "Norms and Ethics in International Relations."

11. Joost Pauwelyn, *Conflict of Norms in Public International Law: How WTO Law Relates to Other Rules of International Law* (Cambridge: Cambridge University Press, 2003), 176.

12. Mathieu Beirlaen, "A Unifying Framework for Reasoning about Normative Conflicts," *The Logica Yearbook* (2011): 1.

13. Abdullatif Elhad, Joost Breuker, and Bob Brouwer, "On the Formal Analysis of Normative Conflicts," *Information & Communications Technology Law* 9, no. 3 (2000): 209.

14. Marko Milanovic, "Norm Conflicts, International Humanitarian Law and Human Rights Law," in *Human Rights and Humanitarian International Law*, ed. Orna Ben-Naftali (Oxford: Oxford University Press, 2010), 8.

15. Jörg Kammerhofer, "Structural Uncertainty through Neo-Kelsenian Consistency: Conflicts of Norms in International Law," *Papers of the European Society of International Law* (2005): 1.

16. Wendt, *Social Theory of International Politics*, 230.

17. Alexander Wendt, "Anarchy Is What States Make of It: The Social Construction of Power Politics," *International Organization* 46, no. 2 (1992): 391–425; Jutta Weldes, "Constructing National Interests," *European Journal of International Relations* 2, no. 3 (1996): 275–318; Dill, *Legitimate Targets?*, 23.

18. Dill, *Legitimate Targets?*, 24.

19. James March and Johan Olsen, "The Logic of Appropriateness," in *The Oxford Handbook of Public Policy*, ed. Michael Moran, Martin Rein, and Robert E. Goodin (Oxford: Oxford University Press, 2006), 689.

20. Wendt, *Social Theory of International Politics*; March and Olsen, "The Logic of Appropriateness"; Finnemore and Sikkink, "International Norm Dynamics and Political Change." For an excellent discussion of the limits entailed in the logic of appropriateness, see Thomas Risse, "'Let's Argue!': Communicative Action in World Politics," *International Organization* 54, no. 1 (2000): 1–39.

21. Ian Hurd, "Legitimacy and Authority in International Politics," *International Organization* 53, no. 2 (1999).

22. Risse, "Let's Argue!," 6; Neta Crawford, *Argument and Change in World Politics: Ethics, Decolonization, and Humanitarian Intervention* (Cambridge: Cambridge University Press, 2002).

23. Risse, "Let's Argue!," 2.

24. Ibid., 10.

25. Ibid., 7.

26. Sandholtz, "The Multiple Path to Norm Replacement," 9.

27. Crawford, *Argument and Change in World Politics*, 31.

28. Kenneth Neal Waltz, *Theory of International Politics* (Boston: McGraw-Hill, 1979), 118; Robert Axelrod, *The Evolution of Cooperation* (New York: Basic,

1984), 6; Robert Keohane, *After Hegemony: Cooperation and Discord in the World Political Economy* (Princeton, N.J.: Princeton University Press, 1984), 64.

29. Ian Hurd, "Constructivism," in *The Oxford Handbook of International Relations*, ed. Christian Reus-Smit and Duncan Snidal (Oxford: Oxford University Press, 2008), 301; Dill, *Legitimate Targets?*, 24.

30. Kratochwil, *Rules, Norms, and Decisions*, 9. For a discussion of the role of justifications in cases of human rights violations, see Jetschke, *Human Rights and State Security*.

31. Andrew Hurrell, "Legitimacy and the Use of Force: Can the Circle Be Squared?," *Review of International Studies* 31 (2005): 24; Ian Hurd, "The Strategic Use of Liberal Internationalism: Libya and the UN Sanctions, 1992–2003," *International Organization* 59, no. 3 (2005): 500; Ian Hurd, "Breaking and Making Norms: American Revisionism and Crises of Legitimacy," *International Politics* 44, no. 2–3 (2007): 196; Christian Reus-Smit, "International Crises of Legitimacy," *International Politics* 44, no. 2–3 (2007): 157–74.

32. David Beetham, *The Legitimation of Power*, 2nd ed. (Houndmills, UK: Palgrave Macmillan, 2013), 75.

33. Hurrell, "Legitimacy and the Use of Force," 24.

34. Jetschke, *Human Rights and State Security*, 4.

35. Hurd, "Breaking and Making Norms," 196.

36. Jetschke, *Human Rights and State Security*, 4.

37. Kratochwil, *Rules, Norms, and Decisions*, 98.

38. Nina Tannenwald, "The Nuclear Taboo: The United States and the Normative Basis of Nuclear Non-Use," *International Organization* 53, no. 3 (1999): 435.

39. Antje Wiener and Uwe Puetter, "The Quality of Norms Is What Actors Make of It : Critical Constructivist Research on Norms," *Journal of International Law and International Relations* 5, no. 1 (2009): 2.

40. Stephen D. Krasner, *Sovereignty: Organized Hypocrisy* (Princeton, N.J.: Princeton University Press, 1999), 7.

41. Mark Suchman, "Managing Legitimacy: Strategic and Institutional Approaches," *Academy of Management Review* 20, no. 3 (1995): 574.

42. Hurrell, "Legitimacy and the Use of Force," 159; Jean-Marc Coicaud, *Legitimacy and Politics: A Contribution to the Study of Political Right and Political Responsibility* (Cambridge: Cambridge University Press, 2002), 2.

43. Hurd, "Breaking and Making Norms," 196.

44. Wendt, "Anarchy Is What States Make of It," 396–97.

45. Andrew Cortell and James Davis, "When Norms Clash: International Norms, Domestic Practices, and Japan's Internalisation of the GATT/WTO," *Review of International Studies* 31, no. 1 (2005): 6.

46. Beetham, *The Legitimation of Power*, xi; Jason Ralph and Adrian Gallagher, "Legitimacy Faultlines in International Society: The Responsibility to Protect and Prosecute after Libya," *Review of International Studies* 41, no. 3 (2015): 557.

47. Hurrell, "Legitimacy and the Use of Force," 16; Hurd, "Legitimacy and Authority in International Politics," 384.

48. Beetham, *The Legitimation of Power*, 29.

49. Ibid., xii.

50. Ian Clark, *Legitimacy in International Society* (New York: Oxford University Press, 2005), 4.

51. Crawford, *Argument and Change in World Politics*, 33; Reus-Smit, "International Crises of Legitimacy," 169.

52. George Modelski, "Kautilya: Foreign Policy and International System in the Ancient Hindu World," *American Political Science Review* 58, no. 3 (1964): 549–60; K. J. Holsti, "National Role Conceptions in the Study of Foreign Policy," *International Studies Quarterly* 14, no. 3 (1970): 247–48; Arndt Michael, *India's Foreign Policy and Regional Multilateralism* (Basingstoke, UK: Palgrave Macmillan, 2013), 24–27; Jürgen Rüland, "Democratizing Foreign-Policy Making in Indonesia and the Democratization of ASEAN: A Role Theory Analysis," *TRaNS: Trans-Regional and -National Studies of Southeast Asia* 5, no. 1 (2017): 53; Finnemore and Sikkink, "International Norm Dynamics and Political Change," 903; Hurd, "Legitimacy and Authority in International Politics," 379.

53. Hurd, "Legitimacy and Authority in International Politics," 386.

54. Hedley Bull, *The Anarchical Society: A Study of Order in World Politics* (New York: Columbia University Press, 1977), 13.

55. Barry Buzan and Ole Wæver, *Regions and Powers: The Structure of International Security* (Cambridge: Cambridge University Press, 2003), 17.

56. Clark, *Legitimacy in International Society*, 5.

57. Ralph and Gallagher, "Legitimacy Faultlines in International Society," 556.

58. Hurd, "The Strategic Use of Liberal Internationalism," 23.

59. Ralph Turner, "Role-Taking, Role Standpoint, and Reference-Group Behavior," *American Journal of Sociology* 61, no. 4 (1956): 316; March and Olsen, "The Logic of Appropriateness," 689.

60. Holsti, "National Role Conceptions in the Study of Foreign Policy," 246.

61. Knut Kirste and Hanns W. Maull, "Zivilmacht und Rollentheorie," *Zeitschrift für Internationale Beziehungen* 3, no. 2 (1996): 284.

62. Rüland, "Democratizing Foreign-Policy Making in Indonesia and the Democratization of ASEAN," 51.

63. Jonathan Mercer, *Reputation and International Politics*, Cornell Studies in Security Affairs (Ithaca, N.Y.: Cornell University Press, 1996), 27; Shiping Tang, "Reputation, Cult of Reputation, and International Conflict," *Security Studies* 14, no. 1 (2005): 38.

64. Thomas Franck, *The Power of Legitimacy among Nations* (Oxford: Oxford University Press, 1990), 191; Henning Boekle, Volker Rittberger, and Wolfgang Wagner, "Norms and Foreign Policy: Constructivist Foreign Policy Theory," *Tübinger Arbeitspapiere zur Internationalen Politik und Friedensforschung* 34a (1999): 11.

65. Institutionalists emphasize a property-based concept of reputation that facilitates the likelihood of international cooperation. Within a framework of repeated interactions, international expectations about legitimate action, which flow from an actor's commitments or promises, matter, as the participating agents consider a good reputation valuable. A good reputation allows actors to predict another actor's future moves during strategic interaction by putting its action in a context of past and future interactions (J. C. Sharman, "Rationalist and Constructivist Perspectives on Reputation," *Political Studies* 55, no. 1 [2007]: 26).

66. George W. Downs and Michael A. Jones, "Reputation, Compliance, and International Law," *Journal of Legal Studies* 31, no. 1 (2002): 96.

67. Hurd, "Breaking and Making Norms," 194.

68. A relational understanding of reputation affects the way in which states can be sanctioned: it is not only material sanctions that matter; immaterial or even symbolic punishments that aim at a state's status as a legitimate member of a group with a shared normative system are also expected to have an effect (Boekle, Rittberger, and Wagner, "Norms and Foreign Policy," 10).

69. Sandholtz, "Explaining International Norm Change," 11.

70. Finnemore and Sikkink, "International Norm Dynamics and Political Change," 902.

71. Jetschke, *Human Rights and State Security*.

72. Robert D. Putnam, "Diplomacy and Domestic Politics: The Logic of Two-Level Games," *International Organization* 42, no. 3 (1988): 434.

73. Boekle, Rittberger, and Wagner, "Norms and Foreign Policy," 11.

74. Beetham, *The Legitimation of Power*, 75; Putnam, "Diplomacy and Domestic Politics," 436.

75. In explaining how governments sometimes get away with human rights violations, Jetschke argues that they can frame their domestic situations differently from human rights organizations. In providing persuasive accounts of why human rights violations occur, they can influence audiences and justify their practices (see Jetschke, *Human Rights and State Security*).

76. Crawford, *Argument and Change in World Politics*, 14–15.

77. Sandholtz, "Explaining International Norm Change," 9; Crawford, *Argument and Change in World Politics*, 15.

78. In her study of human rights violations, Jetschke uses the spiral model developed by Risse et al. showing that international expectations have an impact on governments' decision-making (see Jetschke, *Human Rights and State Security*).

79. Sandholtz, "Explaining International Norm Change," 12; John Ikenberry and Charles Kupchan, "Socialization and Hegemonic Power," *International Organization* 44, no. 3 (1990): 288.

80. As important elements of persuasive power, Sandholtz mentions diplomatic representation, presence in the shared organizations and negotiations as well as access to mass media (Sandholtz, "Explaining International Norm Change," 12).

81. Sandholtz, "Explaining International Norm Change."
82. Boekle, Rittberger, and Wagner, "Norms and Foreign Policy," 11.
83. Panke and Petersohn, "Why International Norms Disappear Sometimes," 721.
84. Krook and True, "Rethinking the Life Cycles of International Norms"; Panke and Petersohn, "Why International Norms Disappear Sometimes."
85. Sandholtz, "The Multiple Path to Norm Replacement," 7.
86. I recognize that a single state cannot replace a norm, as norm replacement constitutes a collective process and requires the acceptance and approval of those states that share the norm within a regional grouping or more broadly within international society. So technically speaking, when saying that a government employs a strategy of general norm replacement, this means that it seeks to contribute to the replacement of a norm. Whether or not a norm is replaced depends on the acceptance and support by others.
87. Hurd, "Legitimacy and Authority in International Politics," 386; Kratochwil, *Rules, Norms, and Decisions*, 9.
88. Sandholtz, "Explaining International Norm Change," 14.
89. Kammerhofer, "Structural Uncertainty through Neo-Kelsenian Consistency: Conflicts of Norms in International Law," 5.
90. Ibid.
91. Giovanni Battista Ratti, "Negation in Legislation," in *Logic in the Theory and Practice of Lawmaking*, ed. Michał Araszkiewicz and Krzysztof Płeszka (Cham, Switzerland: Springer, 2015), 147. To illustrate the point, consider the framing of Responsibility to Protect (RtoP). The principle reconciles two norms, namely nonintervention in the internal affairs of states and collective intervention for humanitarian purposes. It creates a gap within the former "general" norm and reduces legitimate military intervention to instances of genocide, war crimes, crimes against humanity, and ethnic cleansing. While nonintervention as the general norm is expected to be applied as the general standard in interstate affairs, cases of genocide, war crimes, crimes against humanity, and ethnic cleansing create legitimate exceptions to the rule and in fact obligate external players to act when states have failed in their responsibility to protect their populations. The obligation to assist—as a last resort even by military means—supersedes the obligation to not intervene in the internal affairs of other states. On the framing of RtoP, see Alex Bellamy, "The Responsibility to Protect—Five Years On," *Ethics & International Affairs* 24, no. 2 (2010): 143–69; and Alexander Betts and Phil Orchard, "Introduction: The Normative Institutionalization-Implementation Gap," in *Implementation and World Politics: How International Norms Change Practice*, ed. Betts and Orchard (Oxford: Oxford University Press, 2014), 1–20.
92. R. J. Vincent, *Nonintervention and International Order* (Princeton, N.J.: Princeton University Press, 1974).
93. Jennifer Welsh, "Taking Consequences Seriously: Objections to Humanitarian Intervention," in *Humanitarian Intervention and International Relations*, ed. Welsh (Oxford: Oxford University Press, 2004), 6.

94. Wiener, "Contested Compliance"; Krook and True, "Rethinking the Life Cycles of International Norms."

95. Crawford, *Argument and Change in World Politics*, 17.

96. Adrienne Heritier, "Causal Explanation," in *Approaches and Methodologies in the Social Sciences: A Pluralist Perspective*, ed. Donatella Della Porta and Michael Keating (Cambridge: Cambridge University Press, 2008), 61–79; Martha Finnemore, *The Purpose of Intervention: Changing Beliefs about the Use of Force* (Ithaca, N.Y.: Cornell University Press, 2003); Jeffrey T. Checkel, "Why Comply? Social Learning and European Identity Change," *International Organization* 55, no. 3 (2001): 553–88; Jörg Friedrichs and Friedrich Kratochwil, "On Acting and Knowing: How Pragmatism Can Advance International Relations Research and Methodology," *International Organization* 63, no. 4 (2009): 701–31.

97. John Gerring, "Case Selection for Case-Study Analysis: Qualitative and Quantitative Techniques," in *The Oxford Handbook of Political Methodology.*, ed. Janet Box-Steffensmeier, Henry Brady, and David Collier (Oxford: Oxford University Press, 2008), 645–84.

98. David Forsythe, *Human Rights in International Relations* (Cambridge: Cambridge University Press, 2012), 48.

99. James Chin, interview by the author, Kuala Lumpur, 8 October 2016.

100. Amitav Acharya, *Regionalism and Multilateralism: Essays on Cooperative Security in the Asia-Pacific* (Singapore: Times Academic Press, 2002), 225.

101. Dewi Fortuna Anwar, *Indonesia in ASEAN: Foreign Policy and Regionalism* (Singapore: Institute of Southeast Asian Studies, 1994), 167.

102. Gregory Fox and Brad Roth, "Introduction: The Spread of Liberal Democracy and Its Implications for International Law," in *Democratic Governance and International Law*, ed. Fox and Roth (Cambridge: Cambridge University Press, 2000), 1–25; Thomas Carothers, "Democracy and Human Rights: Policy Allies or Rivals?," *Washington Quarterly* 17, no. 3 (1994): 109–20; James Gomez and Robin Ramcharan, "Introduction: Democracy and Human Rights in Southeast Asia," *Journal of Current Southeast Asian Affairs* 33, no. 3 (26 January 2015): 3–17.

103. For extraterritorial human rights concerns in democratizing states, see Herman Joseph Kraft, "Human Rights in Southeast Asia: The Search for Regional Norms," *East-West Center Working Papers* 4 (2005): 1–40; Kraft shows that governments of Indonesia, the Philippines, and Thailand have been critical in pushing the boundaries on the issue of a regional standard of human rights in ASEAN and actively advocated for democracy and human rights standards within the region. On human rights concerns as part of ASEAN state's foreign policy, see also Hiro Katsumata, "Why Is ASEAN Diplomacy Changing? From 'Non-Interference' to 'Open and Frank Discussions,'" *Asian Survey* 44, no. 2 (2004): 237–54; Hiro Katsumata, "ASEAN and Human Rights: Resisting Western Pressure or Emulating the West?," *Pacific Review* 5 (2009): 619–37; Gomez and Ramcharan, "Introduction"; Amitav Acharya, "Democratisation and the Prospects for Participatory Regionalism in Southeast Asia," *Third World Quarterly* 24, no. 2 (2003): 375–90; and Ami-

tav Acharya, "Southeast Asia's Democratic Moment," *Asian Survey* 39, no. 3 (1999): 418–32.

104. Monika Heupel, "How Do States Perceive Extraterritorial Human Rights Obligations? Insights from the Universal Periodic Review," *Human Rights Quarterly* 40, no. 3 (2018): 521–46.

105. Gerring, "Case Selection for Case-Study Analysis."

106. Human Rights Watch, "Burma: Arbitrary Detention of Protesters," 22 August 2007, http://www.hrw.org/news/2007/08/21/burma-arbitrary-detention-protesters.

107. Human Rights Watch, "Crackdown: Repression of the 2007 Popular Protests in Burma," 7 December 2007, 23, http://www.hrw.org/sites/default/files/reports/burma1207web.pdf.

108. "Myanmar's Protests: On the Brink," *The Economist*, 27 September 2007.

109. Amnesty International, "Myanmar Needs a Comprehensive International Arms Embargo," 28 September 2007, https://www.amnesty.org/download/Documents/60000/asa160142007en.pdf.

110. Human Rights Watch, "Crackdown: Repression of the 2007 Popular Protests in Burma," 42.

111. Amnesty International, "Myanmar Demonstrators Defiant in Face of Escalating Repression," 27 September 2007, https://twitter.com/thomas_wiegold/status/1426886216490827782?s=20.

112. "Myanmar: UN Rights Expert to Probe Allegations of Abuses during Crackdown," *UN News*, 24 October 2007, https://www.un.org/apps/news/story.asp?NewsID=24405&Cr=myanmar&Cr1=#.WmiK1LQ-dAY.

113. BBC, "Burma Toll at Least 31, UN Says," 7 December 2007, http://news.bbc.co.uk/2/hi/asia-pacific/7133239.stm.

114. Human Rights Watch, "Burma: China Should Push to Get Aid In," 10 May 2008, http://www.hrw.org/news/2008/05/09/burma-china-should-push-get-aid.

115. Human Rights Watch, "Burma: Cyclone Donors Should Ensure Transparency and Accountability," 23 July 2008, http://www.hrw.org/news/2008/07/22/burma-cyclone-donors-should-ensure-transparency-and-accountability.

116. Amnesty International, "Myanmar Briefing. Human Rights Concerns a Month after Cyclone Nargis," 5 June 2008, http://www.amnesty.org/en/library/asset/ASA16/013/2008/en/85931049-32e5-11dd-863f-e9cd398f74da/asa160132008eng.pdf.

117. Human Rights Watch, "Burma. Postpone Referendum to Save Lives HRW," 9 May 2008, http://www.hrw.org/news/2008/05/07/burma-postpone-referendum-save-lives.

118. "Burma Denies US Access; Relief Supplies from UN Starting to Get Through," *Bangkok Post*, 9 May 2008.

119. Nirmal Ghosh, "Give, but Stay Away," *Straits Times*, 10 May 2008.

120. "Burma Denies US Access; Relief Supplies from UN Starting to Get Through."

121. Human Rights Watch, "Burma: New Rules Further Delay Relief," 12 June 2008, http://www.hrw.org/en/news/2008/06/11/burma-new-rules-further-delay-relief.

122. In April 2012 opposition politicians led by Aung San Suu Kyi entered the Burmese parliament, following historic by-elections.

123. Human Rights Watch, "Burma: Government Forces Targeting Rohingya Muslims HRW," 31 July 2012, http://www.hrw.org/news/2012/07/31/burma-government-forces-targeting-rohingya-muslims-0.

124. Human Rights Watch, "'The Government Could Have Stopped This': Sectarian Violence and Ensuing Abuses in Burma's Arakan State," 1 August 2012, 1, http://www.hrw.org/sites/default/files/reports/burma0812webwcover.pdf.

125. "HRW Cites 'Atrocities' in Myanmar," *Jakarta Post*, 1 August 2012.

126. "State of Emergency Declared for Western Myanmar," *Jakarta Post*, 11 June 2012.

127. "Burma Faces More Unrest in Rakhine State," https://www.bbc.com/news/world-asia-18406370.

128. Human Rights Watch, "Burma: New Violence in Arakan State," 26 October 2012, http://www.hrw.org/news/2012/10/26/burma-new-violence-arakan-state.

129. Human Rights Watch, "'All You Can Do Is Pray': Crimes against Humanity and Ethnic Cleansing of Rohingya Muslims in Burma's Arakan State," April 2013, 146–47, http://www.hrw.org/sites/default/files/reports/burma0413webwcover_0.pdf.

130. Hanna Hindstrom, "Burmese Authorities Targeting Rohingyas, UK Parliament Told," *Democratic Voice of Burma*, 28 June 2012, http://www.dvb.no/news/burmese-authorities-targeting-rohingyas-uk-parliament-told/22676.

131. "UNHCR Country Operations Profile—Myanmar," *UNHCR*, 2014, http://www.unhcr.org/pages/49e4877d6.html.

132. Erik Martinez Kuhonta, Dan Slater, and Tuong Vu, "Introduction. The Contributions of Southeast Asian Political Studies," in *Southeast Asia in Political Science: Theory, Region, and Qualitative Analysis*, ed. Kuhonta, Slater, and Vu (Stanford, Calif.: Stanford University Press, 2008), 7.

133. Alexander George and Andrew Bennett, *Case Studies and Theory Development in the Social Sciences* (Cambridge, Mass.: MIT Press, 2005), 6.

134. Ibid., 206.

135. Darren G. Lilleker, "Interviewing the Political Elite: Navigating a Potential Minefield," *Politics* 23, no. 3 (2003): 208.

136. Beth Leech, "Asking Questions: Techniques for Semistructured Interviews," *PS: Political Science & Politics* 35, no. 4 (2002): 667.

2. Commitment to the Norms

1. Lee Jones, *ASEAN, Sovereignty and Intervention in Southeast Asia* (Basingstoke, UK: Palgrave Macmillan, 2011).

2. Martha Finnemore and Kathryn Sikkink, "International Norm Dynamics and Political Change," *International Organization* 52, no. 4 (1998): 887–917; Ellen Lutz and Kathryn Sikkink, "International Human Rights Law and Practice in Latin America," *International Organization* 54, no. 3 (2000): 633–59; Kathryn Sikkink, *The Justice Cascade: How Human Rights Prosecutions Are Changing World Politics* (New York: Norton, 2011); Jeffrey Checkel, "Norms, Institutions, and National Identity in Contemporary Europe," *International Studies Quarterly* 43, no. 1 (1999): 83–114; Frank Dobbin, Beth Simmons, and Geoffrey Garrett, "The Global Diffusion of Public Policies: Social Construction, Coercion, Competition, or Learning?," *Annual Review of Sociology* 33, no. 1 (2007): 449–72; Sarah Percy, "Mercenaries: Strong Norm, Weak Law," *International Organization* 61, no. 2 (April 2007): 367–97; Jeffrey Legro, "Which Norms Matter? Revisiting the 'Failure' of Internationalism," *International Organization* 51, no. 1 (1997): 31–63.

3. Alexander Betts and Phil Orchard, *Implementation and World Politics: How International Norms Change Practice* (Oxford: Oxford University Press, 2014), 2.

4. Ibid., 4–5; Wayne Sandholtz, "Explaining International Norm Change," in *International Norms and Cycles of Change*, ed. Sandholtz and Stiles Kendall (Oxford: Oxford University Press, 2009), 12.

5. Betts and Orchard, *Implementation and World Politics*, 2–3.

6. Catherine Michelle Renshaw, "Human Rights and Regionalism in Southeast Asia" (Ph.D. diss., University of Sydney, 2014), 11.

7. I will consistently use the term "noninterference" to refer to the ASEAN interpretation of the norm. "Nonintervention" will only be used in reference to the international norm.

8. Rodolfo Severino, *Southeast Asia in Search of an ASEAN Community* (Singapore: ISEAS, 2006), 85–86.

9. Hsien-Li Tan, *The ASEAN Intergovernmental Commission on Human Rights: Institutionalising Human Rights in Southeast Asia* (Cambridge: Cambridge University Press, 2011), 63.

10. Mohammed Ayoob, *The Third World Security Predicament: State Making, Regional Conflict, and the International System* (London: Lynne Rienner, 1995), 3; Robert Jackson, *Quasi-States: Sovereignty, International Relations and the Third World* (Cambridge: Cambridge University Press, 1990), 21–25; Amitav Acharya, "The Evolution of Norms: The Social Construction of Non-Interference in Asian Regionalism," paper presented at the Provincializing Westphalia Conference, Oxford, 2008, 3.

11. Ayoob, *The Third World Security Predicament*, 71.

12. Ibid., 3.

13. Richard Stubbs, "The ASEAN Alternative? Ideas, Institutions and the Challenge to 'Global' Governance," *Pacific Review* 21, no. 4 (2008): 452.

14. Acharya, "The Evolution of Norms," 3.

15. "Final Communiqué of the Asian-African Conference of Bandung" (Bandung: Indonesian Ministry of Foreign Affairs, 24 April 1955), Art. G2 and G4.

16. "Belgrade Declaration of Non-Aligned Countries" (Belgrade: Non-Aligned Countries, September 6, 1961), Art. 14.

17. Maziar Jamnejad and Michael Wood, "The Principle of Non-Intervention," *Leiden Journal of International Law* 22, no. 2 (June 2009): 347.

18. Lauren Dunn, Peter Nyers, and Richard Stubbs, "Western Interventionism versus East Asian Non-Interference: Competing 'Global' Norms in the Asian Century," *Pacific Review* 23, no. 3 (2010): 297; Rodolfo C. Severino, "Will There Be a New ASEAN in the 21st Century?," *Asia Europe Journal* 2, no. 2 (July 2004): 181.

19. Ian Storey, "Thailand. Southern Discomfort: Separatist Conflict in the Kingdom of Thailand," in *Fixing Fractured Nations: The Challenge of Ethnic Separatism in the Asia-Pacific*, ed. Robert Wirsing and Mohammed Ahrari, Critical Studies of the Asia Pacific Series (New York: Palgrave Macmillan, 2010), 49.

20. Dunn, Nyers, and Stubbs, "Western Interventionism versus East Asian Non-Interference," 297–98.

21. Marshall Clark, "Indonesia's Postcolonial Regional Imaginary: From a 'Neutralist' to an 'All-Directions' Foreign Policy," *Japanese Journal of Political Science* 12, no. 2 (2011): 296; Stubbs, "The ASEAN Alternative?," 460.

22. "The ASEAN Declaration" (Bangkok: ASEAN, 8 August 1967), Preamble.

23. Amitav Acharya, *Regionalism and Multilateralism: Essays on Cooperative Security in the Asia-Pacific* (Singapore: Times Academic Press, 2002), 225; Jürgen Haacke, *ASEAN's Diplomatic and Security Culture: Origins, Development and Prospects* (London: Routledge, 2003), 4; Li-ann Thio, "Implementing Human Rights in ASEAN Countries: "Promises to Keep and Miles to Go before I Sleep," *Yale Human Rights and Development Journal* 2, no. 1 (1999): 9; Ang Cheng Guan, "Myanmar: Time for a Unified Approach," *Security Dialogue* 32, no. 4 (2001): 468.

24. John Ciorciari, "Institutionalizing Human Rights in Southeast Asia," *Human Rights Quarterly* 34, no. 3 (2012): 697.

25. Tan, *The ASEAN Intergovernmental Commission on Human Rights*, 145–46.

26. Herman Joseph Kraft, "ASEAN and Intra-ASEAN Relations: Weathering the Storm?," *Pacific Review* 13, no. 3 (2000): 462.

27. "Treaty of Amity and Cooperation in Southeast Asia" (Bali: ASEAN, 24 February 1976), Art. 2.

28. Dewi Fortuna Anwar, *Indonesia in ASEAN: Foreign Policy and Regionalism* (Singapore: Institute of Southeast Asian Studies, 1994), 171.

29. "Charter of the Association of Southeast Asian Nations" (Singapore: ASEAN, 20 November 2007), Preamble.

30. "Terms of Reference ASEAN Intergovernmental Commission of Human Rights" (Jakarta: ASEAN, July 2009), Art. 2, 2.1.

31. "Foreign Policy, Vision and Mission," Indonesian Ministry of Foreign Affairs, 2015, http://www.kemlu.go.id/en/kebijakan/landasan-visi-misi-polugri/Default.aspx.

32. Resolution No. II/MPR/1993 of the People's Consultative Assembly.

33. "Indonesia's Foreign Policy/The Principles of Foreign Policy," Indonesian Embassy DC, 2016, http://www.embassyofindonesia.org/wordpress/?page_id=118.

34. Indonesian Government, "Law of the Republic of Indonesia Concerning Foreign Relations," Pub. L. No. 37 (1999), Preamble.

35. Indonesian Defense Ministry, "Buku Putih Pertahanan Indonesia 2008," 2008, 39–40, https://www.kemhan.go.id/wp-content/uploads/2015/12/04f92fd80ee3d01c8e5c5dc3f56b34e31.pdf.

36. Indonesian Government, "Peraturan Presiden Republik Indonesia Tentang Kebijakan Umum Pertahanan Negara (Presidential Regulations on General Policy Guidelines on State Defense Policy)," Pub. L. No. 7 (2008), Art. 4.

37. Indonesian Defense Ministry, "Buku Putih Pertahanan Indonesia 2008," 40.

38. "Malaysia's Foreign Policy," Foreign Ministry of Malaysia, 2016, https://www.kln.gov.my/web/guest/foreign-policy.

39. Ibid.

40. Ibid.

41. Malaysian Foreign Ministry, "Strategic Plan 2009–2015," 2009, http://www.kln.gov.my/c/document_library/get_file?uuid=bf7282c4-3cad-49cd-a525-15a3e67702a0&groupId=10136, xiii.

42. Ibid., 22.

43. "Malaysia's National Defence Policy" (Putrajaya: Ministry for Defense), accessed February 18, 2016, Preface, http://www.mod.gov.my/phocadownload/DASAR-PERTAHANAN/ndp.pdf (site discontinued).

44. Government of Thailand, "Constitution of the Kingdom of Thailand, B.E. 2550" (2007), Part 2, Section 77.

45. "Policy Statement of the Council of Ministers" (Bangkok: Government of Thailand, 30 December 2008), 7, http://planipolis.iiep.unesco.org/upload/Thailand/Thailand_policy_statement.pdf.

46. Shaun Narine, *Explaining Asean: Regionalism in Southeast Asia* (Boulder, Colo.: Lynne Rienner, 2002); Catherine Drummond, "The ASEAN Intergovernmental Commission on Human Rights (AICHR) and the Responsibility to Protect: Development and Potential," Working Paper on ASEAN and RtoP, 2010, http://www.r2pasiapacific.org/docs/R2P%20Reports/AICHR%20and%20R2P_Report%20No_1%202010.pdf (site discontinued); Haacke, *ASEAN's Diplomatic and Security Culture*; Tan, *The ASEAN Intergovernmental Commission on Human Rights*; Jörn Dosch, *The Changing Dynamics of Southeast Asian Politics* (London: Lynne Rienner, 2007); Robin Ramcharan, "ASEAN and Non-Interference: A Principle Maintained," *Contemporary Southeast Asia* 22, no. 1 (2000): 60–88; Amitav Acharya, *Constructing a Security Community in Southeast Asia: ASEAN and the Problem of Regional Order* (London: Routledge, 2001).

47. Lee Jones, *ASEAN, Sovereignty and Intervention in Southeast Asia* (Basingstoke, UK: Palgrave Macmillan, 2011); Shaun Narine, "ASEAN in the Twenty-First Century: A Sceptical Review," *Cambridge Review of International Affairs* 22, no. 3 (2009): 369–86; Robin Ramcharan, "ASEAN and Non-Interference: A Principle

Maintained," *Contemporary Southeast Asia* 22, no. 1 (2000): 60–88; Li-ann Thio, "Implementing Human Rights in ASEAN Countries: 'Promises to Keep and Miles to Go before I Sleep,'" *Yale Human Rights and Development Journal* 2, no. 1 (1999): 1–86; Kavi Chongkittavorn, "Enforcing the Charter against Rogue Members," *The Nation*, 15 June 2009.

48. Kraft, "ASEAN and Intra-ASEAN Relations," 462.

49. Ibid., 464; "Surin Sees Benefits in Intervention Policy," *The Nation*, 27 June 1998.

50. Jürgen Haacke, "Enhanced Interaction with Myanmar and the Project of a Security Community: Is ASEAN Refining or Breaking with Its Diplomatic and Security Culture?," *Contemporary Southeast Asia* 27, no. 2 (2005): 585–87.

51. "Opening Statement by His Excellency Dr. Surin Pitsuwan Minister of Foreign Affairs of Thailand at the 31st ASEAN Ministerial Meeting, Manila, Philippines, 24 July 1998" (Manila: ASEAN, 3 July 2012), http://asean.org/?static_post=opening-statement-by-his-excellency-dr-surin-pitsuwan-minister-of-foreign-affairs-of-thailand-at-the-31st-asean-ministerial-meeting-manila-philippines-24-july-1998.

52. Herman Joseph Kraft, "Human Rights in Southeast Asia: The Search for Regional Norms," *East-West Center Working Papers* 4 (2005): 14.

53. Kavi Chongkittavorn, "ASEAN Needs 'Flexible Engagement,'" *The Nation*, 21 July 1998.

54. Surin Pitsuwan, interview by the author, Bangkok, 22 June 2016.

55. Kraft, "ASEAN and Intra-ASEAN Relations," 465.

56. Tan, *The ASEAN Intergovernmental Commission on Human Rights*, 146.

57. Thio, "Implementing Human Rights in ASEAN Countries," 51.

58. Kraft, "Human Rights in Southeast Asia," 10–11.

59. "Speech by the Indonesian President Megawati Soekarnoputri at the 58th Session of the General Assembly," UN General Assembly, New York, 23 September 2003, A/58/PV.8.

60. "Speech by the Foreign Minister of Indonesia Hassan Wirajuda at the 63rd Session of the General Assembly," UN General Assembly, New York, 27 September 2008, A/63/PV.14.

61. Ibid.

62. Ibid.

63. "Speech by the Indonesian President Susilo Bambang Yudhoyono at the 67th Session of the General Assembly," UN General Assembly, New York, 25 September 2012, A/67/PV.6.

64. "Speech by the Malaysian Prime Minister Mahathir Mohamad at the 58th Session of the General Assembly," UN General Assembly, New York, 25 September 2003, A/58/PV.11.

65. "Speech by the Malaysian Prime Minister Abdullah Badawi at the 59th Session of the General Assembly," UN General Assembly, New York, 27 September 2004, A/59/PV.11.

66. Ibid.

67. "Speech by the Malaysian Prime Minister Abdullah Badawi at the 62nd Session of the General Assembly," UN General Assembly, New York, 28 September 2007, http://www.un.org/webcast/ga/62/2007/pdfs/malaysia-eng.pdf.

68. Ibid.

69. "Speech by the Foreign Minister of Malaysia Rais Yatim at the 63rd Session of the General Assembly," UN General Assembly, New York, 27 September 2008, A/63/PV.14.

70. Ibid.

71. "Speech by the Foreign Minister of Thailand Surakiart Sathirathai at the 58th Session of the General Assembly," UN General Assembly, New York, 30 September 2003, A/58/PV.17.

72. "Thaksin Warns Foreigners Not to Criticize Crackdown," *Taipei Times*, 2 May 2004, http://www.taipeitimes.com/News/world/archives/2004/05/02/2003153822/1.

73. "Syed Hamid Tells Thaksin: Don't Stop ASEAN from Discussing Southern Thailand," *Malaysiakini*, 27 November 2004.

74. "Speech by the Foreign Minister of Thailand Surapong Tovichakchaikul at the 66th Session of the General Assembly," UN General Assembly, New York, 27 September 2011, A/66/PV.28.

75. Ibid.

76. Acharya, *Regionalism and Multilateralism*, 225.

77. Tan, *The ASEAN Intergovernmental Commission on Human Rights*, 43.

78. Ibid., 26.

79. David Forsythe, *Human Rights in International Relations* (Cambridge: Cambridge University Press, 2012), 30.

80. Ibid., 45.

81. Thio, "Implementing Human Rights in ASEAN Countries," 26.

82. Vidhu Verma, "Debating Rights in Malaysia: Contradictions and Challenges in Democratisation," *Journal of Contemporary Asia* 32, no. 1 (2002): 113.

83. Tan, *The ASEAN Intergovernmental Commission on Human Rights*, 26.

84. These include the Convention on the Elimination of all Discrimination against Women 1981, the Convention on the Rights of the Child 1990, and the Convention on the Rights of Persons with Disabilities 2008.

85. Hiro Katsumata, "ASEAN and Human Rights: Resisting Western Pressure or Emulating the West?," *Pacific Review* 5 (2009): 622.

86. "Joint Communique of the Twenty-Sixth ASEAN Ministerial Meeting Singapore 23–24 July 1993" (Singapore: ASEAN, 24 July 1993), Art. 16–18.

87. Kraft, "Human Rights in Southeast Asia," 11.

88. Ibid., 4.

89. "Charter of the Association of Southeast Asian Nations," Art. 1.7.

90. Ibid., Art. 14.

91. "ASEAN Human Rights Declaration" (Phnom Penh: ASEAN, 18 November 2012).
92. Brian Galligan, "Human Rights in Asia: Comparative Reflections," in *Human Rights in Asia*, ed. Thomas Davis and Galligan (Cheltenham, UK: Edward Elgar, 2011), 215.
93. Ibid.
94. Jeff Herbert, "The Legal Framework of Human Rights in Indonesia," in *Indonesia: Law and Society*, ed. Timothy Lindsey (Annandale, Va.: Federation Press, 2008), 457.
95. Ross Clarke, "Retrospectivity and the Constitutional Validity of the Bali Bombing and East Timor Trials," *Australian Journal of Asian Law* 5, no. 2 (2003): 3.
96. Herbert, "The Legal Framework of Human Rights in Indonesia," 457.
97. Government of Indonesia, "The Law No. 39/1999 Concerning Human Rights," Pub. L. No. 39 (1999), Art. 45–51.
98. Ibid., Art. 98.
99. Ibid., Art. 75.
100. Herbert, "The Legal Framework of Human Rights in Indonesia," 461; Thio, "Implementing Human Rights in ASEAN Countries," 63–69; Tan, *The ASEAN Intergovernmental Commission on Human Rights*, 83.
101. Michele Ford, "International Networks and Human Rights in Indonesia," in *Human Rights in Asia*, ed. Thomas Davis and Brian Galligan (Cheltenham, UK: Edward Elgar, 2011), 43.
102. Michele Ford, "International Networks and Human Rights in Indonesia," in *Human Rights in Asia*, ed. Thomas Davis and Brian Galligan (Cheltenham, UK: Edward Elgar, 2011), 38–55.
103. "Indonesia: Freedom in the World 2007" (Freedom House, 2007), https://freedomhouse.org/sites/default/files/2020-02/Freedom_in_the_World_2007_complete_book.pdf.
104. In 2008 the Constitutional Court declared Articles 154 and 155 of the Indonesian Criminal Code unconstitutional on the ground that they prohibit free expression (see "Indonesia: Freedom in the World 2008" [Freedom House, 2008], https://freedomhouse.org/sites/default/files/2020-02/Freedom_in_the_World_2008_complete_book.pdf).
105. Michael Connors, "Ambivalent about Human Rights: Thai Democracy," in *Human Rights in Asia*, ed. Thomas Davis and Brian Galligan (Cheltenham, UK: Edward Elgar, 2011), 104; Tan, *The ASEAN Intergovernmental Commission on Human Rights*, 101.
106. Government of Thailand, "Constitution of the Kingdom of Thailand 1997" (1997), Sec. 32–69.
107. Government of Thailand, "National Human Rights Commission Act, B.E. 2542" (1999), Sec. 15; Thai Government, "Constitution of the Kingdom of Thailand, B.E. 2550" (2007), Sec. 256–257, https://www.constituteproject.org/constitution/Thailand_2007.pdf.

108. Thai Government, Constitution of the Kingdom of Thailand, B.E. 2550, Sec. 256(1).

109. Theodor Rathgeber, "Human Rights and the Institutionalisation of ASEAN: An Ambiguous Relationship," *Journal of Current Southeast Asian Affairs* 33, no. 3 (2014): 155.

110. Tan, *The ASEAN Intergovernmental Commission on Human Rights*, 108.

111. Human Rights Watch, *World Report 2013: Events of 2012* (New York: Human Rights Watch, 2013), 374, https://www.hrw.org/sites/default/files/wr2013_web.pdf; Human Rights Watch, *World Report 2007: Events of 2006* (New York: Human Rights Watch, 2007), https://www.hrw.org/legacy/wr2k7/wr2007master.pdf.

112. Human Rights Watch, *World Report 2008: Events of 2007* (New York: Human Rights Watch, 2008), 340, https://www.hrw.org/legacy/wr2k8/pdfs/wr2k8_web.pdf.

113. The Government of Malaysia, "Federal Constitution as of 1 November 2010" (2010), Art. 5(1); ibid., Art. 8(2).

114. Tan, *The ASEAN Intergovernmental Commission on Human Rights*, 114.

115. Human Rights Watch, *World Report 2009: Events of 2008* (New York: Human Rights Watch, 2009), 266, https://www.hrw.org/sites/default/files/reports/wr2009_web.pdf.

116. Amnesty International, *Amnesty International Report 2009: The State of the World's Human Rights* (London: Amnesty International, 2009), 199, https://www.hrw.org/legacy/wr2k7/wr2007master.pdf.

117. Human Rights Watch, *World Report 2012: Events of 2011* (New York: Human Rights Watch, 2012), 341, https://www.hrw.org/sites/default/files/reports/wr2012.pdf.

118. Government of Malaysia, "Human Rights Commission of Malaysia Act 1999" (1999), Art. 4.

119. Tan, *The ASEAN Intergovernmental Commission on Human Rights*, 118.

120. Human Rights Watch, *World Report 2007: Events of 2006*, 284.

121. Shamsuddin Taya, "Political Legal Perspective: Evaluating Human Rights in Malaysia," *Asian Journal of Social Science* 38, no. 3 (2010): 4.

122. Anthony Milner, "Contesting Human Rights in Malaysia," in *Human Rights in Asia*, ed. James Davis and Brian Galligan (Cheltenham, UK: Edward Elgar, 2011), 100; Taya, "Political Legal Perspective," 7.

123. Rosalyn Higgins, *Problems and Process: International Law and How We Use It* (Oxford: Oxford University Press, 1995), 34.

124. "2005 World Summit Outcome" (New York: United Nations, October 24, 2005), A/RES/60/1 Para. 138–140.

125. Thomas Davis, "Human Rights in Asia: Institutions, Norms and Politics," in *Human Rights in Asia*, ed. Davis and Brian Galligan (Cheltenham, UK: Edward Elgar, 2011), 2; Tan, *The ASEAN Intergovernmental Commission on Human Rights*, 8.

126. "Charter of the Association of Southeast Asian Nations," Art. 1.7.

127. Tan, *The ASEAN Intergovernmental Commission on Human Rights*, 11.

128. Mathew Davies, "An Agreement to Disagree: The ASEAN Human Rights Declaration and the Absence of Regional Identity in Southeast Asia," *Journal of Current Southeast Asian Affairs* 33, no. 3 (2014): 111.

129. Emirza Adi Syailendra, "Indonesia's Foreign Policy Outlook: Challenges of 2013 and Beyond," *RSIS Commentaries* 19 (2013): 1.

130. Indonesian Government, Law of the Republic of Indonesia Concerning Foreign Relations, Preamble 1.

131. "Strategic Objectives of the Indonesian Foreign Policy," Indonesian Ministry of Foreign Affairs, https://www.kemlu.go.id/en/kebijakan/landasan-visi-misi-polugri/Pages/Strategic-Objectives-of-Indonesian-Foreign-Policy.aspx (site discontinued).

132. Muhammad Wirajuda, "The Impact of Democratisation on Indonesia's Foreign Policy: Regional Cooperation, Promotion of Political Values, and Conflict Management" (Ph.D. diss., London School of Economics and Political Science, 2014), 30.

133. Rizal Sukma, "Indonesia Finds a New Voice," *Journal of Democracy* 22, no. 4 (2011): 111.

134. Ibid., 117.

135. Dewi Fortuna Anwar, "The Impact of Domestic and Asian Regional Changes on Indonesian Foreign Policy," *Southeast Asian Affairs* (2010): 132.

136. "Speech by H. E. Dr. Susilo Bambang Yudhoyono, President of the Republic of Indonesia before the Indonesian Council on World Affairs (ICWA)," Indonesian Ministry of Foreign Affairs, Jakarta, 20 May 2005, https://www.Kemlu.Go.Id/En/Pidato/Presiden/Pages/Speech-by-H.E.-Dr.-Susilo-Bambang-Yudhoyono-President-of-the-Republic-of-Indonesia-before-the-Indone.Aspx (site discontinued).

137. Ibid.

138. Ralf Emmers, "Indonesia's Role in ASEAN: A Case of Incomplete and Sectorial Leadership," *Pacific Review* 27, no. 4 (2014): 556; Tan, *The ASEAN Intergovernmental Commission on Human Rights*, 77.

139. Susilo Bambang Yudhoyono, "Indonesia: Regional Role, Global Reach: Speech at the London School of Economics," London, 31 March 2009, http://www.lse.ac.uk/assets/richmedia/channels/publicLecturesAndEvents/transcripts/20090331_BambangYudhoyono_tr.pdf.

140. Ibid.

141. "Keynote Speech by H. E. Susilo Bambang Yudhoyono, President of the Republic of Indonesia at the ASEAN Forum: Rethinking ASEAN Towards the ASEAN Community 2015, Jakarta, 7 August 2007," ASEAN, 27 July 2012, http://Asean.Org/?Static_post=keynote-Speech-by-He-Susilo-Bambang-Yudhoyono-President-Republic-of-Indonesia-at-the-Asean-Forum-Rethinking-Asean-towards-the-Asean-Community-2015-Jakarta-7-August-2007 (site discontinued).

142. Wirajuda, "The Impact of Democratisation on Indonesia's Foreign Policy"; Ann Marie Murphy, "Indonesia Returns to the International Stage: Good News for the United States," *Orbis* 53, no. 1 (2009): 65–79; Kelley Currie, *Mirage or*

Reality? Asia's Emerging Human Rights and Democracy Architecture (Arlington, Va.: Project 2049 Institute, 2010).

143. Marty Natalegawa, "Annual Press Statement 2011 of the Foreign Minister of the Republic of Indonesia," Jakarta, 7 January 2011.

144. "Commitment and Voluntary Pledges of Indonesia in the Field of Human Rights" (New York: Permanent Mission of the Republic of Indonesia to the UN, April 28, 2006), 306/SOC-101/IV/06.

145. Daniel Lynch, "The (More Than) Half-Full Glass: Thailand's Democracy in Comparative Perspective," paper presented at the Tenth International Conference on Thai Studies, Bangkok, 2008, 9.

146. Ibid.

147. Chai-Anan Samudavanija, *Thailand: State-Building, Democracy, and Globalization* (Bangkok: Institute of Public Policy Studies, 2002), 11.

148. Kavi Chongkittavorn, "Thai Diplomacy an Utter Failure over Past Year," *The Nation*, 26 November 2007.

149. Chongkittavorn, "ASEAN Needs 'Flexible Engagement.'"

150. Kusuma Snitwongse, "Thai Foreign Policy in the Global Age: Principle or Profit?," *Contemporary Southeast Asia* 23, no. 2 (2001): 191.

151. "Speech by the Foreign Minister of Thailand Surakiart Sathirathai at the 58th Session of the General Assembly."

152. "Speech by the Foreign Minister of Thailand Kantathi Suphamongkhon at the 60th Session of the General Assembly," UN General Assembly, New York, 18 September 2005, A/60/PV.12.

153. "Policy Statement of the Council of Ministers" (Bangkok: Government of Thailand, 3 November 2006); "Policy Statement of the Council of Ministers," 30 December 2008.

154. "Annual Report 2012" (Bangkok: Ministry of Foreign Affairs, 2012), 34, http://www.mfa.go.th/main/contents/files/policy-20130903-140114-733766.pdf (site discontinued).

155. Pradap Pibulsonggram, "The Thai Perspective," in *The Making of the ASEAN Charter*, ed. Tommy Koh, Rosario Manalo, and Walter Woon (Singapore: World Scientific Publishing, 2009), 82.

156. "Speech by the Chairman of the Thai Delegation Don Pramudwinai at the 63rd Session of the General Assembly," UN General Assembly, New York, 29 September 2008.

157. Thai Government, "Policy Statement of the Council of Ministers: Delivered by Prime Minister Abhisit Vejjajiva to the National Assembly 30 December B.E. 2551 (2008)," 2008, http://planipolis.iiep.unesco.org/upload/Thailand/Thailand_policy_statement.pdf.

158. Tan, *The ASEAN Intergovernmental Commission on Human Rights*, 160.

159. Naim Musa, "Malaysia in ASEAN: Foreign Policy on Non-Traditional Security Issues," 2012, 61, https://www.academia.edu/4219715/Malaysia_foreign_policy_after_mahathir_era.

160. Syed Hamid Albar, "Building an East Asian Security Community," speech presented at Second East Asia Forum, Kuala Lumpur, December 6, 2004.

161. Mely Caballero-Anthony, "Evolving Regional Governance in East Asia: From ASEAN to an East Asia Community," in *Governance and Regionalism in Asia*, ed. Nicholas Thomas (Abingdon, UK: Routledge, 2009), 55.

162. "Address by the Honourable Dato' Sero Abdullah Ahmad Badawi, Prime Minister of Malaysia at the Opening of the 39th ASEAN Ministerial Meeting Kuala Lumpur, 25 July 2006," Kuala Lumpur, ASEAN, 5 July 2006, http://asean.org/?static_post=address-by-the-honourable-dato-seri-abdullah-ahmad-badawi-prime-minister-of-malaysia-at-the-opening-of-the-39th-asean-ministerial-meeting-kuala-lumpur-25-july-2006-2 (site discontinued).

163. Ibid.

164. "Syed Hamid: Intervene, Don't Interfere," *Malaysiakini*, 14 June 2006.

165. Ibid.

166. Tommy Koh, "The Negotiation Process," in *The Making of the ASEAN Charter*, ed. Koh, Rosario Manalo, and Walter Woon (Singapore: World Scientific Publishing, 2009), 59.

167. Malaysian Foreign Ministry, "Strategic Plan 2009–2015," 21.

168. Ibid., 2.

169. Ibid., 40.

3. Norm Reconciliation in Indonesia

1. Tony Hotland, "RI Urges Military Restraint in Myanmar," *Jakarta Post*, 27 September 2007.

2. Ibid.

3. Ibid.

4. "Singapore's Foreign Minister George Yeo on the Crackdown in Myanmar," *Straits Times*, 28 September 2007.

5. Ibid.

6. Marty Natalegawa, "Myanmar Government Puts ASEAN Charter at Risk," 9 October 2007.

7. "Protesters Rally across Asia against Myanmar," Reuters, 29 September 2007; see also "Disparate Views in ASEAN on Crisis in the Family," *Straits Times*, 10 October 2007.

8. Abdul Khalik, "UN Resolution Crucial to Diffuse Myanmar's Problems," *Jakarta Post*, 6 October 2007.

9. "Transkripsi Keterangan Pers Bersamam Menteri Luar Negeri RI, Dr. N. Hassan Wirajuda, Dan Utusan Khusus PBB, Prof. Ibrahim Gambari," Kementerian luar Negeri, 18 October, 2007, http://kemlu.go.id/Pages/SpeechTranscriptionDisplay.aspx?Name1=Transkripsi&Name2=Menteri&IDP=196&l=id (site discontinued).

10. Moe Zwa Kyaw, "Reconciliation Is Far Away, but a Transition Plan," *Bangkok Post*, 16 October 2007.

11. Urop Hudiono, "Envoy Urges Talks on Myanmar," *Jakarta Post*, 19 October 2007.
12. Abdul Khalik, "RI Won't Raise Myanmar at UNSC," *Jakarta Post*, 27 October 2007.
13. Abdul Khalik and Kornelius Purba, "RI Takes Diplomatic Approach to Junta," *Jakarta Post*, 20 November 2007.
14. Abdul Khalik and Kornelius Purba, "SBY Pursues Alternative Approach to Myanmar," 21 November 2007.
15. "Indonesian President: Burma Should Not Apply Reforms 'by Revolution,'" BBC, 20 November 2007.
16. Khalik and Purba, "SBY Pursues Alternative Approach to Myanmar."
17. "Update Report No. 2: Myanmar," Security Council Report, United Nations, 18 March 2008, http://www.securitycouncilreport.org/update-report/lookup-c-glKWLeMTIsG-b-3961583.php.
18. Abdul Khalik and Desy Nurhayati, "RI Offers $1M in Aid for Myanmar," *Jakarta Post*, 7 May 2008.
19. Ibid.
20. "RI Bantu Myanmar 1 Juta Dollar AS," *Kompas*, 6 May 2008.
21. "Hercules TNI AU Siap Angkut Bantuan Ke Myanmar," *Kompas*, May 2008.
22. ASEAN, "A Humanitarian Call: The ASEAN Response to Cyclone Nargis" (Jakarta: ASEAN Secretariat, July 2010), 80, http://www.asean.org/wp-content/uploads/images/2012/publications/A%20Humanitarian%20Call%20The%20ASEAN%20Response%20to%20Cyclone%20Nargis.pdf.
23. Abdul Khalik and Lilian Budianto, "UN Wants RI to Lead Myanmar Relief Efforts," *Jakarta Post*, 10 May 2008.
24. ASEAN, "A Humanitarian Call: The ASEAN Response to Cyclone Nargis," 19.
25. Umar Hadi, interview by the author, Jakarta, 9 March 2016.
26. Hassan Wirajuda, interview by the author, Jakarta, 15 August 2013.
27. Abdul Khalik, "ASEAN's Task Force to Channel Foreign Aid to Myanmar," *Jakarta Post*, 21 May 2008.
28. Wirajuda, interview.
29. Nirmal Gosh, "Asean Has Grown Stronger after Cyclone: Geroge Yeo," *Straits Times*, 2 July 2008.
30. "Statement by H. E. Dr. N. Hassan Wirajuda Minister of Foreign Affairs of the Republic of Indonesia at the ASEAN-UN International Pledging Conference, Yangon, Myanmar, 15 May 2008," Yangon: Ministry of Foreign Affairs, May 15, 2008, http://www.kemlu.go.id/Pages/SpeechTranscriptionDisplay.aspx?Name1=Pidato&Name2=Menteri&IDP=50&l=en (site discontinued).
31. Margareth Aritonang and Bagus Saragih, "RI Ready to Fight for Rohingya," *Jakarta Post*, 31 July 2012.
32. Bagus Saragih, "Myanmar Trying to Reconcile Groups: SBY," *Jakarta Post*, 5 August 2012.

33. "UN, NGO Staff in Rakhine Released," *The Nation*, 22 August 2012.
34. Saragih, "Myanmar Trying to Reconcile Groups: SBY."
35. Ibid.
36. Novan Iman Santosa, "Myanmar Asks RI to Help Settle Rohingya Problem," *Jakarta Post*, 21 November 2012.
37. Jennifer Welsh, "Taking Consequences Seriously: Objections to Humanitarian Intervention," in *Humanitarian Intervention and International Relations*, ed. Welsh (Oxford: Oxford University Press, 2004), 6.
38. "Indonesia Calls for Long-Term Support for Rohingya," *The Nation*, 10 January 2013.
39. Kurniawan Hari, "Indonesia to Promote Reconciliation in Rakhine," *Jakarta Post*, 9 January 2013.
40. Kurniawan Hari, "Refugees Lives in Myanmar," *Jakarta Post*, 19 January 2013.
41. Ridwan Max Sijabat, "President Asked to Bring Myanmar Issue to the Front at UN Assembly," *Jakarta Post*, 24 September 2007.
42. Ibid.
43. Ibid.
44. Ibid.
45. "In Solidarity with the Struggle for Democracy in Myanmar," AIPMC, 25 September 2007, http://www.aseanmp.org/?p=1225 (site discontinued).
46. Ibid.
47. Ban Ki-Moon, "A Stronger UN for a Better World," speech at 62nd session of the General Assembly, New York, 25 September 2007, https://www.un.org/webcast/ga/62/2007/pdfs/sg-english.pdf.
48. "President Bush Addresses the United Nations General Assembly," The White House, 25 September 2007, https://georgewbush-whitehouse.archives.gov/news/releases/2007/09/20070925-4.html.
49. "AS Bekukan Asset 14 Pejabat Tinggi Myanmar," *Merdeka*, 28 September 2007.
50. "Speech by the President of the United States George W. Bush at the 62nd Session of the General Assembly, New York, 25 September 2007," United Nations, 25 September 2007, http://www.un.org/webcast/ga/62/2007/pdfs/usa-eng.pdf.
51. Dewi Fortuna Anwar, interview by the author, Jakarta, 7 April 2016.
52. Wirajuda, interview.
53. "Human Rights Council Resolution S-5/1, Situation of Human Rights in Myanmar" (Human Rights Council, 2 October 2007), A/HRC/RES/S-5/1.
54. "EU-US Statement on Burma/Myanmar" (European Union at United Nations, 6 September 2007), http://www.eu-un.europa.eu/articles/en/article_7339_en.htm.
55. "In Quotes: Burma Reactions," September 27, 2007, http://news.bbc.co.uk/2/hi/asia-pacific/7014704.stm.
56. "Open Letter to ASEAN Member States on the Situation in Myanmar," Amnesty International, 27 September 2007, https://www.amnesty.org/en/wp-content/uploads/2021/07/asa160112007en.pdf.

57. "ASEAN Expresses 'Revulsion' at Myanmar's Violent Repression," *The Star*, 28 September 2007.
58. "Shame on ASEAN," *Jakarta Post*, 27 September 2007.
59. Ibid.
60. Imron Cotan, interview by the author, Jakarta, 7 April 2016.
61. "ASEAN Expresses 'Revulsion' at Myanmar's Violent Repression."
62. "Foreign Leaders Hail ASEAN's Tough Stand," *Straits Times*, 29 September 2007.
63. Ibid.
64. "Statement by the President of the Security Council" (Security Council, 11 October 2007), S/PRST/2007/37.
65. "Burma: End Attacks on Protesters, Account for Monks" (Human Rights Watch, 28 September 2007), http://www.hrw.org/news/2007/09/27/burma-end-attacks-protestors-account-monks.
66. Hadi, interview.
67. Ibid.
68. Wimar Witolar, interview by the author, Jakarta, 14 March 2016.
69. Amitav Acharya, *Indonesia Matters: Asia's Emerging Democratic Power* (Singapore: World Scientific Publishing, 2015), 2; Hiro Katsumata, "ASEAN and Human Rights: Resisting Western Pressure or Emulating the West?," *Pacific Review* 5 (2009): 620; Paulo Gorjão, "Regime Change and Foreign Policy: Portugal, Indonesia and the Self-Determination of East Timor," *Democratization* 9, no. 4 (2002): 142–58; Giovanni Carbone, "The Consequences of Democratization," *Journal of Democracy* 20, no. 2 (2009): 123–37.
70. See Seng Tan, interview by the author, Singapore, 30 May 2016.
71. Jürgen Rüland, "Democratizing Foreign-Policy Making in Indonesia and the Democratization of ASEAN: A Role Theory Analysis," *TRaNS: Trans-Regional and -National Studies of Southeast Asia* 5, no. 1 (2017): 62.
72. Paige Johnson Tan, "Navigating a Turbulent Ocean: Indonesia's Worldview and Foreign Policy," *Asian Perspective* 31, no. 3 (2007): 147–81.
73. "President Bush Meets President Yudhoyono of Indonesia, Bogor," The White House, 2 October 2007, https://2001-2009.state.gov/p/eap/rls/rm/76326.htm (site discontinued).
74. Human Rights Watch, *World Report 2010: Events of 2009* (New York: Human Rights Watch, 2010), 312, https://www.hrw.org/sites/default/files/world_report_download/wr2010.pdf.
75. Ibid.
76. Cotan, interview.
77. Ibid.
78. Martha Finnemore and Kathryn Sikkink, "International Norm Dynamics and Political Change," *International Organization* 52, no. 4 (1998): 903.
79. Sukma Rizal, "Time for ASEAN to Act against Military Leaders in Yangon," *Jakarta Post*, 1 October 2007.

80. Ibid.
81. "Interfaith Leaders Speak out against Myanmar," *Jakarta Post*, 2 October 2007.
82. Ibid.
83. "Burma's 'Saffron Revolution' Is Not Over" (International Federation for Human Rights, December 2007), https://www.fidh.org/IMG/pdf/BURMA-DEC2007.pdf.
84. Donald Weatherbee, *International Relations in Southeast Asia: The Struggle for Autonomy* (Oxford: Rowman and Littlefield, 2005), 140.
85. Amitav Acharya, *The Quest for Identity: International Relations of Southeast Asia*. (Singapore: Oxford University Press, 2000), 55.
86. Weatherbee, *International Relations in Southeast Asia*, 31.
87. Endy Bayuni, interview by the author, Jakarta, 5 August 2013.
88. Endy Bayuni, "The Hope for Peace in Papua Recedes—for Now," *Jakarta Post*, 22 June 2012.
89. Bayuni, interview.
90. Dewi Fortuna Anwar, "Insurgencies and Communal Conflicts: Governance and Security in Indonesia's Plural Societies," in *Non-Traditional Security Issues in Southeast Asia*, ed. Andrew Tan and Kenneth Boutin (Singapore: Select Publishing for Institute of Defence and Strategic Studies, 2001), 358.
91. Anwar, interview.
92. On the domestic protests in Indonesia following the opening of the West Papua Office in Oxford, UK, on 28 April 2012, see Pierre Marthinus, "Indonesia Protests the Opening of Free West Papua Office in Oxford," *Jakarta Post*, 5 May 2013, http://www.thejakartapost.com/news/2013/05/05/ndonesia-protests-opening-free-west-papua-office-oxford.html.
93. Adrian Pereira, interview by the author, Kuala Lumpur, 26 July 2016.
94. Wiryono Sastrohandoyo, interview by the author, Jakarta, 23 August 2013.
95. "Yudhoyono Rejects Aceh Peace Critics," *Sydney Morning Herald*, 16 August 2005.
96. Ibid.
97. Ibid.
98. Ibid.
99. "Myanmar PM Soe Win Dies after Illness," Reuters, 12 October 2007.
100. Maung Dee, "Activists Groups Urge People to Revive 'Saffron Revolution,'" *Mizzima News*, 27 November 2007; "Monks Vow to Continue Junta Boycott," *DVB*, 19 November 2007.
101. Denis Grey, "If Junta Falls, What Then?," *Irrawaddy*, 25 October 2007.
102. Ibid.
103. Ibid.
104. Any Chew, "Give Myanmar a Big Taste of Democracy," *New Straits Times*, 6 November 2007.
105. Ibid.; Supalak Ganjanakhundee, "Burma Slaps on ASEAN Face," *The Nation*, 20 November 2007.

106. Abdul Khalik and Kornelius Purba, "SBY Declares 'Soft Power' Approach to Myanmar," *Jakarta Post*, 23 November 2007.

107. Ibid.

108. "ASEAN Mired in Burma Quagmire: After Summit," *The Nation*, 21 November 2007.

109. "Allow Humanitarian Aid Organizations Immediate Access into Myanmar," AIPMC, 5 May 2008, http://www.aseanmp.org/?p=1212 (site discontinued).

110. "NGO Indonesia Desak Myanmar Buka Akses Bantuan Asing," *Kompas*, 9 May 2008.

111. Seth Mydans and Helene Cooper, "Aid for Myanmar Mobilizes, Mixed with Criticism," *New York Times*, 7 May 2008.

112. "US Envoy Says Myanmar Should Focus on Cyclone, Not Referendum," *Jakarta Post*, 7 May 2008.

113. Ibid.

114. Steven Erlanger, "UN Is Urged to Force Myanmar to Take Aid; French Official Says Civilians Are Priority," *New York Times*, 8 May 2008.

115. Human Rights Watch, "Burma: China Should Push to Get Aid In," 10 May 2008, http://www.hrw.org/news/2008/05/09/burma-china-should-push-get-aid.

116. "Update Report No. 4: Myanmar," Security Council Report, United Nations, 14 May 2008, http://www.securitycouncilreport.org/update-report/lookup-c-glKWLeMTIsG-b-4130257.php.

117. "Myanmar Opens Its Door—a Bit," *Straits Times*, 18 May 2008.

118. Seth Mydans, "Myanmar to Let ASEAN Coordinate Foreign Aid," *New York Times*, 20 May 2008.

119. "US Official Condemns Myanmar over Relief; But Defense Secretary Opposes the Use of Force to Provide Aid," *New York Times*, 2 June 2008.

120. Catherine Michelle Renshaw, "Human Rights and Regionalism in Southeast Asia" (Ph.D. diss., University of Sydney, 2014), 185.

121. Khalik and Budianto, "UN Wants RI to Lead Myanmar Relief Efforts."

122. Ibid.

123. Dinna Wisnu, interview by the author, Jakarta, 15 March 2016.

124. Khalik and Budianto, "UN Wants RI to Lead Myanmar Relief Efforts."

125. Tom Hotland, "It's Time for ASEAN to Act on Myanmar, Says Analyst," *Jakarta Post*, 13 May 2008.

126. "Supporting Heartless Generals," *Jakarta Post*, 13 May 2008.

127. Cotan, interview.

128. Ibid.

129. Wirajuda, interview.

130. Ibid.

131. Surin Pitsuwan, interview by the author, Bangkok, 22 June 2016.

132. Maynard, "Australia Praises Asean for Unblocking Aid Flow," *Straits Times*, 22 May 2008.

133. Surin, interview.

134. Ibid.
135. Hadi, interview.
136. Khalik, "ASEAN's Task Force to Channel Foreign Aid to Myanmar."
137. "US 'Deeply Concerned' on Myanmar Religious Violence," AFP, 9 June 2012.
138. "U.S. Praises Myanmar's Response to Sectarian Clashes," Reuters, 19 June 2012.
139. Ibid.
140. "EU Welcomes 'Measured' Myanmar Response to Rioting," Reuters, 11 June 2012.
141. Kavi Chongkittavorn, "Rohingya Plight Further Divides ASEAN," *The Nation*, 5 September 2012.
142. "Editorial: Remember the Rohingya," *Jakarta Post*, 19 June 2012.
143. "International Monitoring and Protection of All Civilians from Religious and Ethnic Violence Needed in Western Burma," Burma Partnership, 13 June 2012, http://www.burmapartnership.org/2012/06/international-monitoring-and-protection-of-all-civilians-from-religious-and-ethnic-violence-needed-in-western-burma/.
144. "Indonesian Islamic Hard-Liners Vow Jihad for Myanmar's Rohingyas," *Jakarta Globe*, 13 July 2012.
145. Ulma Haryanto, Ezra Sihitea, and Ismira Lutfia, "Growing Unease in Indonesia over Plight of Rohingya," *Jakarta Globe*, 25 July 2012.
146. Fertile Tjahjono, "PBNU Desak Presiden Selesaikan Masalah Rohingya," *Kompas*, 28 July 2012.
147. Hartawan, "Nurhayati Ali Assegaf Desak IPU Ambil Sikap Tegas," *Kompas*, 24 July 2012.
148. Eva Sundari cited in Haryanto et al., "Growing Unease in Indonesia over Plight of Rohingya," *Jakarta Globe*, 25 July 2012.
149. Herlini Amran cited in Diyoko, "PKS Minta Presiden Beri Suaka Pengungsi Rohingya," *Kompas*, 25 July 2012.
150. Kiki Budi Hartawan, "Ketua DPR: Indonesia Harus Tegur Myanmar," *Kompas*, 25 July 2012.
151. Aritonang and Saragih, "RI Ready to Fight for Rohingya."
152. Ibid.
153. Mochammad Faisal Karim, "ASEAN Responsibility to Protect," *Jakarta Post*, 3 August 2012.
154. Ibid.
155. Rizal Ramli, "Indonesia and the Rohingya," *Jakarta Post*, 7 August 2012.
156. Bayuni, interview.
157. Sandro Gatra, "Pramono: Perjelas Pembelaan Untuk Rohingya," *Kompas*, 1 August 2012.
158. Karim, "ASEAN Responsibility to Protect."

159. Saragih, "Myanmar Trying to Reconcile Groups: SBY."
160. Haris Azhar, interview by the author, Jakarta, 5 August 2013.
161. Verdinand Robertua, "Intervention in the Rohingya Issue," *Jakarta Post*, 6 August 2012.
162. Sandro Gatra, "Etnis Rohingya Minta Intervensi Pemerintah Indonesia," *Kompas*, 13 August 2012.
163. Sastrohandoyo, interview.
164. "ASEAN Mulls Aiding Rohingya," *The Nation*, 10 August 2012.
165. Pichai Chuensuksawadi, "Surin Calls on ASEAN to Act on Rohingya Issue before Minority Becomes Radicalized," *Bangkok Post*, 28 October 2012.
166. "Statement of ASEAN Foreign Ministers on the Recent Developments in the Rakhine State, Myanmar," Burma Partnership, 17 August 2012, http://www.burmapartnership.org/2012/08/statement-of-asean-fms-on-the-recent-developments-in-the-rakhine-state/.
167. "Myanmar Declined Talks Offer on Violence: ASEAN," AFP, 30 October 2012.
168. "Editorial, Wise Words from Mr Surin," *Bangkok Post*, 30 October 2012.
169. Yang Razali Kassim, "Plight of the Rohingya: ASEAN Credibility Again at Stake," *RSIS Commentaries*, 2012, 2.
170. Jeerawat Na Thalang, "ASEAN Chief Urges Relief for Myanmar's Rohingya," *The Nation*, 18 November 2012.
171. "Protestors in Jakarta Demand Indonesia Expel Myanmar Ambassador," *Jakarta Globe*, 9 August 2012.
172. Gatra, "Etnis Rohingya Minta Intervensi Pemerintah Indonesia."
173. Ridwan May Sijabat, "Stop Humanitarian Tragedy in Myanmar: Inter-Religious Intellectuals," *Jakarta Post*, 16 August 2012.
174. Fuadi Pitsuwan, "West Islam Can Unite over Rohingya Cause," *Bangkok Post*, 20 November 2012.
175. "Myanmar Unrest: Amnesty: Rohingyas Being Targeted," *The Nation*, 23 July 2012.
176. Pitsuwan, "West Islam Can Unite over Rohingya Cause."
177. "Myanmar Gives Green Light for Aid to Rohingya," *The Nation*, 13 August 2012.
178. Kiki Budi Hartawan, "Menlu: OKI Harus Ambil Langkah Konkret," *Kompas*, 14 August 2012.
179. Wirajuda, interview.
180. Ibid.
181. Hafid Abbas, "The Rohingya Crisis: ASEAN vs Red Cross," *Jakarta Post*, 6 September 2012.
182. Fabian Kuwado, "Bantuan Dari PMI Tanpa Campur Tangan Pemerintah," *Kompas*, 25 August 2012.

4. Strategic Norm Replacement in Thailand

1. Supalak Ganjanakhundee, "Thailand Expresses Concern over Burma Protest," *The Nation*, 27 September 2007.
2. Achara Ashayagachat, "Govt Neglects Crisis in Burma," *Bangkok Post*, 27 September 2007.
3. "Speech by the Prime Minister of Thailand Surayud Chulanont at the 62nd Session of the General Assembly," UN General Assembly, New York, 27 September 2007, http://www.un.org/webcast/ga/62/2007/pdfs/thailand-en.pdf.
4. Ibid.
5. Kavi Chongkittavorn, "Thailand's Policy of Cowardice on Burma," *The Nation*, 1 October 2007.
6. Ibid.
7. Thomas Fuller, "For Myanmar's Neighbors, Mutual Needs Trump Qualms," *New York Times*, 2 October 2007, sec. Asia Pacific, https://www.nytimes.com/2007/10/02/world/asia/02asia.html.
8. Chongkittavorn, "Thailand's Policy of Cowardice on Burma."
9. Supalak Khundee, "US Leaders Put Burma Woes Ahead of Thailand," *The Nation*, 5 October 2007.
10. Kavi Chongkittavorn, "Time for Thailand to Revisit Its Policy on Burma," *The Nation*, 29 October 2007.
11. Ibid.
12. Maximilian Wechsler, "Election as Scheduled," *Bangkok Post*, 14 October 2007.
13. Supalak Khundee, "Gambari Briefs Nitya on Burma Visit in New York," *The Nation*, 6 October 2007.
14. Ibid.
15. Supalak Khundee, "Burma to Sign Asean Charter," *The Nation*, 20 November 2007.
16. Supalak Khundee, "Burma PM Opposes Asean on UN Envoy," *The Nation*, 21 November 2007.
17. Kavi Chongkittavorn, "Thai Diplomacy an Utter Failure over Past Year," *The Nation*, 26 November 2007.
18. "Bt 3.2 Million in Initial Relief," *The Nation*, 7 May 2008.
19. Miki Honda, "Natural Disaster and Humanitarian Assistance in Asia: The Case of Myanmar," *GIARI Working Paper* 4 (2009): 3.
20. Honda, "Natural Disaster and Humanitarian Assistance in Asia: The Case of Myanmar."
21. "Thailand Sends Aid to Rangoon; Cyclone Nargis Death Toll Soars Past 22,000," *Bangkok Post*, 7 May 2008.
22. "Bt 3.2 Million in Initial Relief."
23. "Race against Time to Help Nargis Victims," *Bangkok Post*, 16 May 2008.
24. "Mixed Signals from Burma over Disaster," *The Nation*, 8 May 2008.

25. "Burma Warned a Week Ago," *The Nation*, 7 May 2008.
26. "Relief Groups Left Waiting; UN Asks Burma to Waive Visas for Aid Workers," *Bangkok Post*, 8 May 2008.
27. "US Begs Thais to Influence Junta," *The Nation*, 9 May 2008.
28. "Burma Denies US Access; Relief Supplies from UN Starting to Get Through," *Bangkok Post*, 9 May 2008.
29. "Thai PM to Go to Rangoon on Sunday," *The Nation*, 9 May 2008.
30. "Burmese Junta Seizes UN Food Aid; Agencies Plead with Generals to Get Access," *Bangkok Post*, 10 May 2008.
31. "Thai Envoy to Seek Access for Western Aid Groups," *The Nation*, 10 May 2008.
32. "Tragedy Compounded," *The Nation*, 10 May 2008.
33. "Burmese Junta Seizes UN Food Aid."
34. "UN Says 102,000 Dead in Burma," *Bangkok Post*, 12 May 2008.
35. Ibid.
36. "UN Calls on Junta to Open Its Door to Aid," *Bangkok Post*, 13 May 2008.
37. "HM Urges Thais to Help Victims," *Bangkok Post*, 14 May 2008.
38. Sai Silp, "Thai PM to Travel to Burma at UN Chief's Request," *Irrawaddy*, 13 May 2008.
39. "Thai PM to Visit Myanmar on May 14," *OneIndia*, 13 May 2008.
40. "HM Urges Thais to Help Victims."
41. "Burma to Allow in Thai Medical Team," *Bangkok Post*, 15 May 2008.
42. Brian Cartan, "Thai Ties Bind Myanmar Cyclone Relief," *Asia Times*, 24 May 2008.
43. "Burma to Allow in Thai Medical Team."
44. "UN Chief to Fly to Burma for Talks with the Generals," *Bangkok Post*, 20 May 2008.
45. "UN Ups Pressure on Burma's Aid-Shy Junta," *The Nation*, 21 May 2008.
46. "Junta Still Delaying Aid Work," *The Nation*, 26 May 2008.
47. "Editorial—'Only Solution' Unacceptable," *Bangkok Post*, 20 July 2012.
48. Achara Ashayagachat, "Thailand, Myanmar Agree to Strengthen Cooperation," *Bangkok Post*, 23 July 2012.
49. "Thein Sein, PM Ink Deal on Sea Port," *Bangkok Post*, 24 July 2012.
50. Ashayagachat, "Thailand, Myanmar Agree to Strengthen Cooperation."
51. Achara Ashayagachat, "Dawei Cooperation Announced," *Bangkok Post*, 19 November 2012.
52. Aaron Stern, "The Limitation on Democratization in Thailand through the Lens of the 2006 Military Coup," *Taiwan Journal of Democracy* 3, no. 1 (2007): 137.
53. Thawilawdee Bureekul and Robert Albritton, "Measuring Democratization in Thailand after Political Reform," paper presented at CSES Plenary Session, Stockholm, 2–3 October 2003, https://cses.org/wp-content/uploads/2019/05/2003 Plenary_panels_BureekulAlbritton.pdf.

54. Suchit Bunbongkarn, "Thailand's Successful Reforms," *Journal of Democracy* 10, no. 4 (1999): 1.

55. "New Govt to Alter Policy on Burma," *The Nation*, 16 February 2001.

56. Bunbongkarn, "Thailand's Successful Reforms," 6.

57. Pavin Chachavalpongpun, "Thailand-Myanmar Relations: Old Animosity in a New Bilateral Setting," in *International Relations in Southeast Asia: Between Bilateralism and Multilateralism*, ed. Narayanan Ganesan and Ramses Amer (Singapore: ISEAS–Yusof Ishak Institute, 2010), 121.

58. Clark Neher, "Democratization in Thailand," *Asian Affairs* 21, no. 4 (1995): 200; Stern, "The Limitation on Democratization in Thailand through the Lens of the 2006 Military Coup," 137; Chantana Banpasirichote Wun'Gaeo and Uchane Cheangsan, "The Tyranny of the Majority and the Coup d'etat in Thailand," in *The State of Resistance: Popular Resistance in the Global South*, ed. Francois Polet (London: Zed, 2007), 161.

59. Human Rights Watch, "Crackdown: Repression of the 2007 Popular Protests in Burma," 7 December 2007, http://www.hrw.org/sites/default/files/reports/burma1207web.pdf.

60. "New Govt to Alter Policy on Burma."

61. Ibid.; "Editorial, New Government Needs New Policy on Burma," *Bangkok Post*, 10 July 2001.

62. Chachavalpongpun, "Thailand-Myanmar Relations: Old Animosity in a New Bilateral Setting," 121.

63. Ibid., 122.

64. Ibid., 125.

65. Richard Ehrlich, "At the Top of Tyranny," *Bangkok Post*, 30 September 2007.

66. Ashayagachat, "Govt Neglects Crisis in Burma."

67. Ibid.

68. James Ockey, "State, Bureaucracy and Polity in Modern Thai Politics," *Journal of Contemporary Asia* 34, no. 2 (2004): 154–55.

69. Following the coup, the military dissolved the acting House of Representatives and Senate and replaced them with the Council for Democratic Reform on which fifty-eight prominent civilians served as advisors to the military.

70. Jon Ungphakorn, "Straight to the Point, the Time to Speak out on Burma Is Now," *Bangkok Post*, 26 September 2007.

71. Ibid.

72. Ibid.

73. "ASEAN Slams Burmese Junta, Dissidents Say over 200 Killed in Crackdown," *Bangkok Post*, 29 September 2007.

74. Ashayagachat, "Govt Neglects Crisis in Burma."

75. Chongkittavorn, "Thai Diplomacy an Utter Failure over Past Year."

76. Achara Ashayagachat, interview by the author, Bangkok, 11 May 2016.

77. Surayud Surapong Jayanama, interview by the author, Bangkok, 15 June 2016.

78. Ibid.
79. Ibid.
80. Chongkittavorn, "Thailand's Policy of Cowardice on Burma."
81. "Editorial: Cut All Support for Evil Regime," *The Nation*, 27 September 2007.
82. "Unrest in Burma to Hit Border Trade, PTTEP Reports Business as Usual," *Bangkok Post*, 27 September 2007; "Cross-Border Trade Normal despite Tension in Burma," *The Nation*, 27 September 2007.
83. "Anxious Watch by Thai Companies," *The Nation*, 26 September 2007.
84. "Effigy of Than Shwe Set on Fire," *The Nation*, 29 September 2007.
85. Ashayagachat, interview.
86. Supalak Khundee, "Thai Role Gets UK Backing Britain Tells Nitya, It Understands Kingdom's Unique Circumstances," *The Nation*, 30 September 2007.
87. Ibid.
88. Phil Robertson, interview by the author, Bangkok, 8 June 2016.
89. Ibid.
90. Chongkittavorn, "Thailand's Policy of Cowardice on Burma."
91. "Burmese Junta Said to Have Jailed 1000 Demonstrators," *The Nation*, 2 October 2007.
92. Adam Cooper, "The Association of Southeast Asian Nations: The Burma Factor; What ASEAN Should Do about Burma," *Bangkok Post*, 16 November 2007.
93. Ibid.
94. Khundee, "US Leaders Put Burma Woes ahead of Thailand."
95. Including Virginia senator Jim Webb, Indiana senator Richard Luger, and California representative Tom Lantos.
96. Emma Chanlett-Avery, Ben Dolven, and Wil Mackey, "Thailand: Background and U.S. Relations," CRS Report (Congressional Research Service, 29 June 2015), 6, https://fas.org/sgp/crs/row/RL32593.pdf.
97. "Obama Visit to Confirm on US Policy on Asia," *The Nation*, 12 November 2012.
98. "Thailand Protest at Burmese Crackdown," *The Nation*, 9 October 2007; Khundee, "US Leaders Put Burma Woes ahead of Thailand."
99. Laurent Meillan, interview by the author, Bangkok, 3 May 2016.
100. "Thailand Protest at Burmese Crackdown."
101. Ibid.
102. Khundee, "Gambari Briefs Nitya on Burma Visit in New York."
103. "Maintaining the Momentum on Burma, Kouchner, Miliband," *The Nation*, 17 October 2007.
104. Ibid.
105. Chongkittavorn, "Thai Diplomacy an Utter Failure over Past Year."
106. Ibid.
107. Achara Ashayagachat, *Bangkok Post* senior editor, interview by the author, Bangkok, 11 May 2016.

108. "Toll to Rise by Thousands," *The Nation*, 6 May 2008.
109. "Burma Denies US Access."
110. "Cyclone Toll Tops 10000; Burma Appeals for International Aid," *Bangkok Post*, 6 May 2008.
111. "US Begs Thais to Influence Junta."
112. "Burma Denies US Access."
113. Ibid.
114. Sunai Phasuk, interview by the author, Bangkok, 17 May 2016.
115. Joshua Kurlantzick, "Thailand," in *Pathways to Freedom: Political and Economic Lessons from Democratic Transitions*, ed. Isobel Coleman and Terra Lawson-Remer (New York: Council on Foreign Relations Press, 2013), 158.
116. Nicholas Farrelly, "Why Democracy Struggles: Thailand's Elite Coup Culture," *Australian Journal of International Affairs* 67, no. 3 (2013): 287.
117. Farrelly, "Why Democracy Struggles."
118. Surapong Jayanama, interview.
119. "Editorial, Junta Must Let in Relief Aid," *Bangkok Post*, 9 May 2008.
120. Ibid.
121. "Burmese Junta Seizes UN Food Aid."
122. Ibid.
123. "UN Calls on Junta to Open Its Door to Aid."
124. Ibid.
125. "Thai PM to Visit Myanmar on May 14."
126. Achara Ashayagachat, "Doing Too Much, Too Soon May Backfire," *Bangkok Post*, 14 May 2008.
127. Ibid.
128. Ibid.
129. Ibid.
130. Ibid.
131. Surapong Jayanama, interview.
132. Tej Bunnag, interview by the author, Bangkok, 24 June 2016.
133. Achara Ashayagachat, "Samak—PM or Spokesperson for Regime in Burma," *Bangkok Post*, 16 May 2008.
134. Sanitsuda Ekachai, "Govt Has Blood on Its Hands, Too," *Bangkok Post*, 15 May 2008.
135. Ibid.
136. "Junta Must Protect the Burmese People," *The Nation*, 15 May 2008.
137. Kavi Chongkittavorn, "UN Must Support ASEAN on Burma," *The Nation*, 16 May 2008.
138. Cartan, "Thai Ties Bind Myanmar Cyclone Relief."
139. Surapong Jayanama, interview.
140. "Airport May Be Relief Hub; UN Seeks Use of Don Mueang for Burma Aid," *Bangkok Post*, 19 May 2008.
141. Ibid.

142. "Call for UN to Intervene in Rohingya 'Genocide,'" *The Nation*, 12 June 2012.
143. Ibid.
144. Ibid.
145. "Editorial, Rakhine Strife Tests Reforms," *Bangkok Post*, 12 June 2012.
146. Ibid.
147. Sanitsuda Ekachai, "Myanmar's Chance to Help Rohingya," *Bangkok Post*, 14 June 2012.
148. "Activists Call for Swift Action on Myanmar Violence," *Bangkok Post*, 14 June 2012.
149. Ibid.
150. Achara Ashayagachat, "UN, ASEAN Urged to Send Team to Rakhine," *Bangkok Post*, 15 June 2012.
151. Phasuk, interview.
152. Ibid.
153. Syeda Naushin Parnini, "The Crisis of the Rohingya as a Muslim Minority in Myanmar and Bilateral Relations with Bangladesh," *Journal of Muslim Minority Affairs* 33, no. 2 (2013): 289.
154. Robertson, interview.
155. "Editorial—'Only Solution' Unacceptable."
156. Achara Ashayagachat, "Refugees Boosted by Suu Kyi Visit," *Bangkok Post*, 5 June 2012.
157. "Editorial—'Only Solution' Unacceptable."
158. Ibid.
159. Ibid.
160. Ibid.
161. "Myanmar Killings Alarm Amnesty," *The Nation*, 21 July 2012.
162. Surapong Jayanama, interview.
163. Ibid.
164. Phasuk, interview.
165. Surapong Jayanama, interview.
166. "Thein Sein, PM Ink Deal on Sea Port."
167. Ibid.
168. "Students: Stop Rohingya Massacre," *Bangkok Post*, 23 July 2012.
169. Muang Kyaw Nu, interview by the author, Bangkok, 24 May 2016.
170. "Suu Kyi Departs on Landmark US Visit," *Bangkok Post*, 16 September 2012.
171. "Editorial: Myanmar Stalked by Ethnic Strife in NY," *Bangkok Post*, 30 September 2012.
172. "Suu Kyi: Thein Sein 'Keen' on Change," *Bangkok Post*, 19 September 2012.
173. "3 Dead in Myanmar Communal Clashes," *Bangkok Post*, 23 October 2012.
174. "Thousands Flee Myanmar Strife," *Bangkok Post*, 27 October 2012.

175. Ibid.
176. "UN 'Alarmed' by New Myanmar Unrest," *Bangkok Post,* 25 October 2012.
177. "Communal Violence Rocks Myanmar, Many Dead," *Bangkok Post,* 26 October 2012.
178. Ibid.
179. "Editorial, Wise Words from Mr Surin," *Bangkok Post,* 30 October 2012.
180. "Editorial, The Two Ills of Myanmar," *Bangkok Post,* 6 November 2012.

5. From Norm Reconciliation to Conflict Denial in Malaysia

1. Azhar Abu Samah, "KL Mahu Yangon Elak Kekerasan," *Berita Harian,* 27 September 2007. "Myanmar Protests Threaten Turmoil: Malaysian Minister," *Malaysiakini,* 25 September 2007.
2. Ibid.
3. Ibid.
4. Ibid.
5. Foo Yee Ping, "Unrest in Myanmar Affects ASEAN, Says Foreign Minister," *The Star,* 26 September 2007.
6. Samah, "KL Mahu Yangon Elak Kekerasan."
7. "Surayud Lays into Burmese Junta at UN," *The Nation,* 29 September 2007.
8. Ibid.
9. "Speech by the Malaysian Prime Minister Abdullah Badawi at the 62nd Session of the General Assembly," UN General Assembly, New York, 28 September 2007, http://www.un.org/webcast/ga/62/2007/pdfs/malaysia-eng.pdf.
10. Ibid.
11. "Collective ASEAN Stand Warranted," *New Straits Times,* 30 September 2007.
12. Ibid.
13. Foo Yee Ping, "PM: ASEAN's Constructive Engagement with Junta Has Failed," *The Star,* 28 September 2007.
14. Azhar Abu Samah, "ASEAN Desak Myanmar Hentikan Krisis Secara Aman," *Berita Harian,* 29 September 2007.
15. Ping, "PM: ASEAN's Constructive Engagement with Junta Has Failed."
16. Samah, "ASEAN Desak Myanmar Hentikan Krisis Secara Aman."
17. "PM: Yangon Should Release Detainees," *New Straits Times,* 29 September 2007.
18. "ASEAN to Coax Yangon to Co-Operate with UN," *New Straits Times,* 17 October 2007.
19. Ibid.
20. Ibid.
21. "ASEAN Setuju PBB Selesai Krisis Dalaman Myanmar," *Berita Harian,* 17 October 2007.
22. Syed Nazri, "Sanctions No Solution to Myanmar Problem," *New Straits Times,* 25 October 2007.

23. Ibid.
24. Ibid.
25. Mutazar Abd Ghani, "ASEAN Bakal Bentuk Identiti Sendiri," *Berita Harian*, 19 November 2007.
26. Ahmad Pazil Md Isa, "Rundingan Myanmar, PBB Disokong," *Berita Harian*, 22 November 2007.
27. "Najib: Govt Ready to Send Aid If Asked," *New Straits Times*, 8 May 2008.
28. Johan Afandi and Amin Ridzuan Ridzuan, "Malaysia Tawar Bantuan (HL)," *Berita Harian*, 8 May 2008.
29. Ibid.
30. "Govt Sends Aid to Myanmar," *New Straits Times*, 11 May 2008.
31. "RM4 Juta Bantu Rakyat Myanmar," *Berita Harian*, 11 May 2008.
32. "Malaysian Aid on the Way to Nargis Victims," *New Straits Times*, 13 May 2008; Anwar Husin, "Bantuan Kemanusiaan Ke Myanmar," *Berita Harian*, 13 May 2008.
33. "Yangon Terharu Sumbangan KL," *Berita Harian*, 14 May 2008.
34. Ibid.
35. "ASEAN to Co-Ordinate International Relief Effort," *New Straits Times*, 20 May 2008.
36. Jan Dahinten and Ovais Subhani, "Malaysia Says ASEAN Wants Bigger Role in Myanmar Cyclone Relief," *Reuters*, 1 June 2008.
37. Vasudevan, "Let ASEAN Give More Aid, Najib Urges Myanmar," *New Straits Times*, 2 June 2008.
38. Ibid.
39. Ibid.
40. Ibid.
41. "Malaysia Effort to Provide Assistance to Myanmar," South-South Information Gateway, 12 June 2012, http://www.ssig.gov.my/blog/2012/06/13/malaysia-effort-to-provide-assistance-to-myanmar/.
42. "Malaysia Concerned with Ethnic Violence in Rakhine," *Bernama*, 17 June 2012.
43. "Press Statement by the Minister of Foreign Affairs of Malaysia on the Development in Rakhine, Myanmar," Foreign Ministry of Malaysia, 20 June 2012, https://www.kln.gov.my/archive/content.php?t=3&articleId=2169760.
44. "Burma Turns down M'sian Aid for Strife-Torn Rakhine State," *Malaysiakini*, 21 June 2012.
45. Ibid.
46. "Press Statement by the Minister of Foreign Affairs of Malaysia on the Development in Rakhine, Myanmar."
47. "Burma Turns down M'sian Aid for Strife-Torn Rakhine State."
48. "Sukar Bantu, Etnik Rohingya Tidak Diiktiraf," *Berita Harian*, 11 September 2012.
49. "Putra 1Malaysia to Aid Rohingya," *New Straits Times*, 12 August 2012.

50. Moer Hisham Zulkifli, "Rakyat Malaysia Pemurah," *Berita Harian*, 1 September 2012.

51. "Sukar Bantu, Etnik Rohingya Tidak Diiktiraf."

52. "Myanmar Benar Malaysia Beri Bantuan," *Berita Harian*, 17 September 2012.

53. Ibid.

54. Ahmad Zaini Kamaruzzaman, "Darah, Air Mata Sittwe," *Berita Harian*, 11 October, 2012.

55. "Myanmar Benar Malaysia Beri Bantuan."

56. Mohd Nasaruddin Parzi, "14 Sukarelawan Ke Myanmar," *Berita Harian*, 20 September 2012.

57. Lum Chee Hong, "Kapal Sewa Bawa Bantuan Rohingya," *Berita Harian*, n.d.

58. "Misi Rakhine Bukti Malaysia Peka," *Berita Harian*, 26 September 2012.

59. "KP1M Sifatkan Misi Ke Myanmar Paling Sukar," *Berita Harian*, 13 October 2012.

60. Ibid.

61. "Mercy Malaysia Rancang Baik Pulih Hospital Di Myanmar," *Berita Harian*, 10 October 2012.

62. Chuman, "We're Ready to Help Myanmar," *New Straits Times*, 10 October 2012.

63. Fazli Abudllah, "ASEAN Perlu Sepakat Tangani Isu Rohingya," *Berita Harian*, 18 November 2012.

64. "Violence against Burmese Monks Lambasted," *Malaysiakini*, 26 September 2007.

65. Ibid.

66. Ibid.

67. Ibid.

68. Mohammad Agus Yusoff, Azmi Awang, and Leo Agustino, "Democratic Reforms in Malaysia: Where It's Heading To?," *Jurnal Kebijakan Dan Administrasi Publik* 14, no. 1 (2015): 24; Gaik Cheng Khoo, "The Rise of Constitutional Patriotism in Malaysian Civil Society," *Asian Studies Review* 38, no. 3 (2014): 330; Chai Ai Reen, Khairiah Salwa Mokhtar, and Paramjit Singh Jamir Sing, "Administration in Malaysia. Reformation under Abdullah Ahmad Badawi," *NIDA Case Research Journal* 4, no. 2 (2012): 179.

69. Naim Musa, "Malaysia in ASEAN: Foreign Policy on Non-Traditional Security Issues." (2012), 60, https://www.academia.edu/4219715/Malaysia_foreign_policy_after_mahathir_era.

70. Johan Saravanamuttu, *Malaysia's Foreign Policy. The First Fifty Years.* (Singapore: ISEAS, 2010), 234; Reen, Mokhtar, and Sing, "Administration in Malaysia. Reformation under Abdullah Ahmad Badawi." It was thus under Badawi's leadership and in his function as ASEAN chair that the Malaysian government created some space for NGOs to take part at the sidelines of the 2005 ASEAN summit in Kuala Lumpur.

71. Lim Kit Siang, "Malaysian Parliamentary Caucus on Democracy in Myanmar to Be Formed," 8 April 2004, https://limkitsiang.com/archive/2004/apr04/lks2963.htm.

72. "Myanmar Protests Threaten Turmoil: Malaysian Minister."

73. Johan Saravanamuttu, "ASEAN in Malaysian Foreign Policy Discourse and Practice, 1967–1997," *Asian Journal of Political Science* 5, no. 1 (1997): 35–51; Mirzan Mahathir and Fazil Irwan, "Malaysia's Role in Asian Regional Cooperation: A Look at Foreign Policy Themes," *Asia-Pacific Review* 14, no. 2 (2007): 97–111.

74. Jörn Dosch, "Mahathirism and Its Legacy in Malaysia's Foreign Policy," *European Journal of East Asian Studies* 13, no. 1 (2014): 5; Khadijah Md Khalid, "Malaysia's Foreign Policy under Najib: A Comparison with Mahathir," *Asian Survey* 51, no. 3 (2011): 430–31.

75. Elina Noor and T. N. Qistina, "Great Power Rivalries, Domestic Politics and Malaysian Foreign Policy," *Asian Security* 13, no. 3 (2017): 204.

76. Dosch, "Mahathirism and Its Legacy in Malaysia's Foreign Policy," 7.

77. Ruhanas Harun, "In Pursuit of National Interest: Change and Continuity in Malaysia's Foreign Policy towards the Middle East," *International Journal of West Asian Studies* 1, no. 0 (2009): 23–38.

78. Syed Hamid Albar, interview by the author, Kuala Lumpur, 2 September 2016.

79. Reen, Mokhtar, and Sing, "Administration in Malaysia: Reformation under Abdullah Ahmad Badawi," 182.

80. Sivamurugan Pandian, Rusdi Omar, and Mohd Azizuddin Mohd Sani, "'Work with Me, Not for Me': Malaysia under Abdullah Ahmad Badawi (2003–2009)," *Asian Culture and History* 2, no. 1 (2010): 104.

81. Ahmad Fauzi Abdul Hamid and Muhamad Takiyuddin Ismail, "Abdullah Ahmad Badawi: A Malaysian Neo-Conservative?," *Japanese Journal of Political Science* 13, no. 3 (2012): 394; Musa, "Malaysia in ASEAN: Foreign Policy on Non-Traditional Security Issues," 47.

82. "Speech by the Foreign Minister of Malaysia Syed Hamid Albar at the 60th Session of the General Assembly New York," UN General Assembly, New York, 19 September 2005, A/60/PV.13.

83. Ioannis Gatsiounis, "Islam Hadhari in Malaysia," Hudson Institute, February 16, 2006, 79, https://www.hudson.org/research/9811-islam-hadhari-in-malaysia.

84. Albar, interview.

85. "Collective ASEAN Stand Warranted."

86. Ibid.

87. Albar, interview.

88. Azhar Abu Smah, "Bush Berhelah Isu Pelepasan Gas Rumah Hijau," *Berita Harian*, 2 October 2007.

89. Wan Azizah Wan Ismail, "Time for ASEAN to Kick Burma Out," *Malaysiakini*, 2 October 2007.

90. Ibid.
91. David Miliband, "ASEAN Nations Have Vital Role," *New Straits Times*, 4 October 2007.
92. Albar, interview.
93. Ping, "Unrest in Myanmar Affects ASEAN, Says Foreign Minister."
94. Ibid.
95. Brian Yap, "It Is Hard to Keep Looking the Other Way," *New Straits Times*, 3 October 2007.
96. Ibid.
97. Ismail, "Time for ASEAN to Kick Burma Out."
98. "Thousands Protest Again against Burmese Junta," *Malaysiakini*, 2 October 2007.
99. "Gambari Tells ASEAN: Turn Rhetoric into Real Action," *Malaysiakini*, 17 October 2007.
100. "ASEAN Will Never Suspend Burma, Says M'sia," *Malaysiakini*, 16 October 2007.
101. Rastam Mohd Isa, interview by the author, Kuala Lumpur, 11 August 2016.
102. Jeffrey Hays, "Malaysia under Prime Minister Abdullah Ahmad Badawi," 2008, http://factsanddetails.com/southeast-asia/Malaysia/sub5_4a/entry-3629.html.
103. Bridget Welsh, "Malaysia's Glasnost," in *The Report: Malaysia 2007*, ed. Oxford Business Group (Oxford: Oxford Business Group, 2007), 29.
104. Lee Hock Guan, "Malaysia in 2007: Abdullah Administration under Siege," *Southeast Asian Affairs* (200): 188.
105. Welsh, "Malaysia's Glasnost," 29.
106. Guan, "Malaysia in 2007," 188.
107. Ibid., 198.
108. Ibid., 190; see also "Malaysia 2008, Freedom in the World," 2008, https://freedomhouse.org/report/freedom-world/2008/malaysia.
109. Chew Cy, interview by the author, Kuala Lumpur, 22 July 2016.
110. "Burma Objects, UN Briefing Cancelled," *Malaysiakini*, 20 November 2007.
111. Mutazar Abdul Ghani and Johan Afandi, "Sidang Berjaya Capai Matlamat: Abdullah," *Berita Harian*, 22 November 2007.
112. Saravanamuttu, *Malaysia's Foreign Policy. The First Fifty Years.* 239.
113. Yusoff, Awang, and Agustino, "Democratic Reforms I Malaysia," 21–22.
114. Suaram, *Malaysia Human Rights Report 2008* (Petaling Jaya: Suaram Kommunikasi, 2009), 10.
115. "Yangon Urged to Let in Experts," *New Straits Times*, 11 May 2008.
116. "Call to Delay Referendum," *New Straits Times*, 13 May 2008.
117. Ibid.
118. "Postpone Referendum," *New Straits Times*, 8 May 2008.

119. "Usul Wan Azizah Ditolak," *Berita Harian*, 13 May 2008.
120. Ibid.
121. "No Regrets in Supporting Burma to Join ASEAN," *Malaysiakini*, 22 May 2008.
122. Ibid.
123. Ibid.
124. Ibid.
125. Albar, interview.
126. Frank Schimmelfennig, "The Community Trap: Liberal Norms, Rhetorical Action, and the Eastern Enlargement of the European Union," *International Organization* 55, no. 1 (2001): 47–80, 66.
127. "Speech by the Foreign Minister of Malaysia Rais Yatim at the 63rd Session of the General Assembly," UN General Assembly, New York, 27 September 2008, A/63/PV.14.
128. Khaidir Majid, "Ribut Nargis Dedah Krisis Kemanusiaan," *Berita Harian*, 9 May 2008.
129. Albar, interview.
130. "ASEAN to Co-Ordinate International Relief Effort."
131. Azril Mohd Amin, "A Plea for the Rohingyas," *Malaysiakini*, 13 June 2012.
132. Ibid.
133. "PAS Leaders Distance Selves from Nasha's Statement," *Malaysiakini*, 10 October 2012.
134. Susan Loone, "SEA May Turn into Killing Field over Rohingya Deaths," *Malaysiakini*, 12 August 2012.
135. *Pakatan Rakyat* is an informal Malaysian political coalition of opposition parties.
136. Aidila Razak, "Pressure Your Gov't to Halt Violence against Rohingyas," *Malaysiakini*, 10 August 2012.
137. "Dr. M: Rohingya Issues Can Be Handled Diplomatically," *New Straits Times*, 16 August 2012.
138. Nigel Aw, "PM Should Speak out for Rohingya, Says Dr M," *Malaysiakini*, 17 September 2012.
139. "Recognise Rohingya as Citizens, Dr M Tells Myanmar," *New Straits Times*, 18 September 2012.
140. MAPIM is an association of several NGOs that fight for the aspirations of Muslims in Malaysia.
141. "MAPIM Minta PM Bela Nasib Umat Islam Di Myanmar," *Berita Harian*, 17 June 2012.
142. Ibid.
143. Ibid.
144. "Sedia Bantu Etnik Rohingya," *Berita Harian*, 24 August 2012.
145. Chuman, "We're Ready to Help Myanmar."
146. Ibid.

147. Cy, interview.
148. Tian Chua, interview by the author, Kuala Lumpur, 15 August 2016.
149. Kian Ming Ong, interview by the author, Kuala Lumpur, 18 August 2016.
150. Razali Ismail, interview by the authorm Kuala Lumpur, 12 August 2016.
151. Zulkofli Jamaludin, "Konflik Syria, Etnik Rohingya Dibincang," *Berita Harian*, 13 August 2012.
152. "Malaysia Sokong OIC Gantung Syria," *Berita Harian*, 16 August 2012.

Conclusion

1. Amitav Acharya, *Regionalism and Multilateralism: Essays on Cooperative Security in the Asia-Pacific* (Singapore: Times Academic Press, 2002), 225.
2. Luke Glanville, *Sovereignty and the Responsibility to Protect: A New History* (Chicago: University of Chicago Press, 2014), 108; Davide Rodogno, *Against Massacre: Humanitarian Interventions in the Ottoman Empire, 1815–1914* (Princeton, N.J.: Princeton University Press, 2012), 12.
3. Martha Finnemore and Kathryn Sikkink, "International Norm Dynamics and Political Change," *International Organization* 52, no. 4 (1998): 887–917.
4. Hiro Katsumata, "ASEAN and Human Rights: Resisting Western Pressure or Emulating the West?," *Pacific Review* 5 (2009): 619–37.

Bibliography

Acharya, Amitav. *Constructing a Security Community in Southeast Asia: ASEAN and the Problem of Regional Order.* London: Routledge, 2001.
———. "Democratisation and the Prospects for Participatory Regionalism in Southeast Asia." *Third World Quarterly* 24, no. 2 (2003): 375-90.
———. "The Evolution of Norms: The Social Construction of Non-Interference in Asian Regionalism." Paper presented at the Provincializing Westphalia conference, Oxford, 2008.
———. "How Ideas Spread: Whose Norms Matter? Norm Localization and Institutional Change in Asian Regionalism." *International Organization* 58, no. 2 (2004): 239-75.
———. *Indonesia Matters: Asia's Emerging Democratic Power.* Singapore: World Scientific Publishing, 2015.
———. *The Quest for Identity. International Relations of Southeast Asia.* Singapore: Oxford University Press, 2000.
———. *Regionalism and Multilateralism: Essays on Cooperative Security in the Asia-Pacific.* Singapore: Times Academic Press, 2002.
———. "Southeast Asia's Democratic Moment." *Asian Survey* 39, no. 3 (1999): 418-32.
Alexandra, Lina. "Indonesia and the Responsibility to Protect." *Pacific Review* 25, no. 1 (2012): 51-74.
Amnesty International. *Amnesty International Report 2009: The State of the World's Human Rights.* London: Amnesty International, 2009. https://www.hrw.org/legacy/wr2k7/wr2007master.pdf.
———. "Myanmar Briefing: Human Rights Concerns a Month after Cyclone Nargis." 5 June 2008. http://www.amnesty.org/en/library/asset/ASA16/013/2008/en/85931049-32e5-11dd-863f-e9cd398f74da/asa160132008eng.pdf.
———. "Myanmar Demonstrators Defiant in Face of Escalating Repression." 27 September 2007. https://www.amnesty.org/download/Documents/60000/asa160102007en.pdf.
———. "Myanmar Needs a Comprehensive International Arms Embargo." 28 September 2007. http://www.amnesty.org/en/library/asset/ASA16/010/2007/en/8f053137-d366-11dd-a329-2f46302a8cc6/asa160102007en.pdf.

———. "Open Letter to ASEAN Member States on the Situation in Myanmar." 27 September 2007. https://www.amnesty.org/download/Documents/60000/asa160112007en.pdf.

Anwar, Dewi Fortuna. "The Impact of Domestic and Asian Regional Changes on Indonesian Foreign Policy." *Southeast Asian Affairs* (2010): 126–41.

———. *Indonesia in ASEAN: Foreign Policy and Regionalism*. Singapore: Institute of Southeast Asian Studies, 1994.

———. "Insurgencies and Communal Conflicts: Governance and Security in Indonesia's Plural Societies." In *Non-Traditional Security Issues in Southeast Asia*, edited by Andrew Tan and Kenneth Boutin, 349–76. Singapore: Select Publishing for Institute of Defence and Strategic Studies, 2001.

ASEAN. "Address by the Honourable Dato' Sero Abdullah Ahmad Badawi, Prime Minister of Malaysia at the Opening of the 39th ASEAN Ministerial Meeting Kuala Lumpur, 25 July 2006." Kuala Lumpur, 25 July 2006. http://asean.org/?static_post=address-by-the-honourable-dato-seri-abdullah-ahmad-badawi-prime-minister-of-malaysia-at-the-opening-of-the-39th-asean-ministerial-meeting-kuala-lumpur-25-july-2006-2.

———. *The ASEAN Declaration*. Bangkok: ASEAN, 8 August 1967.

———. *ASEAN Human Rights Declaration*. Phnom Penh: ASEAN, 18 November 2012.

———. *Charter of the Association of Southeast Asian Nations*. Singapore: ASEAN, 20 November 2007.

———. "A Humanitarian Call: The ASEAN Response to Cyclone Nargis." Jakarta: ASEAN Secretariat, July 2010. http://www.asean.org/wp-content/uploads/images/2012/publications/A%20Humanitarian%20Call%20The%20ASEAN%20Response%20to%20Cyclone%20Nargis.pdf.

———. *Joint Communique of the Twenty-Sixth ASEAN Ministerial Meeting*. Singapore: ASEAN, July 24, 1993.

———. *Terms of Reference: ASEAN Intergovernmental Commission on Human Rights*. Jakarta: ASEAN, July 2009.

———. *Treaty of Amity and Cooperation in Southeast Asia*. Bali: ASEAN, 24 February 1976.

Axelrod, Robert. *The Evolution of Cooperation*. New York: Basic, 1984.

Ayoob, Mohammed. *The Third World Security Predicament: State Making, Regional Conflict, and the International System*. London: Lynne Rienner, 1995.

Beetham, David. *The Legitimation of Power*. 2nd ed. Houndmills, UK: Palgrave Macmillan, 2013.

Beirlaen, Mathieu. "A Unifying Framework for Reasoning about Normative Conflicts." *The Logica Yearbook* (2011): 1–14.

Bellamy, Alex. "The Responsibility to Protect—Five Years On." *Ethics & International Affairs* 24, no. 2 (2010): 143–69.

Bellamy, Alex, and Mark Beeson. "The Responsibility to Protect in Southeast Asia: Can ASEAN Reconcile Humanitarianism and Sovereignty?" *Asian Security* 6, no. 3 (2010): 262–79.
Betts, Alexander, and Phil Orchard. *Implementation and World Politics: How International Norms Change Practice.* Oxford: Oxford University Press, 2014.
———. "Introduction. The Normative Institutionalization-Implementation Gap." In *Implementation and World Politics: How International Norms Change Practice,* edited by Betts and Orchard, 1–20. Oxford: Oxford University Press, 2014.
Björkdahl, Annika. "Norms in International Relations: Some Conceptual and Methodological Reflections." *Cambridge Review of International Affairs* 15, no. 1 (2010): 9–23.
Boekle, Henning, Volker Rittberger, and Wolfgang Wagner. "Norms and Foreign Policy: Constructivist Foreign Policy Theory." *Tübinger Arbeitspapiere zur Internationalen Politik und Friedensforschung* 34a (1999): 1–46.
Bull, Hedley. *The Anarchical Society: A Study of Order in World Politics.* New York: Columbia University Press, 1977.
Bunbongkarn, Suchit. "Thailand's Successful Reforms." *Journal of Democracy* 10, no. 4 (1999): 54–68.
Bureekul, Thawilawdee, and Robert Albritton. "Measuring Democratization in Thailand after Political Reform." Paper presented at CSES Plenary Session, Stockholm, 2–3 October 2003. https://cses.org/wp-content/uploads/2019/05/2003Plenary_panels_BureekulAlbritton.pdf.
Buitelaar, Tom, and Gisela Hirschmann. "Criminal Accountability at What Cost? Norm Conflict, UN Peace Operations, and the International Criminal Court," *European Journal of International Relations* #?, no. 27 (2021): 548–71.
Buzan, Barry, and Ole Wæver. *Regions and Powers: The Structure of International Security.* Cambridge: Cambridge University Press, 2003.
Caballero-Anthony, Mely. "Evolving Regional Governance in East Asia: From ASEAN to an East Asia Community." In *Governance and Regionalism in Asia,* edited by Nicholas Thomas, 32–65. Abingdon, UK: Routledge, 2009.
Capie, David. "Localization as Resistance: The Contested Diffusion of Small Arms Norms in Southeast Asia." *Security Dialogue* 39, no. 6 (2008): 637–58.
Carbone, Giovanni. "The Consequences of Democratization." *Journal of Democracy* 20, no. 2 (2009): 123–37.
Carothers, Thomas. "Democracy and Human Rights: Policy Allies or Rivals?" *Washington Quarterly* 17, no. 3 (1994): 109–20.
Chachavalpongpun, Pavin. "Thailand-Myanmar Relations: Old Animosity in a New Bilateral Setting." In *International Relations in Southeast Asia: Between Bilateralism and Multilateralism,* edited by Narayanan Ganesan and Ramses Amer, 117–42. Singapore: ISEAS–Yusof Ishak Institute, 2010.
Chanlett-Avery, Emma, Ben Dolven, and Wil Mackey. *Thailand: Background and U.S. Relations.* CRS Report. Congressional Research Service, 29 June 2015. https://fas.org/sgp/crs/row/RL32593.pdf.

Checkel, Jeffrey T. "Norms, Institutions, and National Identity in Contemporary Europe." *International Studies Quarterly* 43, no. 1 (1999): 83–114.

———. "Why Comply? Social Learning and European Identity Change." *International Organization* 55, no. 3 (2001): 553–88.

Ciorciari, John. "Institutionalizing Human Rights in Southeast Asia." *Human Rights Quarterly* 34, no. 3 (2012): 695–725.

Clark, Ian. *Legitimacy in International Society*. New York: Oxford University Press, 2005.

Clark, Marshall. "Indonesia's Postcolonial Regional Imaginary: From a 'Neutralist' to an 'All-Directions' Foreign Policy." *Japanese Journal of Political Science* 12, no. 2 (2011): 287–304.

Clarke, Ross. "Retrospectivity and the Constitutional Validity of the Bali Bombing and East Timor Trials." *Australian Journal of Asian Law* 5, no. 2 (2003): 1–32.

Coicaud, Jean-Marc. *Legitimacy and Politics: A Contribution to the Study of Political Right and Political Responsibility*. Cambridge: Cambridge University Press, 2002.

Connors, Michael. "Ambivalent about Human Rights: Thai Democracy." In *Human Rights in Asia*, edited by Thomas Davis and Brian Galligan, 103–22. Cheltenham, UK: Edward Elgar, 2011.

Cortell, Andrew, and James Davis. "When Norms Clash: International Norms, Domestic Practices, and Japan's Internalisation of the GATT/WTO." *Review of International Studies* 31, no. 1 (2005): 3–25.

Crawford, Neta. *Argument and Change in World Politics: Ethics, Decolonization, and Humanitarian Intervention*. Cambridge: Cambridge University Press, 2002.

Currie, Kelley. *Mirage or Reality? Asia's Emerging Human Rights and Democracy Architecture*. Arlington: Project 2049 Institute, 2010.

Dahinten, Jan, and Ovais Subhani. "Malaysia Says ASEAN Wants Bigger Role in Myanmar Cyclone Relief." *Reuters*, 1 June 2008.

Davies, Mathew. "An Agreement to Disagree: The ASEAN Human Rights Declaration and the Absence of Regional Identity in Southeast Asia." *Journal of Current Southeast Asian Affairs* 33, no. 3 (2014): 107–29.

Davis, Thomas. "Human Rights in Asia: Institutions, Norms and Politics." In *Human Rights in Asia*, edited by Davis and Brian Galligan, 1–24. Cheltenham, UK: Edward Elgar, 2011.

Dill, Janina. *Legitimate Targets? Social Construction, International Law and US Bombing*. New York: Cambridge University Press, 2015.

Dobbin, Frank, Beth Simmons, and Geoffrey Garrett. "The Global Diffusion of Public Policies: Social Construction, Coercion, Competition, or Learning?" *Annual Review of Sociology* 33, no. 1 (2007): 449–72.

Dosch, Jörn. *The Changing Dynamics of Southeast Asian Politics*. London: Lynne Rienner, 2007.

———. "Mahathirism and Its Legacy in Malaysia's Foreign Policy." *European Journal of East Asian Studies* 13, no. 1 (2014): 5–32.

Downs, George W., and Michael A. Jones. "Reputation, Compliance, and International Law." *Journal of Legal Studies* 31, no. 1 (2002): 95–114.

Drummond, Catherine. "The ASEAN Intergovernmental Commission on Human Rights (AICHR) and the Responsibility to Protect: Development and Potential." Working Paper on ASEAN and RtoP, 2010. http://www.r2pasiapacific.org/docs/R2P%20Reports/AICHR%20and%20R2P_Report%20No_1%20 2010.pdf (site discontinued).

Dunn, Lauren, Peter Nyers, and Richard Stubbs. "Western Interventionism versus East Asian Non-Interference: Competing 'Global' Norms in the Asian Century." *Pacific Review* 23, no. 3 (2010): 295–312.

Elhad, Abdullatif, Joost Breuker, and Bob Brouwer. "On the Formal Analysis of Normative Conflicts." *Information & Communications Technology Law* 9, no. 3 (2000): 207–17.

Emmers, Ralf. "Indonesia's Role in ASEAN: A Case of Incomplete and Sectorial Leadership." *Pacific Review* 27, no. 4 (2014): 543–62.

Farrelly, Nicholas. "Why Democracy Struggles: Thailand's Elite Coup Culture." *Australian Journal of International Affairs* 67, no. 3 (2013): 281–96.

Fen, Lilianne, and Hanna Krebs. "Regional Organisations and Humanitarian Action: The Case of ASEAN." HPG Working Paper, 2014, 1–19.

Finnemore, Martha. *The Purpose of Intervention: Changing Beliefs about the Use of Force*. Ithaca, N.Y.: Cornell University Press, 2003.

Finnemore, Martha, and Kathryn Sikkink. "International Norm Dynamics and Political Change." *International Organization* 52, no. 4 (1998): 887–917.

Florini, Ann. "The Evolution of International Norms." *International Studies Quarterly* 40, no. 3 (1996): 363–89.

Foot, Rosemary. *Rights beyond Borders: The Global Community and the Struggle over Human Rights in China*. Oxford: Oxford University Press, 2000.

Ford, Michele. "International Networks and Human Rights in Indonesia." In *Human Rights in Asia*, edited by Thomas Davis and Brian Galligan, 38–55. Cheltenham, UK: Edward Elgar, 2011.

Forsythe, David. *Human Rights in International Relations*. Cambridge: Cambridge University Press, 2012.

Fox, Gregory, and Brad Roth. "Introduction: The Spread of Liberal Democracy and Its Implications for International Law." In *Democratic Governance and International Law*, edited by Fox and Roth, 1–25. Cambridge: Cambridge University Press, 2000.

Franck, Thomas. *The Power of Legitimacy among Nations*. Oxford: Oxford University Press, 1990.

Freedom House. "Malaysia 2008, Freedom in the World." 2008. https://freedomhouse.org/report/freedom-world/2008/malaysia.

Friedrichs, Jörg, and Friedrich Kratochwil. "On Acting and Knowing: How Pragmatism Can Advance International Relations Research and Methodology." *International Organization* 63, no. 4 (2009): 701–31.

Galligan, Brian. "Human Rights in Asia: Comparative Reflections." In *Human Rights in Asia*, edited by Thomas Davis and Galligan, 212–25. Cheltenham, UK: Edward Elgar, 2011.
Gatsiounis, Ioannis. "Islam Hadhari in Malaysia." Hudson Institute. February 16, 2006. https://www.hudson.org/research/9811-islam-hadhari-in-malaysia.
George, Alexander, and Andrew Bennett. *Case Studies and Theory Development in the Social Sciences*. Cambridge, Mass.: MIT Press, 2005.
Gerring, John. "Case Selection for Case-Study Analysis: Qualitative and Quantitative Techniques." In *The Oxford Handbook of Political Methodology*, edited by Janet Box-Steffensmeier, Henry Brady, and David Collier, 645–84. Oxford: Oxford University Press, 2008.
Glanville, Luke. *Sovereignty and the Responsibility to Protect: A New History*. Chicago: University of Chicago Press, 2014.
Goertz, Gary, and Paul Diehl. "Toward a Theory of International Norms: Some Conceptual and Measurement Issues." *Journal of Conflict Resolution* 36, no. 4 (1992): 634–64.
Gomez, James, and Robin Ramcharan. "Introduction: Democracy and Human Rights in Southeast Asia." *Journal of Current Southeast Asian Affairs* 33, no. 3 (2015): 3–17.
Gorjão, Paulo. "Regime Change and Foreign Policy: Portugal, Indonesia and the Self-Determination of East Timor." *Democratization* 9, no. 4 (2002): 142–58.
Guan, Ang Cheng. "Myanmar: Time for a Unified Approach." *Security Dialogue* 32, no. 4 (2001): 467–80.
Guan, Lee Hock. "Malaysia in 2007: Abdullah Administration under Siege." *Southeast Asian Affairs* (2008): 187–206.
Haacke, Jürgen. *ASEAN's Diplomatic and Security Culture: Origins, Development and Prospects*. London: Routledge, 2003.
———. "Enhanced Interaction with Myanmar and the Project of a Security Community: Is ASEAN Refining or Breaking with Its Diplomatic and Security Culture?" *Contemporary Southeast Asia* 27, no. 2 (2005): 188–216.
Hamid, Ahmad Fauzi Abdul, and Muhamad Takiyuddin Ismail. "Abdullah Ahmad Badawi: A Malaysian Neo-Conservative?" *Japanese Journal of Political Science* 13, no. 3 (2012): 379–99.
Harun, Ruhanas. "In Pursuit of National Interest: Change and Continuity in Malaysia's Foreign Policy towards the Middle East." *International Journal of West Asian Studies* 1 (2009): 23–38.
Herbert, Jeff. "The Legal Framework of Human Rights in Indonesia." In *Indonesia: Law and Society*, edited by Timothy Lindsey. Annandale, Va.: Federation Press, 2008.
Heritier, Adrienne. "Causal Explanation." In *Approaches and Methodologies in the Social Sciences: A Pluralist Perspective*, edited by Donatella Della Porta and Michael Keating, 61–79. Cambridge: Cambridge University Press, 2008.

Heupel, Monika. "How Do States Perceive Extraterritorial Human Rights Obligations? Insights from the Universal Periodic Review." *Human Rights Quarterly* 40, no. 3 (2018): 521–46.

Higgins, Rosalyn. *Problems and Process: International Law and How We Use It.* Oxford: Oxford University Press, 1995.

Hindstrom, Hanna. "Burmese Authorities Targeting Rohingyas, UK Parliament Told." *Democratic Voice of Burma*, 28 June 2012. http://www.dvb.no/news/burmese-authorities-targeting-rohingyas-uk-parliament-told/22676.

Holsti, K. J. "National Role Conceptions in the Study of Foreign Policy." *International Studies Quarterly* 14, no. 3 (1970): 233–309.

Honda, Miki. "Natural Disaster and Humanitarian Assistance in Asia: The Case of Myanmar." *GIARI Working Paper* 4 (2009): 1–14.

Human Rights Watch. "'All You Can Do Is Pray': Crimes against Humanity and Ethnic Cleansing of Rohingya Muslims in Burma's Arakan State." April 2013. http://www.hrw.org/sites/default/files/reports/burma0413webwcover_0.pdf.

———. "Burma: Arbitrary Detention of Protesters." 22 August 2007. http://www.hrw.org/news/2007/08/21/burma-arbitrary-detention-protesters.

———. "Burma: China Should Push to Get Aid In." 10 May 2008. http://www.hrw.org/news/2008/05/10/burma-china-should-push-get-aid.

———. "Burma: Cyclone Donors Should Ensure Transparency and Accountability." 23 July 2008. http://www.hrw.org/news/2008/07/22/burma-cyclone-donors-should-ensure-transparency-and-accountability.

———. "Burma: End Attacks on Protesters, Account for Monks." 28 September 2007. https://www.hrw.org/news/2007/09/28/burma-end-attacks-protestors-account-monks.

———. "Burma: Government Forces Targeting Rohingya Muslims HRW." 31 July 2012. https://www.hrw.org/news/2012/07/31/burma-government-forces-targeting-rohingya-muslims.

———. "Burma: New Rules Further Delay Relief." 12 June 2008. http://www.hrw.org/en/news/2008/06/11/burma-new-rules-further-delay-relief.

———. "Burma: New Violence in Arakan State." 26 October 2012. http://www.hrw.org/news/2012/10/26/burma-new-violence-arakan-state.

———. "Burma: Postpone Referendum to Save Lives HRW." 9 May 2008. http://www.hrw.org/news/2008/05/07/burma-postpone-referendum-save-lives.

———. "Crackdown: Repression of the 2007 Popular Protests in Burma." 7 December 2007. http://www.hrw.org/sites/default/files/reports/burma1207web.pdf.

———. "'The Government Could Have Stopped This': Sectarian Violence and Ensuing Abuses in Burma's Arakan State." 1 August 2012. https://www.hrw.org/report/2012/07/31/government-could-have-stopped/sectarian-violence-and-ensuing-abuses-burmas-arakan.

———. *World Report 2007: Events of 2006.* New York: Human Rights Watch, 2007. https://www.hrw.org/legacy/wr2k7/wr2007master.pdf.

———. *World Report 2008: Events of 2007*. New York: Human Rights Watch, 2008. https://www.hrw.org/legacy/wr2k8/pdfs/wr2k8_web.pdf.
———. *World Report 2009: Events of 2008*. New York: Human Rights Watch, 2009. https://www.hrw.org/sites/default/files/reports/wr2009_web.pdf.
———. *World Report 2010: Events of 2009*. New York: Human Rights Watch, 2010. https://www.hrw.org/sites/default/files/world_report_download/wr2010.pdf.
———. *World Report 2012: Events of 2011*. New York: Human Rights Watch, 2012. https://www.hrw.org/sites/default/files/reports/wr2012.pdf.
———. *World Report 2013: Events of 2012*. New York: Human Rights Watch, 2013. https://www.hrw.org/sites/default/files/wr2013_web.pdf.
Huntington, Samuel P. *The Third Wave: Democratization in the Late Twentieth Century*. Norman: University of Oklahoma Press, 1991.
Hurd, Ian. "Breaking and Making Norms: American Revisionism and Crises of Legitimacy." *International Politics* 44, no. 2–3 (2007): 194–213.
———. "Constructivism." In *The Oxford Handbook of International Relations*, edited by Christian Reus-Smit and Duncan Snidal, 299–316. Oxford: Oxford University Press, 2008.
———. "Legitimacy and Authority in International Politics." *International Organization* 53, no. 2 (1999): 379–408.
———. "The Strategic Use of Liberal Internationalism: Libya and the UN Sanctions, 1992–2003." *International Organization* 59, no. 3 (2005): 495–526.
Hurrell, Andrew. "Legitimacy and the Use of Force: Can the Circle Be Squared?" *Review of International Studies* 31 (2005): 15–32.
———. "Norms and Ethics in International Relations." In *Handbook of International Relations*, edited by Walter Carlsnaes, Thomas Risse-Kappen, and Beth Simmons. London: SAGE, 2002.
Ikenberry, John, and Charles Kupchan. "Socialization and Hegemonic Power." *International Organization* 44, no. 3 (1990): 283–315.
Jackson, Robert. *Quasi-States: Sovereignty, International Relations and the Third World*. Cambridge: Cambridge University Press, 1990.
Jamnejad, Maziar, and Michael Wood. "The Principle of Non-Intervention." *Leiden Journal of International Law* 22, no. 2 (2009): 345–81.
Jetschke, Anja. *Human Rights and State Security*. Philadelphia: University of Pennsylvania Press, 2011.
Jones, Lee. *ASEAN, Sovereignty and Intervention in Southeast Asia*. Basingstoke, UK: Palgrave Macmillan, 2011.
———. "ASEAN's Albatross: ASEAN's Burma Policy, from Constructive Engagement to Critical Disengagement." *Asian Security* 4, no. 3 (2008): 271–93.
Jose, Betcy. *Norm Contestation: Insights into Non-Conformity with Armed Conflict Norms*. Springer Briefs in Political Science. Cham, Switzerland: Springer International, 2018.

Kammerhofer, Jörg. "Structural Uncertainty through Neo-Kelsenian Consistency: Conflicts of Norms in International Law." *Papers of the European Society of International Law* (2005): 1–25.
Kassim, Yang Razali. "Plight of the Rohingya: ASEAN Credibility Again at Stake." *RSIS Commentaries* (2012): 1–2.
Katsumata, Hiro. "ASEAN and Human Rights: Resisting Western Pressure or Emulating the West?" *Pacific Review* 5 (2009): 619–37.
———. "Why Is ASEAN Diplomacy Changing? From 'Non-Interference' to 'Open and Frank Discussions'?" *Asian Survey* 44, no. 2 (2004): 237–54.
Katzenstein, Peter. "Introduction: Alternative Perspectives on National Security." In *The Culture of National Security: Norms and Identity in World Politics*, edited by Katzenstein, 1–32. New York: Columbia University Press, 1996.
Keohane, Robert. *After Hegemony: Cooperation and Discord in the World Political Economy*. Princeton, N.J.: Princeton University Press, 1984.
Khalid, Khadijah Md. "Malaysia's Foreign Policy under Najib: A Comparison with Mahathir." *Asian Survey* 51, no. 3 (2011): 429–52.
Khoo, Gaik Cheng. "The Rise of Constitutional Patriotism in Malaysian Civil Society." *Asian Studies Review* 38, no. 3 (2014): 325–44.
Kirste, Knut, and Hanns W. Maull. "Zivilmacht und Rollentheorie." *Zeitschrift für Internationale Beziehungen* 3, no. 2 (1996): 283–312.
Koh, Tommy. "The Negotiation Process." In *The Making of the ASEAN Charter*, edited by Koh, Rosario Manalo, and Walter Woon, 47–68. Singapore: World Scientific Publishing, 2009.
Kraft, Herman Joseph. "ASEAN and Intra-ASEAN Relations: Weathering the Storm?" *Pacific Review* 13, no. 3 (2000): 453–72.
———. "Human Rights in Southeast Asia. The Search for Regional Norms." *East-West Center Working Papers* 4 (2005): 1–40.
Krasner, Stephen D. *Sovereignty: Organized Hypocrisy*. Princeton, N.J.: Princeton University Press, 1999.
Kratochwil, Friedrich. *Rules, Norms, and Decisions: On the Conditions of Practical and Legal Reasoning in International Relations and Domestic Affairs*. Cambridge: Cambridge University Press, 1991.
Krook, Mona Lena, and Jacqui True. "Rethinking the Life Cycles of International Norms: The United Nations and the Global Promotion of Gender Equality." *European Journal of International Relations* 18, no. 1 (2012): 103–27.
Kuhonta, Erik Martinez, Dan Slater, and Tuong Vu. "Introduction: The Contributions of Southeast Asian Political Studies." In *Southeast Asia in Political Science: Theory, Region, and Qualitative Analysis*, edited by Kuhonta, Slater, and Vu. Stanford, Calif.: Stanford University Press, 2008.
Kurlantzick, Joshua. "Thailand." In *Pathways to Freedom: Political and Economic Lessons from Democratic Transitions*, edited by Isobel Coleman and Terra Lawson-Remer, 157–80. New York: Council on Foreign Relations Press, 2013.

Leech, Beth. "Asking Questions: Techniques for Semistructured Interviews." *PS: Political Science & Politics* 35, no. 4 (2002): 665–68.
Legro, Jeffrey. "Which Norms Matter? Revisiting the 'Failure' of Internationalism." *International Organization* 51, no. 1 (1997): 31–63.
Lilleker, Darren G. "Interviewing the Political Elite: Navigating a Potential Minefield." *Politics* 23, no. 3 (2003): 207–14.
Lutz, Ellen, and Kathryn Sikkink. "International Human Rights Law and Practice in Latin America." *International Organization* 54, no. 3 (2000): 633–59.
Lynch, Daniel. "The (More Than) Half-Full Glass: Thailand's Democracy in Comparative Perspective." Paper presented at the Tenth International Conference on Thai Studies, Bangkok, 2008.
Mahathir, Mirzan, and Fazil Irwan. "Malaysia's Role in Asian Regional Cooperation: A Look at Foreign Policy Themes." *Asia-Pacific Review* 14, no. 2 (2007): 97–111.
March, James, and Johan Olsen. "The Logic of Appropriateness." In *The Oxford Handbook of Public Policy*, edited by Michael Moran, Martin Rein, and Robert E. Goodin, 689–707. Oxford: Oxford University Press, 2006.
Mercer, Jonathan. *Reputation and International Politics*. Cornell Studies in Security Affairs. Ithaca, N.Y.: Cornell University Press, 1996.
Michael, Arndt. *India's Foreign Policy and Regional Multilateralism*. Basingstoke, UK: Palgrave Macmillan, 2013.
Milanovic, Marko. "Norm Conflicts, International Humanitarian Law and Human Rights Law." In *Human Rights and Humanitarian International Law*, edited by Orna Ben-Naftali, 1–36. Oxford: Oxford University Press, 2010.
Milner, Anthony. "Contesting Human Rights in Malaysia." In *Human Rights in Asia*, edited by James Davis and Brian Galligan, 91–102. Cheltenham, UK: Edward Elgar, 2011.
Modelski, George. "Kautilya: Foreign Policy and International System in the Ancient Hindu World." *American Political Science Review* 58, no. 3 (1964): 549–60.
Murphy, Ann Marie. "Indonesia Returns to the International Stage: Good News for the United States." *Orbis* 53, no. 1 (2009): 65–79.
Musa, Naim. "Malaysia in ASEAN: Foreign Policy on Non-Traditional Security Issues." 2012. https://www.academia.edu/4219715/Malaysia_foreign_policy_after_mahathir_era.
Narine, Shaun. "ASEAN in the Twenty-First Century: A Sceptical Review." *Cambridge Review of International Affairs* 22, no. 3 (2009): 369–86.
———. *Explaining ASEAN: Regionalism in Southeast Asia*. Boulder, Colo.: Lynne Rienner, 2002.
Noor, Elina, and T. N. Qistina. "Great Power Rivalries, Domestic Politics and Malaysian Foreign Policy." *Asian Security* 13, no. 3 (2017): 200–219.
Ockey, James. "State, Bureaucracy and Polity in Modern Thai Politics." *Journal of Contemporary Asia* 34, no. 2 (2004): 143–62.

Pandian, Sivamurugan, Rusdi Omar, and Mohd Azizuddin Mohd Sani. "'Work with Me, Not for Me': Malaysia under Abdullah Ahmad Badawi (2003–2009)." *Asian Culture and History* 2, no. 1 (2010): 97–107.
Panke, Diana, and Ulrich Petersohn. "Why International Norms Disappear Sometimes." *European Journal of International Relations* 18, no. 4 (2012): 719–42.
Parnini, Syeda Naushin. "The Crisis of the Rohingya as a Muslim Minority in Myanmar and Bilateral Relations with Bangladesh." *Journal of Muslim Minority Affairs* 33, no. 2 (2013): 281–97.
Pauwelyn, Joost. *Conflict of Norms in Public International Law: How WTO Law Relates to Other Rules of International Law*. Cambridge: Cambridge University Press, 2003.
Percy, Sarah. "Mercenaries: Strong Norm, Weak Law." *International Organization* 61, no. 2 (2007): 367–97.
Pibulsonggram, Pradap. "The Thai Perspective." In *The Making of the ASEAN Charter*, edited by Tommy Koh, Rosario Manalo, and Walter Woon, 70–94. Singapore: World Scientific Publishing, 2009.
Price, Richard. "Reversing the Gun Sights: Transnational Civil Society Targets Land Mines." *International Organization* 52, no. 3 (1998): 613–44.
Putnam, Robert D. "Diplomacy and Domestic Politics: The Logic of Two-Level Games." *International Organization* 42, no. 3 (1988): 427–60.
Ralph, Jason, and Adrian Gallagher. "Legitimacy Faultlines in International Society: The Responsibility to Protect and Prosecute after Libya." *Review of International Studies* 41, no. 3 (2015): 553–73.
Ramcharan, Robin. "ASEAN and Non-Interference: A Principle Maintained." *Contemporary Southeast Asia* 22, no. 1 (2000): 60–88.
Rathgeber, Theodor. "Human Rights and the Institutionalisation of ASEAN: An Ambiguous Relationship." *Journal of Current Southeast Asian Affairs* 33, no. 3 (2014): 131–65.
Ratti, Giovanni Battista. "Negation in Legislation." In *Logic in the Theory and Practice of Lawmaking*, edited by Michał Araszkiewicz and Krzysztof Płeszka, 137–57. Cham, Switzerland: Springer, 2015.
Reen, Chai Ai, Khairiah Salwa Mokhtar, and Paramjit Singh Jamir Sing. "Administration in Malaysia: Reformation under Abdullah Ahmad Badawi." *NIDA Case Research Journal* 4, no. 2 (2012): 175–83.
Renshaw, Catherine Michelle. "Human Rights and Regionalism in Southeast Asia." Ph.d. diss., University of Sydney, 2014.
Reus-Smit, Christian. "International Crises of Legitimacy." *International Politics* 44, no. 2–3 (2007): 157–74.
Risse, Thomas. "'Let's Argue!': Communicative Action in World Politics." *International Organization* 54, no. 1 (2000): 1–39.
Risse, Thomas, Stephen Ropp, and Kathryn Sikkink. *The Power of Human Rights: International Norms and Domestic Change*. Cambridge: Cambridge University Press, 1999.

Rodogno, Davide. *Against Massacre: Humanitarian Interventions in the Ottoman Empire, 1815–1914.* Princeton, N.J.: Princeton University Press, 2012.
Rüland, Jürgen. "ASEAN and the Asian Crisis: Theoretical Implications and Practical Consequences for Southeast Asian Regionalism." *Pacific Review* 13, no. 3 (2000): 421–51.
———. "Democratizing Foreign-Policy Making in Indonesia and the Democratization of ASEAN: A Role Theory Analysis." *TRaNS: Trans-Regional and -National Studies of Southeast Asia* 5, no. 1 (2017): 49–73.
Samudavanija, Chai-Anan. *Thailand: State-Building, Democracy, and Globalization.* Bangkok: Institute of Public Policy Studies, 2002.
Sandholtz, Wayne. "Explaining International Norm Change." In *International Norms and Cycles of Change*, edited by Sandholtz and Stiles Kendall, 1–18. Oxford: Oxford University Press, 2009.
———. "The Multiple Path to Norm Replacement." Paper presented at the International Studies Association meeting, Atlanta, Georgia, 2016.
Saravanamuttu, Johan. "ASEAN in Malaysian Foreign Policy Discourse and Practice, 1967–1997." *Asian Journal of Political Science* 5, no. 1 (1997): 35–51.
———. *Malaysia's Foreign Policy: The First Fifty Years.* Singapore: ISEAS, 2010.
Sartor, Giovanni. "Normative Conflicts in Legal Reasoning." *Artificial Intelligence and Law* 1, no. 2–3 (1992): 209–35.
Severino, Rodolfo. *Southeast Asia in Search of an ASEAN Community.* Singapore: ISEAS, 2006.
———. "Will There Be a New ASEAN in the 21st Century?" *Asia Europe Journal* 2, no. 2 (2004): 179–84.
Sharman, J. C. "Rationalist and Constructivist Perspectives on Reputation." *Political Studies* 55, no. 1 (2007): 20–37.
Sikkink, Kathryn. *The Justice Cascade: How Human Rights Prosecutions Are Changing World Politics.* New York: Norton, 2011.
Snitwongse, Kusuma. "Thai Foreign Policy in the Global Age: Principle or Profit?" *Contemporary Southeast Asia* 23, no. 2 (2001): 189–212.
Stern, Aaron. "The Limitation on Democratization in Thailand through the Lens of the 2006 Military Coup." *Taiwan Journal of Democracy* 3, no. 1 (2007): 127–41.
Storey, Ian. "Thailand. Southern Discomfort: Separatist Conflict in the Kingdom of Thailand." In *Fixing Fractured Nations: The Challenge of Ethnic Separatism in the Asia-Pacific*, edited by Robert Wirsing and Mohammed Ahrari, 36–56. Critical Studies of the Asia Pacific Series. New York: Palgrave Macmillan, 2010.
Stubbs, Richard. "The ASEAN Alternative? Ideas, Institutions and the Challenge to 'Global' Governance." *Pacific Review* 21, no. 4 (2008): 451–68.
Suaram. *Malaysia Human Rights Report 2008.* Petaling Jaya: Suaram Kommunikasi, 2009.
Suchman, Mark. "Managing Legitimacy: Strategic and Institutional Approaches." *Academy of Management Review* 20, no. 3 (1995): 571–610.

Sukma, Rizal. "Indonesia Finds a New Voice." *Journal of Democracy* 22, no. 4 (2011): 110–23.
Syailendra, Emirza Adi. "Indonesia's Foreign Policy Outlook: Challenges of 2013 and Beyond." *RSIS Commentaries* 19 (2013): 1–3.
Tan, Hsien-Li. *The ASEAN Intergovernmental Commission on Human Rights: Institutionalising Human Rights in Southeast Asia.* Cambridge: Cambridge University Press, 2011.
Tan, Paige Johnson. "Navigating a Turbulent Ocean: Indonesia's Worldview and Foreign Policy." *Asian Perspective* 31, no. 3 (2007): 147–81.
Tang, Shiping. "Reputation, Cult of Reputation, and International Conflict." *Security Studies* 14, no. 1 (2005): 34–62.
Tannenwald, Nina. "The Nuclear Taboo: The United States and the Normative Basis of Nuclear Non-Use." *International Organization* 53, no. 3 (1999): 433–68.
Taya, Shamsuddin. "Political Legal Perspective: Evaluating Human Rights in Malaysia." *Asian Journal of Social Science* 38, no. 3 (2010): 485–504.
Thio, Li-ann. "Implementing Human Rights in ASEAN Countries: 'Promises to Keep and Miles to Go before I Sleep.'" *Yale Human Rights and Development Journal* 2, no. 1 (1999): 1–86.
Turner, Ralph. "Role-Taking, Role Standpoint, and Reference-Group Behavior." *American Journal of Sociology* 61, no. 4 (1956): 316–28.
Verma, Vidhu. "Debating Rights in Malaysia: Contradictions and Challenges in Democratisation." *Journal of Contemporary Asia* 32, no. 1 (2002): 108–30.
Vincent, R. J. *Nonintervention and International Order.* Princeton, N.J.: Princeton University Press, 1974.
Waltz, Kenneth Neal. *Theory of International Politics.* Boston: McGraw-Hill, 1979.
Weatherbee, Donald. *International Relations in Southeast Asia: The Struggle for Autonomy.* Oxford: Rowman amd Littlefield, 2005.
Weldes, Jutta. "Constructing National Interests." *European Journal of International Relations* 2, no. 3 (1996): 275–318.
Welsh, Bridget. "Malaysia's Glasnost." In *The Report: Malaysia 2007,* edited by Oxford Business Group, 28–31. Oxford: Oxford Business Group, 2007.
Welsh, Jennifer. "Taking Consequences Seriously: Objections to Humanitarian Intervention." In *Humanitarian Intervention and International Relations,* edited by Welsh, 1–24. Oxford: Oxford University Press, 2004.
Wendt, Alexander. "Anarchy Is What States Make of It: The Social Construction of Power Politics." *International Organization* 46, no. 2 (1992): 391–425.
———. *Social Theory of International Politics.* Cambridge: Cambridge University Press, 1999.
Wiener, Antje. "Contested Compliance: Interventions on the Normative Structure of World Politics." *European Journal of International Relations* 10, no. 2 (2004): 189–234.
———. *The Invisible Constitution of Politics: Contested Norms and International Encounters.* Cambridge: Cambridge University Press, 2008.

Wiener, Antje, and Uwe Puetter. "The Quality of Norms Is What Actors Make of It: Critical Constructivist Research on Norms." *Journal of International Law and International Relations* 5, no. 1 (2009): 1–16.

Wirajuda, Muhammad. "The Impact of Democratisation on Indonesia's Foreign Policy: Regional Cooperation, Promotion of Political Values, and Conflict Management." Ph.d. diss, London School of Economics and Political Science, 2014.

Wun'Gaeo, Chantana Banpasirichote, and Uchane Cheangsan. "The Tyranny of the Majority and the Coup d'etat in Thailand." In *The State of Resistance: Popular Resistance in the Global South,* edited by Francois Polet, 160–66. London: Zed, 2007.

Yusoff, Mohammad Agus, Azmi Awang, and Leo Agustino. "Democratic Reforms in Malaysia: Where It's Heading To?" *Jurnal Kebijakan Dan Administrasi Publik* 14, no. 1 (2015): 19–30.

Index

Page numbers in italics refer to tables.

Abdul Azeez, 132, 133
Abdullah, King of Saudi Arabia, 87
Abdullah Badawi: commencement of premiership, 42, 49, 125; commitment to human rights protection, 53, 54; commitment to noninterference, 40, 42; and Cyclone Nargis, 129; domestic legitimacy crisis, 143–45, 146, 158; resignation, 150; and Saffron Revolution, 127–28, 135–36, 137, 138–42, 145
Abdul Rahim Bakri, 147
Abhisit Vejjajiva, 53
Aceh, 59, 60, 72, 74, 78, 81
Achara Ashayagachat, 102–3, 104, 106, 110
Acharya, Amitav, 35, 39
Adams, Brad, 78
adoption of norms. *See* formal norm adoption
AICHR (ASEAN Intergovernmental Commission on Human Rights), 37, 45, 50, 51, 53, 54, 69
AIPMC (ASEAN Inter-Parliamentary Myanmar Caucus), 64, 77, 103, 134–35, 147
Alatas, Ali, 40, 79
Amnesty International, 29, 82, 118–19, 120
Anifah Aman, 131, 132, 133, 153
Anwar, Dewi Fortuna, 65, 73

Anwar Ibrahim, 49, 151
appropriateness, logic of, 11, 14
Apriradi Tantraporn, 105
Arbour, Louise, 66
arguing, logic of, 11–12, 14
ASEAN (Association of Southeast Asian Nations): democratization, challenges arising from, 1, 10–11; establishment, 36; human rights implementation at member-state level, 45–49; human rights implementation at regional level, 45, 50–54; human rights norm adoption, 43–44; noninterference compliance, 39–41; noninterference conceptualization, *27*, 27–28, 36–37; noninterference implementation at member-state level, 37–39; response to Cyclone Nargis, 60–61, 77, 78, 79–82, 97–98, 114–15, 130–31, 147–49; response to Rakhine Riots, 82–83, 86, 87, 116–17, 121, 132, 151; response to Saffron Revolution, 57, 59, 63, 64, 65, 66–67, 70, 76, 93, 94, 103, 104–5, 108–9, 126–28, 134–36, 138–42, 145–46, 157, 168–69, 170–71
ASEAN Charter, 37, 45, 50, 51, 53, 128
ASEAN Human Rights Declaration, 45, 50

ASEAN Intergovernmental Commission on Human Rights (AICHR), 37, 45, 50, 51, 53, 54, 69
ASEAN Inter-Parliamentary Myanmar Caucus (AIPMC), 64, 77, 103, 134–35, 147
Ashton, Catherine, 82
Asian-African Conference, 35–36
Asian financial crisis (1997), 40, 52, 100–101
Assegaf, Nurhayati Ali, 83
Association of Southeast Asian Nations. *See* ASEAN
Aung San Suu Kyi, 29, 57, 64, 94, 118, 120, 126, 127, 128, 139
Australia, 80
Aye Myint, 130

Bali Democracy Forum, 51–52
Banbury, Tony, 112
Bangkok Declaration, 36
Bangkok Post (newspaper), 96, 102, 104, 112, 113, 114, 116, 118, 120, 121
Bangladesh, 95
Ban Ki-Moon, 64, 87, 94, 97, 108, 113, 115, 116
Bayuni, Endy, 72, 84–85
behaviorism, 3, 11
Berita Harian (newspaper), 130, 133, 139
Betts, Alexander, 33
Boonsang Niampradit, 97
Brown, Gordon, 66, 78
Brown, Malloch, 80
Buddhist monks, Saffron Revolution, 29, 56, 66, 67, 93, 94, 105–6
Buddhist-Muslim conflict. *See* Rakhine Riots
Bull, Hedley, 16
Bush, George W., 64, 69, 77
Bush, Laura, 95
Buzan, Barry, 16–17

Cambodia, 39, 40, 67
Canada, 112

Charan Kullavanijaya, 94
Chew Cy, 145, 154
Child Act (Malaysia), 48
China, 44, 95, 107
choice, logics of action in situations of, 11–14
Chuan Leekpai, 52, 101, 166
Clarke, Ross, 46
colonialism, 36, 72
conflict denial: as concept, 25–26; in Malaysian response to norm conflict, 158–59, 172–74
consequences, logic of, 13, 14
consequentialist but socially embedded logic of norm following: as concept, 3, 13–14; concern for domestic legitimacy, 15–16; concern for international reputation, 16–18
constructivism, 2–3, 9, 11, 16, 17–18
Cotan, Imron, 67, 69, 79
Crawford, Neta, 12
Cyclone Nargis (2008): overview, 29–30; Indonesia's response to, 59–61, 77–82; Malaysia's response to, 129–31, 146–50; Thailand's response to, 95–98, 110–16

Davutoglu, Ahmet, 87
democracy and democratization, 10–11, 28, 45, 50–51, 69, 89, 103, 137–38
Djalal, Dino Patti, 58, 59
Djoko Susilo, 63
domestic expectations and legitimacy costs: overview, 15–16, 18–20, 175–76; in Indonesian norm reconciliation, 90–91, 163–65; in Indonesia's response to Cyclone Nargis, 77; in Indonesia's response to Rakhine Riots, 82–85, 86–87, 88; in Indonesia's response to Saffron Revolution, 63–64, 66, 68, 70–71; in Malaysian conflict denial, 158–59, 173–74; in Malaysia's political

crises, 143–45, 146, 153–54, 171; in Malaysia's response to Cyclone Nargis, 146–47, 148; in Malaysia's response to Rakhine Riots, 150–53, 154–56; in Malaysia's response to Saffron Revolution, 135–36, 139, 145; in Thailand's response to Cyclone Nargis, 110, 114, 115; in Thailand's response to Rakhine Riots, 116–20, 121–22; in Thailand's response to Saffron Revolution, 100, 102, 103–4, 105–6, 109; in Thai-Myanmar economic and military relationship, 100–102; in Thai strategic norm replacement, 122–23, 165–66

East Timor (Timor Leste), 39–40, 72
economy: Asian financial crisis (1997), 40, 52, 100–101; impacted by Saffron Revolution, 105; in Thai-Myanmar relationship, 100–102, 107, 119, 166
Erdogan, Emine, 87
ESCAP (UN Economic and Social Commission for Asia and the Pacific), 78
ethnic conflict: and anti-immigration views in Malaysia, 155–56; and legitimacy crisis in Malaysia, 143–44, 146, 153–54, 171. *See also* Rakhine Riots
European Union (EU), 66, 78, 82, 113

Finnemore, Martha, 18
Florini, Ann, 3
formal norm adoption: defined, 34; of human rights, 43–44; of noninterference, 35–36; scholarship on, 33
FPI (Islamic Defenders Front), 83
France, 66, 67, 78, 108–9, 111

Gambari, Ibrahim, 58–59, 76, 94, 106, 108, 126, 128, 141, 145

Gates, Robert, 78
general norm replacement, as concept, 21–22

Hadi, Umar, 67–68, 81
Hatta, Mohammad, 37
Heupel, Monika, 28
Heyzer, Noeleen, 78
Hizbut Tahrir Indonesia, 83
Holmes, John, 98
Holsti, K. J., 17
Horsey, Richard, 112
HRW (Human Rights Watch), 29–30, 31, 67, 69, 78, 121
humanitarian aid: in Malaysia's framing of Cyclone Nargis, 129–31, 147–50, 172; in Malaysia's framing of Rakhine Riots, 131–34, 156, 173; in Thailand's framing of Cyclone Nargis, 95–98, 110, 113–15
Human Rights Commission of Malaysia (SUHAKAM), 48–49
human rights protection and promotion: and democratization, 28, 45; expectations in Indonesia's response to Rakhine Riots, 82–88; expectations in Malaysia's response to Cyclone Nargis, 146–47; expectations in Malaysia's response to Rakhine Riots, 150–53; expectations in Thailand's response to Cyclone Nargis, 95–97, 110–15; expectations in Thailand's response to Rakhine Riots, 116–17, 118, 119–21; expectations in Thailand's response to Saffron Revolution, 102–4, 105–6, 109; implementation at member-state level, 45–49; in Indonesian norm reconciliation, 89–90, 162–65; international adoption of, 43–44; international defense of, 49–54; in Malaysian norm reconciliation, 140–41, 142, 157, 170–71; prioritized in Indonesia's response to Cyclone

Nargis, 59–61, 77–82; prioritized in Indonesia's response to Saffron Revolution, 56–58, 63–71; prioritized in Malaysia's response to Saffron Revolution, 126–29, 134–42; in Thai strategic norm replacement, 123, 165–68
Human Rights Watch (HRW), 29–30, 31, 67, 69, 78, 121
Hurd, Ian, 3

ideal speech situations, 12
IKIAM (Malaysian Institute of International Islamic Cooperation), 152
India, 95, 107
Indonesia: as ASEAN founding member, 36; criticism of UDHR, 44; defense of human rights internationally, 50–52, 54; defense of noninterference internationally, 41–42; foreign policy documents, 37–38, 50; human rights implementation, 45, 46–47; and noninterference compliance, 40; norm reconciliation approach, 89–91, 162–65; response to Cyclone Nargis, 59–61, 77–82; response to Rakhine Riots, 61–62, 82–88; response to Saffron Revolution, prioritization of human rights, 56–58, 63–71; response to Saffron Revolution, prioritization of noninterference, 58–59, 71, 75–77; secessionist conflicts in, 39, 71–74, 86, 163–64; sovereignty principles, 35
Indonesian Red Cross, 88
Internal Security Act (ISA; Malaysia), 48, 49, 145
international expectations and reputation costs: overview, 16–20, 175–76; human rights, adoption of, 43–44; human rights, defense of, 49–54; in Indonesian norm reconciliation, 90–91, 164; in Indonesia's response to Cyclone Nargis, 77–80, 81; in Indonesia's response to Rakhine Riots, 87, 88; in Indonesia's response to Saffron Revolution, 64–69; in Malaysian conflict denial, 158, 172, 173; in Malaysia's response to Cyclone Nargis, 148–49; in Malaysia's response to Rakhine Riots, 153, 156; in Malaysia's response to Saffron Revolution, 136–37, 139; noninterference, adoption of, 35–36; noninterference, defense of, 41–43; in Thailand's response to Cyclone Nargis, 110–16; in Thailand's response to Rakhine Riots, 120, 121–22; in Thailand's response to Saffron Revolution, 102–3, 104–5, 106–10; in Thai strategic norm replacement, 123–24, 167–68
international relations theory (IRT), 2–3, 9, 11–14, 33, 178
international societies, 16–17
Iran, 87, 153
Iraq War (2003–2011), 42, 43
ISA (Internal Security Act; Malaysia), 48, 49, 145
Islam Hadhari, 137
Islamic Defenders Front (FPI), 83
Islamic solidarity, 87, 150–52, 153, 173–74. *See also* Rakhine Riots

Jakarta Post (newspaper), 58, 66, 72, 82–83, 84
Japan, 66
Jayakumar, Shunmugam, 40
Jemaah Anshorut Tauhis, 83
Jetschke, Anja, 13, 19
John, Eric, 96, 111
Jon Ungphakorn, 103

Kalla, Jusuf, 88
Kampuchea (Cambodia), 39, 40, 67

Khaalilzad, Zalmay, 58
Khazaee, Mohammad, 87
Khin Ohmar, 119–20
Kocijanic, Maja, 82
Komnas HAM (National Human Rights Commission; Indonesia), 46
Kompas (newspaper), 85
Kouchner, Bernard, 66, 67, 78, 80, 108–9, 111, 149
Kraisak Choonhavan, 103–4
Krasner, Stephen D., 13, 15

Laos, 40, 67
Lee Hsien Loong, 76, 145–46
legitimization process, 13. *See also* domestic expectations and legitimacy costs; international expectations and reputation costs
Lewa, Chris, 121
Lim Kit Siang, 147
Lintner, Bertil, 75
logics of action, 11–14
Lynch, Daniel, 52

Mahathir Mohamad, 42, 44, 49, 53, 135, 136, 137, 151, 173–74
Malaysia: as ASEAN founding member, 36; conflict denial approach, 158–59, 172–74; criticism of UDHR, 44; defense of human rights internationally, 53–54; defense of noninterference internationally, 42; domestic legitimacy crises, 143–45, 146, 153–54, 158–59, 171; foreign policy documents, 38–39; human rights implementation, 48–49; migration concerns, 155–56; and noninterference compliance, 40; norm reconciliation approach, 140–41, 142, 157, 170–71; response to Cyclone Nargis, 129–31, 146–50; response to Rakhine Riots, 131–34, 150–56; response to Saffron Revolution, prioritization of human rights, 126–29, 134–42; response to Saffron Revolution, prioritization of noninterference, 129, 143, 145–46; sovereignty principles, 35
Malaysian Consultative Council for the Islamic Organization (MAPIM), 151–52
Malaysian Institute of International Islamic Cooperation (IKIAM), 152
Marzuki Ali, 84, 85
Megawati Sukarnoputri, 50
Meillan, Laurent, 108
Mercy Malaysia, 133
Miliband, David, 66, 106, 108–9, 111, 139
Mohd Azmi Abdul Hamid, 151–52
Muang Aye, 96
Muang Kyaw Nu, 120
Muhammad Hatta Abd Aziz, 130
Muhyiddin Yassin, 133
Mujahid Yusuk Rawa, 151
Mukhriz Mahathir, 146
Muslim Lawyers Association of Malaysia, 150
Muslim solidarity, 87, 150–52, 153, 173–74. *See also* Rakhine Riots
Myanmar. *See* Cyclone Nargis; Rakhine Riots; Saffron Revolution

Najib Razak: and Cyclone Nargis, 129, 130–31, 133; domestic legitimacy crisis, 153–54; and ISA, 48; and Rakhine Riots, 150, 151, 156; and Saffron Revolution, 128
NAM (Non-Aligned Movement), 35, 36, 132
Natalegawa, Marty, 52, 57, 61–62, 79, 84
Nation (newspaper), 93–94, 101, 102, 105, 108–9, 114
National Human Rights Commission (Komnas HAM; Indonesia), 46
National Human Rights Commission (NHRC; Thailand), 47

National League for Democracy (NLD; Myanmar), 29, 63, 119
negative sovereignty, 35
New Guinea (Papua), 72, 73–74, 86
Niphat Thonglek, 96
Nitya Pibulsonggram, 93, 94, 106–8
Non-Aligned Movement (NAM), 35, 36, 132
noninterference: ASEAN's compliance with, 39–41; ASEAN's conceptualization of, 27, 27–28, 36–37; implementation at member-state level, 37–39; in Indonesian norm reconciliation, 89–90, 162–65; international adoption of, 35–36; international defense of, 41–43; in Malaysian conflict denial, 158–59, 172–74; prioritized in Indonesia's response to Rakhine Riots, 61–62, 82–88; prioritized in Indonesia's response to Saffron Revolution, 58–59, 71, 75–77; prioritized in Malaysia's response to Cyclone Nargis, 129–31, 146–50; prioritized in Malaysia's response to Rakhine Riots, 131–34, 150–56; prioritized in Malaysia's response to Saffron Revolution, 129, 143, 145–46; prioritized in Thailand's response to Cyclone Nargis, 95–98, 110–16; prioritized in Thailand's response to Rakhine Riots, 98–99, 116–22; prioritized in Thailand's response to Saffron Revolution, 92–95, 100, 102–10; in Thai strategic norm replacement, 122–24, 165–69. *See also* sovereignty and territorial integrity
nonintervention, 35–36
Noppadon Pattama, 95, 97–98, 113, 115
normative leadership, 20, 21, 23, 24, 26, 157, 164, 165, 170
norm commitment: scholarship on, 33; threefold measure of, 34
norm compliance: domestic and international expectations for, 3–4, 15–18; logics of action in situations of choice, 11–14; with noninterference, 39–41; in threefold measure of norm commitment, 34
norm conflict: as concept, 1–2; as decision-making problem, 9–10, 178; refinement of theoretical framework, 174–78; response types, 4, 19–26, *26*; scholarship on, 2–3, 9, 11–14, 178
norm contestation, 25
norm implementation: defined, 34; of human rights at member-state level, 45–49; of human rights at regional level, 45, 50–54; of noninterference at member-state level, 37–39
norm prioritization, as concept, 20–21
norm reconciliation: as concept, 23–24; in Indonesian response to norm conflict, 89–91, 162–65; in Malaysian response to norm conflict, 140–41, 142, 157, 170–71
norms, as static and changing, 9–10
Norway, 112
Nyan Win, 57, 95, 115, 130

OIC (Organization of Islamic Cooperation), 86–87, 88, 153, 156
Ong, Kian Ming, 155
Orchard, Phil, 33

Pancasila (Indonesian state philosophy), 37
Pandikar Amin Mulia, 147
Papua (New Guinea), 72, 73–74, 86
Pasha, Julian Aldrin, 84
Pauwelyn, Joost, 10
Pereira, Adrian, 73–74
Persons with Disabilities Act (Malaysia), 48
persuasive power, 20, 22, 23, 24, 25, 90, 91, 123, 157, 164, 165
Petcharamesree, Sriprapha, 53

Philippines, 36, 44, 45, 54, 106
Pinheiro, Paulo Sérgio, 29
positive sovereignty, 35
Pramono Anung, 85
process tracing, as research method, 31
Putnam, Robert D., 19
Putra 1Malaysia Club, 132–33

al-Qaradawi, Yusuf, 152

Rais Yatim, 130, 148
Rakhine Riots (2012): overview, 30–31; Indonesia's response to, 61–62, 82–88; Malaysia's response to, 131–34, 150–56; Thailand's response to, 98–99, 116–22
Rastam Mohd Isa, 142
Razali Ismail, 155–56
realism, 2
Red Cross, Indonesian, 88
regional expectations. *See* ASEAN
religious conflict. *See* Rakhine Riots
reputation. *See* international expectations and reputation costs
Responsibility to Protect (RtoP), 49–50, 79, 80, 149
Rice, Condoleezza, 67, 136
Risley, Paul, 112
Risse, Thomas, 12
Rizal Ramli, 84
Robertson, Phil, 106, 117
Rohingya persecution. *See* Rakhine Riots
role conceptions, 17
RtoP (Responsibility to Protect), 49–50, 79, 80, 149
Rudd, Kevin, 80
Russo-Georgian War (2008), 41

Saffron Revolution (2007): overview, 29; Indonesia's response to, prioritization of human rights, 56–58, 63–71; Indonesia's response to, prioritization of noninterference, 58–59, 71, 75–77; Malaysia's response to, prioritization of human rights, 126–29, 134–42; Malaysia's response to, prioritization of noninterference, 129, 143, 145–46; Thailand's response to, 92–95, 100, 102–10
Samak Sundaravej, 95, 96–97, 110, 111–14
Sambuaga, Theo, 63
Sandholtz, Wayne, 10, 20
Sanitsuda Ekachai, 114
Sarasin Viraphol, 105
Sarkozy, Nicolas, 66
Saudi Arabia, 87, 153
secessionism, 70, 71–77, 85–86, 163–64
Security Offences Act (Malaysia), 48
Sihasak Phungketkeow, 118
Sikkink, Kathryn, 18
Silverberg, Kirsten, 136
Singapore, 36, 40, 76, 79–80, 107
Skavdal, Terje, 111
Smith, Stephen, 80
Soe Win, 75
soft power, 20, 22, 23, 24, 26, 90, 91, 157, 165, 170
Solana, Javier, 66, 78
Sonthi Boonyaratglin, 93, 102
Soorian Arjuan, 141
South China Sea conflict, 41–42
sovereignty and territorial integrity: ASEAN commitment to, 37, 42; in foreign policy documents, 38, 39; and international adoption of nonintervention, 35–36, 41. *See also* secessionism
State Peace and Development Council (SPDC; Myanmar), 29
Stothard, Debbie, 117
strategic norm replacement: as concept, 22–23; in Thai response to norm conflict, 122–24, 165–69
Suchman, Mark, 15
Sudarsono, Juwono, 58

SUHAKAM (Human Rights Commission of Malaysia), 48–49
Suharto, 37, 38, 46, 68
Sukma, Rizal, 70–71
Sunai Phasuk, 111, 112, 117, 119
Sundari, Eva, 83–84
Surakiart Sathirathai, 52–53, 101
Surapong Jayanama, 104, 112, 113–14, 115
Surapong Tovitchakchaikul, 98, 119
Surayud Chulanont, 92, 93–94, 100, 102–3, 105, 108, 109
Surin Pitsuwan, 40, 52, 80, 86, 97, 114, 121, 167
Suriya Prasatbuntitya, 118
Susetyo, Benny, 71
Syamsuddin, Din, 71
Syed Hamid Albar: commitment to human rights protection, 54, 137; and Cyclone Nargis, 148, 149; and Saffron Revolution, 126, 128, 138, 139–40, 141–42, 145, 170–71

Tan, Hsien-Li, 40, 49
Tan, See Seng, 68
Tej Bunnag, 114
territorial integrity. *See* sovereignty and territorial integrity
Thailand: as ASEAN founding member, 36; defense of human rights internationally, 52–53, 54; defense of noninterference internationally, 42–43; foreign policy documents, 39, 52, 53; human rights implementation, 45, 47–48; Myanmar's economic and military relationship with, 100–102, 107, 119, 166; and noninterference compliance, 40; response to Cyclone Nargis, 95–98, 110–16; response to Rakhine Riots, 98–99, 116–22; response to Saffron Revolution, 92–95, 100, 102–10; sovereignty principles, 35; strategic norm replacement approach, 122–24, 165–69; United States' relationship with, 107–8, 111–12; UN membership, 44
Thaksin Shinawatra, 43, 101–2, 110, 111
Than Shwe, 93–94, 96, 102, 108
Thant Myint-U, 75
Thein Htay, 62
Thein Sein: and Cyclone Nargis, 79, 96, 97, 113; and Rakhine Riots, 98–99, 116, 118, 119, 120, 156; and Saffron Revolution, 58–59, 75, 76, 94, 109
Thurston, Michael, 82
Timor Leste (East Timor), 39–40, 72
Treaty of Amity and Cooperation (1976), 37
Treaty of Westphalia (1648), 35. *See also* Westphalian norms
Turkey, 87, 153

UDHR (Universal Declaration of Human Rights), 44, 46
UK (United Kingdom), 66, 78, 109–10, 111, 113
UN (United Nations): and Cyclone Nargis, 77–78, 97, 110–11, 115, 149; and international noninterference, 41, 42, 43; and Rakhine Riots, 83, 116–17, 121, 153; and Saffron Revolution, 63, 64, 65, 66, 67, 76, 93, 104, 108–9, 128, 136, 145
UN Charter, 35, 41
UN Economic and Social Commission for Asia and the Pacific (ESCAP), 78
UN Human Rights Council, 52, 57, 65, 70
UN Security Council, 58, 64, 67, 69, 76
UN World Summit Outcome Document (2005), 49–50
United Kingdom (UK), 66, 78, 109–10, 111, 113
United States (US): criticism of Indonesian territorial disputes, 74; and Cyclone Nargis, 77–78, 95–96,

111, 112–13; praise for Indonesian democracy, 69; and Rakhine Riots, 82, 120; and Saffron Revolution, 64, 66, 67, 107, 108, 136; Thailand's relationship with, 107–8, 111–12

Vietnam, 39, 40, 67
Villarosa, Shari, 107

Wæver, Ole, 16–17
Wan Azizah Wan Ismail, 139, 141, 147
Wendt, Alexander, 3
Westphalian norms, 35, 41, 42, 43, 148
WFP (World Food Programme), 112, 115
Wichianchot Sukchotrat, 96
Widjojo, Agus, 75–76
Wirajuda, Hassan: and Cyclone Nargis, 60–61, 80, 81, 115; on democracy, 50–51; and Rakhine Riots, 87–88; and Saffron Revolution, 57, 58, 65, 75

Wiryono Sastrohandoyo, 74, 85–86
Witolar, Wimar, 68
Wunna Maung Lawin, 132

Yeo, George, 61
Yingluck Shinawatra, 98–99, 117–18, 119, 120
Yudhoyono, Susilo Bambang: commitment to human rights protection, 51; commitment to noninterference, 41, 42; and Cyclone Nargis, 59, 60; praise of, 69; and Rakhine Riots, 62; and Saffron Revolution, 58, 63, 66, 76; and secessionism, 74
Yusuf, Slamet Effendy, 83

Zahidi Zainul Abidin, 152
Zaid Ibrahim, 135
Zawacki, Benjamin, 119, 120